PRAEGER LIBRARY OF U.S. GOVERNMENT DEPARTMENTS AND AGENCIES

The Tennessee Valley Authority

Consulting Editors

ERNEST S. GRIFFITH

Former University Professor and Dean Emeritus, School of International Service, American University; former Director, Legislative Reference Service, Library of Congress; and author of *The American System of Government* and *The Modern Government in Action*

HUGH LANGDON ELSBREE

Former Chairman, Department of Political Science, Dartmouth College; former Managing Editor, *American Political Science Review;* former Director, Legislative Reference Service, Library of Congress

THE U.S. GOVERNMENT today is a maze of departments and agencies engaged in a world-wide range of programs and activities. Some departments are as old as the government itself; others are newly created or have been expanded or redirected by recent legislation. The books in this series describe the origin, development, function, methods, and structure of specific departments or agencies and explain how far their activities extend and how they relate to other branches of the government and to the public. All are written by authors with firsthand knowledge of their subjects.

The *Praeger Library of U.S. Government Departments and Agencies* is the only comprehensive, detailed source of such information. More than seventy titles are planned for the series; a list of those already published appears at the back of this volume.

—THE EDITORS

The
Tennessee Valley
Authority

Marguerite Owen

PRAEGER PUBLISHERS
New York • Washington • London

PRAEGER PUBLISHERS
111 Fourth Avenue, New York, N.Y. 10003, U.S.A.
5, Cromwell Place, London SW7 2JL, England

Published in the United States of America in 1973
by Praeger Publishers, Inc.

© 1973 by Praeger Publishers, Inc.

Library of Congress Catalog Card Number: 72–85985

This book is No. 35 in the series
Praeger Library of U.S. Government Departments and Agencies

Printed in the United States of America

The urgings of my brother, Kenneth M. Owen, prompted me to write something about TVA. In his memory, and for his sons, my nephews, the task has been concluded.

Preface

This book is about the Tennessee Valley Authority, but it is not a history of that singular agency of the federal government. The circumstances that resulted in the creation of a unique instrument for resource development are only sketched, and the chronicle of events is limited to the ones that stand out as milestones. Even those are telescoped in presentation, their complexities ignored out of compassion for the reader. The distinguishing features of the remarkable statute hammered out by Congress are identified. Some of the activities undertaken under its provisions are described, and by illustration the methods adopted for achievement are indicated. Accomplishments are summarized, and answers to some of the questions most frequently asked about TVA are provided.

With questions I am acquainted. The Washington office, where I worked for many years, was bombarded with inquiries every day. TVA's administrative as well as its legal headquarters are in the Tennessee Valley. Its work is carried on in the region, but to facilitate communication with other government agencies, with the Office of the President, with Congress, and with the general public a small office is maintained in Washington. One of its many functions is to serve as a kind of information center.

Inquiries come from the White House and from members of Congress. Students writing papers and professors planning seminars drop in. Job hunters come for interviews, and representatives from foreign embassies planning visits for their nationals are received. With no warning or introduction a variety of questions are submitted by telephone. The caller may want to know the number of persons employed by TVA, or the date on which a certain project will be completed. A manufacturer's representative may ask how to apply for an invitation to bid on items TVA proposes to purchase. A surprising number of people are interested in the precise amount of in-lieu tax payments received from TVA by the states and counties in the region, the total sum Congress has appropriated for the agency's use, and an up-to-date report on the monies paid from TVA proceeds to the Treasury of the United States. They may be ready to record the number of consumers served by the distributors of power from TVA, the kinds of fertilizer produced and the means adopted to make it available to farmers. People are concerned about the status of litigation. They are eager to know the results of experiments in forest genetics or of the investigations seeking the elimination of aquatic weeds.

To answer the limitless range of inquiries, the small staff of the Washington office must keep abreast of all the agency's activities in the region. That requires the reading of reports and briefs, of letters and interoffice memoranda, conferences with TVA officials called to Washington, visits to the Valley, and countless conversations by telephone. It demands some understanding of the TVA statute and familiarity with the methods employed to promote its purposes. Experience reduces some inquiries to routine, so frequently are they repeated. There is no way to prepare for others, or to know, when the buzzer calls for attention, whether the voice will be harsh or friendly, the subject one to provoke hilarity or consternation.

Members of Congress call to inquire why TVA is requesting exemption from pending legislation or to seek an expert witness to testify before a committee. Sometimes they have a special problem. An agitated representative, hoarse with the excitement of debate, once telephoned to whisper, "Quick, what's the difference between a kilowatt and a kilowatt-hour?" It was a pleasure to say, "Just think of the difference between a man and a man-hour," grateful for the inspiration that suggested a substitute for a presentation of the distinction between measurements of capacity and energy—an explanation that, under the circumstances, might not have been well received.

No such pat and superficial answer was at hand when another member of Congress reported a catastrophe. It was long after midnight when, using the home telephone number available after office hours, he described the emergency. The generating plant in his hometown in Tennessee had just been demolished by a bolt of lightning. The community was without electricity. The water filtration plant could not be operated. Sewage treatment facilities were shut down. Essential equipment in hospitals was idle. The streets were dark, and when the people arose in the morning they would discover that their electric ranges, hot water heaters, and refrigerators were useless. Even their toasters would not work.

The municipality was not then a distributor of power from TVA or connected with its facilities, but a call to Chattanooga, where the regional power system is monitored around the clock, brought reassurance. The disaster had been reported. Crews were already out in the stormy night working to bring power from TVA to the stricken city. Help was on the way, and except to relieve the anguish of the representative there was no need for communication with Washington. TVA is not managed from the nation's capital.

There were other cries for aid. One of those remembered occurred some years ago, when the coal supply of a Midwestern city was approaching exhaustion and a strike prevented replenishment. Then a senator called to plead for the release from TVA's stockpiles of enough fuel for a temporary supply for the city's hospitals, where the need was acute. The solon was not an admirer of TVA and had often expressed his skepticism about its value. Because he was conscious of his strictures, his embarrassment was almost as great as his concern as he portrayed the desperate situation. Another call to the Valley provided comfort, and, just as it had been a satisfaction to tell the friendly representative that succor was approaching his storm-ravaged community, it was gratifying to advise the critical senator that coal would be despatched, that it was being loaded, and, in response to his request, to discover and report the identifying numbers on the cars, the point of departure, the hour they would leave, and the route the railroad proposed to take for delivery.

The role of the Washington office was small in these affairs, but it was enough to give a lively sense of participation, and to increase our pride that we represented an agency able to respond effectively in an emergency. There was no red tape to unwind. Arrangements for reimbursement came later. Prevention of suffering had priority, and trust prevailed whether the claimant was friend or foe.

We did not always bear good tidings or assuage distress, and sometimes our share in events was more significant. There were times of anxiety and apprehension in the Washington office of TVA, days of strain, and nights when sleep was foregone that memoranda might be ready for the early morning information of embattled legislators. We were the first to know of dangers threatening in Congress, the first to be advised of data required, and the first to hear the result of votes in committees and on the floor of Senate and House. It was exhilarating to report good news, and there were many such felicitous occasions. It was sobering, however, to advise the Board of Directors of problems and perils emerging, and that had to be done with dismaying frequency in TVA's early years. Then crisis seemed to follow crisis, with no rest between. Somehow they passed, one by one. Difficulties were surmounted and battles won, forgotten now by all but a few participants.

In the course of writing this book, I consulted a number of my former colleagues who read early drafts of the manuscript and helped greatly with suggestions. To them I am deeply indebted. Their generosity came as no surprise to me. I had long relied upon it, and my appreciation for this particular assistance only deepens my endless gratitude that I had the good fortune to work with them and for TVA over the years. I hope I have been able to convey to the reader at least a little of the excitement, as well as the sense of purpose shared by the staff of TVA, and to suggest to a younger generation that working for the government can be great.

MARGUERITE OWEN

Washington, D.C.
November, 1972

Contents

Organization charts appear on pages 60 and 62.
Sections of photographs follow pages 84 and 148.

The
Tennessee
Valley
Authority

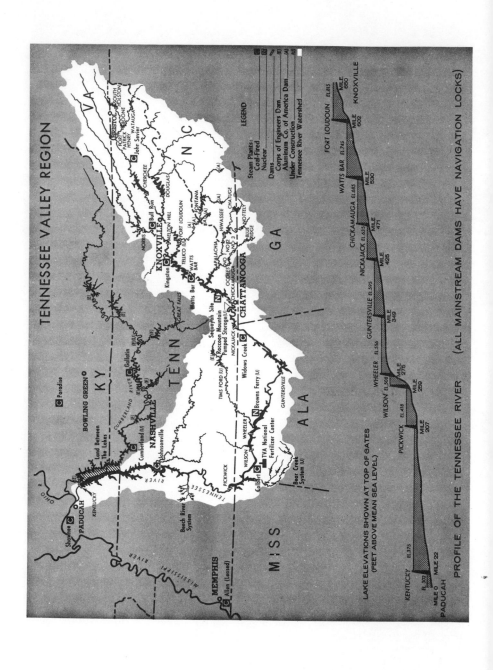

TENNESSEE VALLEY REGION

PROFILE OF THE TENNESSEE RIVER (ALL MAINSTREAM DAMS HAVE NAVIGATION LOCKS)

LAKE ELEVATIONS SHOWN AT TOP OF GATES
(FEET ABOVE MEAN SEA LEVEL)

LEGEND

Steam Plants:
  Coal-Fired
  Nuclear
Dams
  Corps of Engineers Dam
  Aluminum Co. of America Dam
  Under Construction
  Tennessee River Watershed

I

More than a Century to Wait

The Valley of the Tennessee River is beautiful in springtime. The drenching rains diminish, and the fresh new green of woods and pastures becomes a background for the prodigal displays of flowering trees and shrubs. Water tumbles swiftly down in mountain streams and rises high in broad and tranquil lakes. Every prospect pleases. And in the fullness of the season, just as spring prepares to yield to summer, the birthday of an agency of government is celebrated throughout the area. On May 18, 1933, President Franklin D. Roosevelt signed the Act creating the Tennessee Valley Authority (TVA), and every year posters appear in store windows, meetings of recognition are organized, and editorials in the local papers take note of the anniversary. In 1963, President John F. Kennedy journeyed to Muscle Shoals in Alabama to address an audience of some fifteen thousand gathered to honor the thirtieth birthday of TVA.

The day of approval of the statute is remembered, but June 16 goes unremarked. In a way this seems a pity, for that was the date in 1933 when the three men selected by the President to be the new agency's directors met together to face the responsibilities they had undertaken. That was when the life of TVA really began. The statute reads, "The board of directors first appointed shall be deemed the incorporators, and the incorporation shall be

3

held to have been effected from the date of the first meeting of the board."

The incorporators were Arthur E. Morgan, an engineer and president of Antioch College in Ohio, who had been designated Chairman of the Board; another Morgan, unrelated to his colleague, Harcourt A., an agriculturalist then president of the University of Tennessee; and David E. Lilienthal, a lawyer and member of the Public Service Commission of Wisconsin. All three were men of exceptional talents, qualified by training and experience for the job ahead, and even more importantly by their enthusiasm for the new enterprise. Enthusiasm was essential, for they had assumed obligations beyond those they accepted as directors of a public corporation. They were trustees of the devotion and the effort invested in the statute they would administer. With the charter, they inherited a legacy of hope and expectation accumulated over many years.

Their gift from the past was great, for, unlike much of the precedent-shattering legislation adopted in the triumphant "hundred days" of the new Administration, the TVA statute had a long legislative history. Other measures were designed to meet the crisis of the time, to correct abuses made blindingly visible by the stock market crash of 1929, or to ameliorate the suffering of the somber years that followed. They were enacted to feed the hungry, to provide jobs for the despairing idle, to stimulate the recovery of industry, to restore prosperity to agriculture, and to provide safeguards against another cycle of boom and bust. Bills were drafted by experts, submitted to the new Congress by the new Administration, and adopted in the heady atmosphere of excitement and achievement that characterized the first session of the Seventy-third Congress.

The creation of TVA contributed to the general sense of vitality and change, the burgeoning hope. Like other measures adopted, it would give jobs to the jobless and foster economic growth. But, unlike its companions in the legislative process of that buoyant spring and early summer, it had not been initiated in response to the desperate emergency. The major programs it embodied were not new for Congress to consider. They had been debated for more than a decade, discussed in committee hearings, in cloakrooms, and on the floor of both houses. For the thrust that ultimately resulted in the establishment of TVA did not come out of the shock of the market collapse or the despair of the Depression. It came from the necessity for decision with respect to the disposal of properties marked as surplus to defense requirements when World War I was ended. TVA's roots were deep in the past, but the final sequence of events that culminated in the statute of 1933 began when President Woodrow Wilson signed the National Defense Act on June 3, 1916.

Section 124 of that Act authorized the President to select a site and choose a method for production of the nitrates required for munitions in time of war and fertilizers in years of peace. The United States was then dependent on Chile for its supply. For a long time, there had been discontent with that foreign source, and, when prowling German submarines threatened to interrupt shipments, nitrate production within national boundaries was regarded as essential. In September, 1917, some five months after the United States had entered the war, it was announced that an area called Muscle Shoals on the Tennessee River in northern Alabama had been selected as the site, and that a major plant would be constructed there to produce nitrates by the well-known cyanamid process, which required large amounts of power. A smaller facility would be built nearby to experiment in the synthetic method then known to be used in Germany, but alien to technology in the United States. Two steam generating stations were to be constructed to provide initial power service to the plants; two hydroelectric dams would follow in the full development planned by the U.S. Army Corps of Engineers. Construction of the first dam (then called Dam No. 2, later named Wilson) was ordered in February, 1918.*

In the South, designation of Muscle Shoals as a production site was hailed as a tremendous victory, for it meant that when defense requirements eased the plants would be available to supply nitrates for agricultural use in what was then the great fertilizer-consuming area of the nation. Nitrate production at Muscle Shoals had been a goal for more than a decade, discussed in the press and debated in Congress ever since the power potential of this stretch of the river was recognized. Earlier, the thirty-odd miles of the Tennessee

* Dam No. 1 was a navigation dam, two miles downstream from Wilson, completed in 1926. It has been by-passed by later channel improvements.

as it plunged through northern Alabama had been regarded simply as a barrier to navigation, an impediment to progress. In that reach, where the bed of the river dropped almost 140 feet, the turbulent water covered the reefs and hid the shoals during the high-water season. In the months of low rainfall, they were exposed, revealing their threat to the passage of river boats.

The obstacle to navigation was an old problem. It had been a concern of government since 1824, when President James Monroe transmitted with his annual message to Congress a report from his Secretary of War, John C. Calhoun, urging, among other internal improvements, a survey of this stretch of the Tennessee River. A survey was made in 1828 and a recommended canal completed in 1839. It was constructed by the state of Alabama, with the federal government contributing 400,000 acres of public land to be sold to provide revenues to finance the project. Unfortunately, the improvement proved to be inadequate, and, following the recommendation of another survey, ordered in 1871, the United States itself took over the job of building a more ambitious canal, which was opened in 1890. Like its predecessor, this one too was ineffective, and the shoals continued to thwart development of navigation on the river.

In the years that followed, new surveys were made, and slowly technological developments changed a liability into an allurement. As men discovered how the force of flowing water could produce electrical energy to be transmitted to markets over high-voltage lines, the drop in the bed of the river became an asset. Power could be generated there. From about the turn of the century, various private companies applied for franchises to develop the hydroelectric potential of this reach of the Tennessee, and bills approving private ventures were adopted by Congress in 1899, 1903, and 1906. The permits approved in 1899 and 1906 lapsed because of the failure of the corporations to which they were granted to take advantage of their terms, and the bill of 1903 was vetoed by President Theodore Roosevelt. Interest in the shoals did not diminish, however; the power potential of the river was increasingly attractive. More surveys were reported by the Corps of Engineers, and new offers for private development were received. Use of water power to produce fertilizers was the common theme. One proposal was under consideration in the summer of

1916, but negotiations with private interests were suspended after the Defense Act was signed. Then the expectations of the area were focused on the opportunity offered by its Section 124.

In northern Alabama, announcement of the project location was greeted with ceremonial bonfires and community barbecues. There might be criticism elsewhere, but to the people of the area it was the triumph of almost a century of struggle and a guarantee that an era of prosperity would begin. When the dams were built, the river's shoals would be flooded out. The hazard to navigation would be reduced, and, then most desirable of all to the South, an abundant supply of nitrates would be available for farmers as soon as the war was over. These were exciting prospects but, like earlier plans, destined for frustration. The armistice ending World War I had been agreed to and the need for munitions ended before the project was completed. The nitrate plants had been built, but the experimental plant, No. 1, was found to be inoperable as American technicians discovered that their knowledge of the synthetic method was incomplete. Plant No. 2, designed to use the cyanamid process, was subjected to a test run in January, 1919, accepted by the government, and then shut down, to be kept in "stand-by" condition by the Army and activated in the event defense demands should recur. The villages built to receive the anticipated labor force became instant ghost towns. The huge dam No. 2 was only well started when hostilities ended. When the nitrate plant it was intended to serve appeared destined to be idle, a skeptical Congress suspended appropriations for a time, delaying the dam's completion until 1925. Then the Army, which had custody, began to sell the energy produced in its powerhouse to the private company serving the area. Nothing was changed. Once more the shoals asserted their sullen domination of the river and the region.

Except for one provision in the Defense Act, the idle chemical plants, the dam, the houses, and all the supporting facilities might have been sold. In July, 1918, under 40 Stat 850, the President had been authorized to sell, through the head of any executive department, war supplies "and any buildings, plant or factory acquired since April 6, 1917, including the lands upon which the plant or factory may be situated." The properties at Muscle Shoals could not be offered. Section 124 had included a prohibition stating, "The plant or plants provided for under this Act shall be constructed and operated solely by the government and not in conjunction with any other industry or enterprise carried on by private capital." Because of this provision, Congress had to determine the disposition of the properties, and years of controversy were required to settle the question. More than a decade would pass before three men would gather in a room at the Willard Hotel in Washington to accept responsibility for utilizing the facilities at Muscle Shoals as the heart of a broad program to develop the resources of the region.

Under the new statute, the Board of Directors of the Tennessee Valley Authority was given a charter far broader than administration of the existing government properties. Through the stormy years new ideas had been introduced, new concepts debated. The conservation movement was growing, introducing an awareness of the importance of all natural resources, and emphasizing the prodigal waste of the past. The increasing importance of electricity, its use thwarted in some areas and denied to many because of high rates, was receiving national attention. At the same time, the administration of federal functions in the field was being critically examined. These public considerations competed for support with private offers to purchase the properties. The most celebrated, that of Henry Ford, made the name Muscle Shoals known throughout the nation. Like all the offers, the Ford proposal was complex, but because the sponsor was something of a folk hero it was widely publicized with predictions that, if it were accepted, this area in the South would become the Ruhr of America. Other bids were received. In all, more than a hundred bills and resolutions relating to Muscle Shoals were introduced in Congress in the 1920's. Dozens of volumes record the lengthy hearings held by committees of House and Senate. Uncounted hours and days were spent in debate; in *The Coming of the New Deal,* Arthur M. Schlesinger, Jr., reports, "No issue, it has been estimated, consumed so much time in Congress during the twenties." At one point, a special Board of Inquiry was appointed by the President, at another a Joint Committee of House and Senate members investigated the problem. But nothing was settled, no recommendation accepted. The struggle went on.

Two major areas of conflict arose and were sustained throughout the decade: First, should the properties remain in possession of the government to be operated for public benefit as Congress had provided in the Act of 1916, or be sold or leased to private concerns? Second, to what purpose should the facilities be devoted, whether under public or private management? There was no doubt that the original intention had been to use the power from Wilson Dam to operate Plant No. 2 to produce nitrates for munitions in war and fertilizers in peace. There was no disagreement about the necessity of maintaining the plant in standby condition for possible defense requirements in the future. But there agreement ended. Heated controversy was generated by Southern insistence that the plant be operated as contemplated, although the facilities were built to use a process obsolete when the war was over. Then the synthetic method of nitrogen fixation, the Haber process used in Germany, became available to American industry. While the cyanamid process required large amounts of power, the new method did not, and a growing body of opinion held that it would be absurd for the electricity generated at Wilson Dam to be absorbed by already outmoded manufacturing procedure and denied to the homes and farms of the area.

The issues were ceaselessly debated. Congress wearied of the controversy, and out of impatience or fatigue some one of the proposals for private acquisition might have been accepted except for the circumstance that, in the Senate, bills relating to Muscle Shoals were referred to the Committee on Agriculture. George W. Norris, the senior Senator from Nebraska, was a member of that committee during the entire period, its chairman for five crucial years. In his autobiography, *Fighting Liberal,* the Senator, referring to the fact that bills relating to Muscle Shoals were sent to the committee of which he was chairman rather than to the Military Affairs Committee, which had jurisdiction in the House, somewhat plaintively wrote, "I never have known how it [the Muscle Shoals controversy] came to be dumped upon my lap." The responsibility was assigned to him, however, and Norris reported, "I went to work."

First, he undertook an impressive program of self-education. Many of the issues raised were relatively new to him. He studied reports and consulted experts. He journeyed to Muscle Shoals and traveled to Canada to investigate the operations of Ontario Hydro, then the largest publicly owned power system on the continent. Looking backward, he wrote, "I entered upon that study without deeply rooted prejudices. I think I can say I had an open mind." His convictions were developed as his inquiries proceeded and his zeal increased. He was greatly impressed by the Ontario experience, and in detail he described to his colleagues the program of rural electrification under way in the Canadian province.

In support of his belief that the properties at Muscle Shoals should be operated by the government and the power generated at Wilson Dam made available to the people, Norris presented the rates at which electricity was marketed by the public agency in Ontario. They were dramatically lower than those prevailing in the United States. He enlivened debate and underscored his points by displaying copies of actual bills paid for the same amount of electricity in Niagara Falls, Ontario, and in Washington, D.C. In the Canadian city, the consumer had paid the public supplier $3.55, in Washington the bill from the private company was $23.18. He cited the contrast in the cost of lighting the International Bridge at Niagara Falls. A private company served the United States half, Ontario Hydro the Canadian side. According to the Senator, for identical lamps and using power from the same source, the private company bill for an average month would be $43 and that rendered by the Canadian public system only $8.43.

Such disclosures aroused considerable interest in the Senate and in the press. They did not go unchallenged. To the clamorous responses of the private power companies, an apparently impartial voice was added in dissent. On January 18, 1925, just a month after Senator Norris had described the achievements of Ontario Hydro to the Senate, a monograph entitled "Niagara Falls, Its Power Possibilities and Preservation" was published by the Smithsonian Institution. The author was one Samuel S. Wyer, an associate of the Institution, and the document boasted an introduction by Charles D. Walcott, Secretary, endorsing the study. One chapter of the publication purported to prove that the Ontario system was unsound, that its low rates were subsidized, its reports misleading. Debate on one of the proposals to lease the Muscle Shoals properties was under way in the Senate when the brochure was released, and members of Congress receiving the document were astonished to discover the respected Smithsonian involved in the highly controversial situation, willing to endeavor to discredit a government operation in a friendly neighboring country in order to undermine the thesis of a Senator.

There was an uproar. Sir Adam Beck, then Chairman of Ontario Hydro, protested in a pamphlet attacking both the accuracy and propriety of the Smithsonian publication. This, too, was distributed to members of Congress and the press. On March 18, Senator Norris analyzed the fallacies of the Wyer report in the Senate. The ways in which credulous Smithsonian officials had been duped were exposed by enterprising reporters. There was no apology from the Institution but Walcott withdrew the monograph from circulation and ordered the plates destroyed. Wyer's association with the Smithsonian was terminated, although its officials stated they had no reason to believe that his purposes were not honest—and as a kind of extenuation they offered the intelligence that the writer himself had paid for the printing of the report.

Four years later, it appeared that even that statement was not entirely accurate. In the course of a Federal Trade Commission investigation into the propaganda activities of utility companies, Wyer testified on May 11, 1929. Under oath, he acknowledged that in 1924 he had been retained by the Duquesne Light and Power Company, and the printing of the Smithsonian pamphlet had in fact been financed by the private power company. The brochure was reprinted and distributed by the National Electric Light Association, then the trade association of private utilities. It was quoted extensively in *Nation's Business,* a magazine published by the U.S. Chamber of Commerce, and, even though discredited, it provided ammunition for those who were opposed to government operation of Muscle Shoals.

Senator Norris intensified his efforts. He defended the record of Ontario Hydro in the production and sale of power. He conferred with engineers and chemists skilled in the technology of nitrate production and inspected the new synthetic nitrogen plants built by private companies. Fortified by the information he acquired, he became the leader in the fight to save the properties at Muscle Shoals for public service. Relentlessly he exposed the fallacies of the various private offers, the "windfalls" involved. Although he was fighting to provide benefits he believed the people of the area should be able to enjoy, his efforts were not applauded by everyone in the South. Because of his opposition to the Ford proposal, Norris was burned in effigy in Alabama, and he reported that threats against his life "were quite common." Some of the violent protests came from the victims of land speculators who had exploited the Ford offer by selling lots in a nonexistent community to people throughout the United States, but there were others who believed that the Senator had frustrated the realization of a major industrial complex and that he was preventing the abundant production of nitrates for use on Southern farms.

Senator Norris was sure he was right. He was compassionate and understanding of the opposition, but he was stubborn. He never gave up. One by one, he convinced his colleagues that the power generated at Wilson Dam should be used in the homes and on the farms of the area and should not be captive to any industry. One by one, he persuaded them that the government itself should manage the enterprise. The hearings over which he presided were seminars, and the floor of the Senate became a classroom where a patient teacher went over his arguments again and again. He had great legislative skill and was highly esteemed by his colleagues. Slowly, Congress and the country responded, as a man from the Midwestern plains invested all his talents in a cause he had adopted as his own. No one could use the pejorative "pork barrel" to describe his championship of the development of the Tennessee River and the resources of its valley. Years later, in 1961, Senator Lister Hill of Alabama referred to this circumstance when he spoke at a ceremony honoring the centennial anniversary of Senator Norris's birth. Memories of his long association with the Nebraskan prompted the memorial tribute.

> TVA exists today because some auspicious fate decreed that George Norris should be chairman of the committee of the Senate to which bills for the disposal of these properties were referred. There is no better illustration of the simple way this noble man accepted the consequences of his complete dedication to public service. Evasion of responsibility would have been easy for a politician with a normal instinct for self-preservation. The issue was bound to be controversial and the properties were not located in his own state. But for George Norris there could be no hiding place, for him no peace in non-involvement. He was obliged to act in behalf of the people—the people of my State, the people of adjacent states—far from the state he represented.

I like to think that TVA will forever bear the mark of his rare and selfless spirit. I believe, in some mysterious fashion, it makes a difference that the enterprise was not born of parochial concern, or in response to local political pressure, and that no man's ambition was advanced by its creation. Its lineage is pure.

When private offers to purchase or plans to lease the properties had been defeated or withdrawn, Senator Norris pushed bills embodying his own program of development. Twice his proposals for government operation of the properties were adopted by Congress only to fail of executive approval. The first, passed in May, 1928, received a pocket veto from a silent President Calvin Coolidge. On March 3, 1931, the second was returned to Congress by President Herbert Hoover with a vehement message of disapproval.

On December 9 of the same year, the indomitable Norris introduced a new bill. No action was taken. It would have been futile since the President who vetoed a similar measure in March was still in office. The introduction was simply the senator's way of saying the fight would continue, and in the next few months a powerful ally emerged. As a candidate for the Presidency in 1932, Franklin D. Roosevelt warmly sponsored the idea of government operation of the properties. His was no casual campaign endorsement, no passing pre-election approval. He cared about the issue and the region, and in January, 1933, the President-elect, prior to his inauguration in March, took the long train ride to north Alabama. (Muscle Shoals was then more than eighteen hours away from Washington.) A distinguished group of advisers, including members of the Senate and House, accompanied him. According to Clarence Dill, then a senator from Washington, and one of the party, various members of the group would be summoned to his drawing room for private conferences with the President-elect. In a personal letter to TVA's former Manager of Power, G. O. Wessenauer, Dill described how Senator Norris emerged from one such visit, his face glowing with delight, confiding to his colleague, "I am walking on air. I never expected to live to see a man with such a dream in the White House."

The dream was TVA. It was outlined in speeches in the South, and developed further when the President sent a message to Congress on April 10, 1933, saying:

The continued idleness of a great national investment in the Tennessee Valley leads me to ask the Congress for legislation necessary to enlist this project in the service of the people.

It is clear that the Muscle Shoals development is but a small part of the potential public usefulness of the entire Tennessee River. Such use, if envisioned in its entirety, transcends mere power development: it enters the wide fields of flood control, soil erosion, afforestation, elimination from agricultural use of marginal lands, and distribution and diversification of industry. In short, this power development of war days leads logically to national planning for a complete river watershed involving many States and the future lives and welfare of millions. It touches and gives life to all forms of human concerns.

I, therefore, suggest to the Congress legislation to create a Tennessee Valley Authority—a corporation clothed with the power of government but possessed of the flexibility and initiative of a private enterprise. It should be charged with the broadest duty of planning for the proper use, conservation, and development of the natural resources of the Tennessee River drainage basin and its adjoining territory for the general social and economic welfare of the Nation. This authority should also be clothed with the necessary power to carry these plans into effect. Its duty should be the rehabilitation of the Muscle Shoals development and the coordination of it with the wider plan.

Many hard lessons have taught us the human waste that results from lack of planning. Here and there a few wise cities and counties have looked ahead and planned. But our Nation has "just grown." It is time to extend planning to a wider field, in this instance comprehending in one great project many States directly concerned with the basin of one of our greatest rivers.

This in a true sense is a return to the spirit and vision of the pioneer. If we are successful here we can march on, step by step, in a like development of other great natural territorial units within our borders.

FRANKLIN D. ROOSEVELT.

THE WHITE HOUSE, April 10, 1933

No draft of legislation was transmitted from the White House with the message. It was not needed; the Muscle Shoals question was an old one for Congress to consider. There were veterans to draft the enabling act. Representative, later Senator, Lister Hill introduced the bill adopted by the House. Senator Norris was the author in the Senate. Both sat on the Committee of Conference that adjusted the differences between the two versions and determined the final terms of the statute. The familiar provisions of earlier measures were included, and the concept of total resource development, the unified approach, was added.

Full development of the river system itself had been accepted as a goal by Senator Norris in some of his earlier proposals, and at long last, the recommendations of the National Waterways Commission in 1912 were embodied in legislation. One comment in the report of that Commission read in part, "With the increasing unity of our national life and the growing necessity of securing for human needs the maximum beneficial use of the waters of every stream it will become increasingly necessary to treat every stream with all its tributaries as a unit." The Army Corps of Engineers had presented plans for the development of the Tennessee River system in a report to Congress, in 1930, and the vetoed Norris bills had illustrated the principle by including authorization for construction of Cove Creek Dam on the Clinch River in Tennessee. The site was almost 300 miles above Muscle Shoals, but construction of that project on a tributary would, by streamflow regulation, increase the energy that could be generated at Wilson Dam in Alabama, a clear example of the advantage of treating a river and its tributaries as one system. This was one of the ideas long promoted by conservation leaders to be incorporated in the TVA statute. There was another.

Scientists and conservationists recognized the indivisibility of nature. They lectured and wrote about it. On occasions, politicians accepted the truth. In March, 1907, President Theodore Roosevelt created an Inland Waterways Commission (a body predating the Commission quoted above). It was directed "to prepare and report a comprehensive plan for the improvement and control of the river systems of the United States." The development of waterways for navigation was the dominant issue to be considered by the Commission, but one paragraph of the instrument setting out the assignment read:

> It is not possible to properly frame so large a plan as this for the control of our rivers without taking account of the orderly development of other natural resources. Therefore, I ask that the Inland Waterways Commission shall consider the relations of the streams to the use of all the great permanent natural resources and their conservation for the making and maintenance of prosperous homes."

The unity of a river system and the interrelationship of resources, the "seamless web" of nature, had been officially acknowledged, but rivers continued to be developed piecemeal and responsibility for other resources to be divided among different government agencies. Until the statute creating TVA was adopted there had been no reflection in legislation of the growing ecological awareness. Then, for the first time, Congress determined that the water, the land, and the trees should be considered together. Under the unified approach, one agency was empowered to see the job of development as a whole, to join agricultural and industrial growth as objectives, to repudiate the fragmentation of the past. As a pioneering innovation in federal legislation, a river basin emerged as a basic administrative unit. The area of TVA's responsibility was defined by geography, not limited by subject matter as in traditional government organization.

The boundaries of jurisdiction were not exact in every particular, and benefits were expected to be realized beyond the watershed. Although TVA's authority to manage streamflow for flood abatement was confined to the Tennessee and its tributaries,* one of its objectives was to reduce flood crests on the Ohio and lower Mississippi rivers, and the power generated at the structures built to control the waters' flow was to be made available to communities desiring it, if they were located "within transmission distance," outside as well as within the river's drainage basin. In the President's message and in the Act itself, there are references to the agency's responsibility to plan for the development of "adjoining territory" as well as the watershed proper, and the products of the chemical plant were to be available across the nation. Nevertheless, the Valley of the Tennessee was the area where TVA activities would be concentrated. That was its home.

The title of the TVA statute reflected the broadened assignment. The Norris bill of 1931 began:

> Joint resolution to provide for the national defense by the creation of a corporation for the operation of the Government properties at and near Muscle Shoals in the State of Alabama; . . .

* TVA now owns and operates one small dam outside the watershed, the Great Falls Dam, on the Caney Fork, a tributary of the Cumberland River. It was included in the purchase of certain private utility properties in 1939, an acquisition approved by Congress.

The Act of 1933 set out its larger purposes this way:

> To improve the navigability and to provide for the flood control of the Tennessee River; to provide for reforestation and the proper use of marginal lands in the Tennessee Valley; to provide for the agricultural and industrial development of said valley; to provide for the national defense by the creation of a corporation for the operation of Government properties at and near Muscle Shoals in the State of Alabama, and for other purposes.

Some sections were added, a few changes were made, but much of the Tennessee Valley Authority Act of 1933 was a restatement of the provisions of the Norris bills. Fertilizer production was still a primary purpose, but the Board was not limited to use of the cyanamid process. It was directed to experiment in producing "new forms" of fertilizer, authorized to modify and improve existing facilities and to construct new plants. Freed from the preoccupations of the past, the program it was to administer could keep pace with the advance of science.

The freedom to choose methods is an overriding characteristic of the TVA Act. Objectives are clear, established by Congress. But the selection of means to achieve the stated purposes was to be the business of management. To affirm this distinction between general policy determinations and the day-to-day decisions required for their implementation, the corporate form of earlier bills was retained. The designation was symbolic. In fact, every authority given to TVA, every freedom from traditional restriction, could be made available to any federal agency if Congress decided to do so. By creating a corporation, Congress underlined its intent, which was supported by its actions. In the basic Act of 1933, for example, and in certain clarifying amendments adopted in 1935, Congress told the Board to make the river navigable by providing a 9-foot channel from its mouth at Paducah, Kentucky, to its source at Knoxville, Tennessee—some 640 river miles; to control its floods; and to generate as much power as was consistent with those primary objectives. It did not, however, tell the Board how many dams should be built or, with the exception of Cove Creek, where they should be located. In the sale of power, Congress told the Board to give preference to public and nonprofit agencies

within transmission distance and to establish rates that would increase the use and lower the cost of electricity to domestic and
rural consumers, but it did not say what the rates should be. That
was the responsibility of management. It directed the Board to
produce fertilizers, but did not limit the kind of plant food they
might contain. Congress gave the Board the right to choose its own
employees, "without regard to the provisions of Civil Service
laws," but at the same time made certain that political considerations should never prevail in selection. Section 6 of the Act was
clear.

> In the appointment of officials and the selection of employees for
> said corporation, and in the promotion of any such employees or
> officials, no political test or qualification shall be permitted or given
> consideration, but all such appointments and promotions shall be
> given and made on the basis of merit and efficiency. Any member
> of said board who is found by the President of the United States to
> be guilty of a violation of this section shall be removed from office
> by the President of the United States, and any appointee of said
> board who is found by the board to be guilty of a violation of this
> section shall be removed from office by said board.

The Board was not only to be responsible for the selection and
promotion of employees; it was authorized to "fix their compensation, define their duties, . . . and provide a system of organization to fix responsibility and promote efficiency." The objective of
organization was defined, but the directors were not told how efficiency should be accomplished. TVA could buy the land and materials it required, and dispose of the surplus. It could use its
revenues "in conducting its business." It could sue and be sued
in the courts.

The corporation was to be independent, not a part of any central
government department but responsible directly to the President
and to Congress. The directors, appointed by the President and
subject to Senate confirmation, were expected to establish their
headquarters in the region, not in Washington, and while cooperation with local agencies was encouraged in a variety of places
throughout the Act, there was no formula to follow. It was clear
that Congress intended to create an independent nonpolitical
agency, to establish a decentralized administration, to set out certain specific goals as well as general objectives, and to provide

authority equal to responsibility. It could hold the Board accountable for results.

The chance to prove whether such an enlightened plan would work was, on June 16, 1933, in the hands of the three new directors who were required to be "persons who profess a belief in the feasibility and wisdom" of the Act. The hopes and plans of a century were entrusted to them. Old problems, new solutions were their responsibility to consider. The problems were formidable, the opportunities great. The Valley itself, the drainage basin of the Tennessee River, encompassed nearly 41,000 square miles and included portions of seven states—Alabama, Georgia, Kentucky, Mississippi, North Carolina, Tennessee, and Virginia. Almost 3 million people lived within its boundaries, and the depleted resource base was mirrored in their low incomes—in 1933 only about 45 per cent of the national average.

Once magnificent forests had been ravished by fire and the exuberant cutting practices that left desolation in their wake. The economy was based on agriculture and the soil had been mined of its fertility by the cropping systems of the past. Some 350,000 farms with an average size of only seventy acres absorbed the energies of 62 per cent of the labor force of the Valley when TVA began. The rainfall, an average of fifty-two inches a year, which should have been the region's greatest asset, was instead its gravest problem. For it was heavy in winter when much of the land was bare, and the precious topsoil was carried in the runoff of the rainfall to the river, which ran brown on its course to the sea. There were floods in winter and in early spring, but in the autumn the creeks were desolate and dry. This was the Tennessee Valley, where malaria was endemic and where a total program of development was about to start. The river would be controlled, and the resources with which nature had endowed its basin would be developed for the benefit of men. The wait of more than a century was over.

The meager minutes of the first Board meeting report that it lasted almost eight hours. When it adjourned, the story of TVA had begun.

II

Half a Decade to Begin

Incorporation of the new agency had "been effected" at the meeting of June 16. TVA was in the hands of its directors, and they were on their own. There were no traditions to guide them and no precedents to follow. Never before had there been an agency just like TVA. Three men had to devise programs to achieve the objectives of the statute and at the same time create an organization to carry out the plans. They had to arrange for office space and furniture while they established relations with other federal agencies, with the governments of states, towns, cities, and counties, and with the people of the region.

Options before the Board were many. Options can be traps as well as opportunities, and it is a tribute to extraordinary wisdom or phenomenal luck that the choices of nearly forty years ago have provided a durable foundation for achievement. The decisions of the first Board in the first five years of TVA's existence determined the shape and fixed the style that have distinguished the agency for almost four decades. In the beginning, it is unlikely that the directors gave much consideration to their function as pioneers, or reflected greatly on their imprint on the future of the organization. They had to act on demanding problems. Queues of jobless in the streets made it imperative to start building Cove Creek Dam without delay.

Congress had recognized the urgency, and, with no Board yet in office the Act provided that the President might order construction to be undertaken by the Corps of Engineers, the Bureau of Reclamation, or by an engineer selected from private life. By Executive Order 6162 dated June 8, 1933, a week before the first Board meeting, the President had named Arthur E. Morgan, the man he had already designated Chairman of the Board, to supervise the construction for which TVA itself would be responsible. Earlier the same day, by Executive Order 6161, he had selected the Board to be the agency to undertake the responsibilities outlined in Sections 22 and 23 of the new Act, the "planning" sections drafted in response to the theme of his message.

Those sections authorized the President "by such means or methods as he may deem proper" to undertake "such studies, experiments, or demonstrations" as might be useful to Congress and the several states in determining the nature of public programs suitable to serve "the general purpose of fostering an orderly and proper physical, economic, and social development" of the area, and directed that recommendations be made to Congress not only with respect to the specific statutory purposes enumerated, but also others designed to promote "the economic and social well-being of the people living in said river basin." Whatever uncertainties members of Congress may have entertained, the President had none. He intended the responsibilities of the Board to be undiluted, the range of its concern to be restricted only by the Act. He "deemed" the directors of TVA to be the "proper" means to carry out the assignments of Sections 22 and 23.

It was probably fortunate that none of the new officials was conditioned by prior federal service to feel at home in traditional procedures. They had no urge to continue accustomed ways. Without the embarrassment of earlier commitments, they could adopt whatever measures appeared to be best suited to accomplish each particular task. At a meeting on July 29, the Board determined that TVA should depart from common government practice in major construction projects. Instead of letting the job out to contract, the agency itself would build Cove Creek Dam. Under a system known as "force account," bulldozer operators and steamfitters, bricklayers and hod carriers, skilled and common laborers would be employees of the government, selected under a merit system just as managers, scientists, and engineers were chosen. Responsibility for the labor force would not be delegated to a contractor.

Clearly, force account would result in a saving of time and money, an advantage compounded as the number of river control projects grew and the procedures initiated at the first project were extended to others. Construction could start before final designs were completed, men and equipment could be moved from site to site with efficiency and economy. It had other effects. TVA itself had to accept additional responsibilities, beginning with recruitment of a full staff of engineers. Housing had to be provided in isolated areas, a program of employee health and safety developed. Hospitals were required at some locations, and schools for the children of workmen, as well as facilities for training and for recreation.

The consequences were far reaching. As a labor relations policy was formulated, a pioneering venture in the application of collective bargaining procedures to public employment emerged and an apprentice training program was initiated. Adoption of force account as a method of construction has permitted TVA to contribute to the growth of a responsible labor movement in the region and at the same time to influence the standard of performance in a variety of public activities. The libraries, medical programs, and schools established for workmen and their families were, by agreement with local agencies, associated with neighboring facilities, and acted as a prod to upgrade the services available to all the people. The decision of the first Board to build by force account has been pervasive in its influence on the agency and the region throughout the life of TVA. It was not dictated by the statute. It was the free choice of the directors.

In July, the Board named Cove Creek Dam "Norris" in honor of the Senator from Nebraska. From the Corps of Engineers, TVA had inherited surveys and proposals for the development of the river together with preliminary plans for this structure. While, by arrangement with the Bureau of Reclamation, the work of final project design was under way in Denver, in Knoxville, where TVA administrative headquarters had been established, plans for a new town to be built near the dam site were progressing. The directors had decided to build a permanent community rather than a temporary camp, and the hot summer of 1933 was a time of frenetic preparation to permit construction of the dam to begin in October. Land had to be purchased, problems of access determined, and highway changes negotiated with state and county officials. Houses for families and dormitories for single men had to be designed and built, examinations conducted, programs and facilities for training and recreation developed. Every task was new and the Board was rejecting traditional patterns just as firmly as Congress had ignored them. In Volume I of his published journals, then Director David E. Lilienthal tells of the labor relations advice offered by an engineer associated with a private construction company. The expert warned a TVA staff member busy with preparations:

> . . . if you start any of this educational monkey business, you'll have trouble. They'll begin reading books, books on economics, and the first thing you know, you'll have discontentment and trouble with your labor forces. The way we did it . . . was to give them a place to play cards and put in a couple of gamblers who could take all of their money away from them on Saturday, and to have prostitutes camping all around the place to take care of them. In that way they didn't have any money after Saturday night and our labor turnover was low.

The voice of experience was unheeded, and TVA proceeded to plan for a somewhat more antiseptic employment of leisure time than the one described. An excellent library was in process of organization. Space for basketball was incorporated in the design of construction facilities. A theater where movies would be shown and other entertainment offered was included. Ping-pong tables were to be provided and an area reserved for checker playing. Community square dances would be held every week when work began, and classes in arithmetic, in drafting, woodworking and a variety of other subjects were to be open to workmen. Planning for construction of the dam and operation of the town absorbed the excited attention of a growing staff whose lively sense of participation apparently created problems for the directors. At an early meeting, the minutes disclose, the Board felt it necessary to adopt the following policy:

> That no employee of the Tennessee Valley Authority make statements respecting matters of future policies or activities of the Corporation before such policies or activities have been brought before the Board and action taken thereon, . . .

and to direct that all members of the staff be notified of the directors' action.

Employees had to be disciplined, automobiles purchased, and leases for space negotiated while pressure for decision on major programs increased. Initiation of the power program could not be delayed. On September 1, 1933, Wilson Dam and its powerhouse would be turned over to TVA, and the contract with the Alabama Power Company under which the Army had marketed power during the years of its custody would terminate in December. Even before the first Board meeting in June, officials of municipalities were writing to inquire about the possibility of obtaining power. Delegations were seeking audience with the Board. Policies and procedures had to be developed, rates established, and contracts drafted to promote the objectives of the statute. The mandate from Congress was plain. The power program of TVA was not to be undertaken as a device to produce revenues for the government, although the proceeds received from the sale of electricity were expected to cover actual production costs. It was not to be a commercial operation, managed to obtain the maximum income. It was part of the total plan for regional resource development.

Under the TVA Act, electricity was to be used as a tool to strengthen the region. Section 10 had specifically authorized cooperative efforts to assure "the application of electric power to the fuller and better balanced development of the resources of the region." It was to be used to enhance the lives of the people, to ease their burdens and expand their opportunities. The same section added that "the board is hereby authorized and directed to make studies, experiments, and determinations to promote the wider and better use of electric power for agricultural and domestic use," and Section 11 underscored the point when it stated that "the projects herein provided for shall be considered primarily as for the benefit of the people of the section as a whole and particularly the domestic and rural consumers." They were to be served "at the lowest possible rates" and their increased use of electricity was to be encouraged. In fact, what might be described as social purposes are more frequently mentioned in the sections of the Act relating to power than elsewhere. Senator Norris, who drafted them, was not an economist or a business man. He had

had no experience in power system management. He was simply a great humanitarian. People were his concern, and he was determined that the power produced by TVA should be used for their benefit. That was an idea contrary to the prevailing view, which regarded electricity only as a commodity to be sold, not as a developmental or social force.

The conventional point of view was illustrated by the language President Herbert Hoover had used in 1931 when he vetoed the Norris bill, in which many of the power provisions of the later TVA Act were included. In part, he advised Congress, "I hesitate to contemplate the future of our institutions, of our government, and of our country if the preoccupation of its officials is to be no longer the promotion of justice and equal opportunity but is to be devoted to barter in the markets. That is not liberalism, it is degeneration."

It is probable that President Hoover had not read the proposed statute with much care and almost certain that he had heard none of the debates in Congress. He may not have understood that the objective of the bill he vetoed was not "to barter in the markets" but in fact to promote "justice and equal opportunity." On page after page in the record of congressional proceedings, the statements of Senator Norris appear. With compassion and concern, he described the hardships of country life that a supply of electricity could relieve. There was no justice, he pointed out, when rural areas were deprived of power, and opportunity was not equal when the people who lived on farms were denied the fruits of advancing technology in the United States. Rural electrification was one of the great purposes to be served by government operation of Wilson Dam. It was one of the major benefits contemplated in the TVA Act, an objective the Board was committed to advance.

If "barter in the markets" had been the goal, the task of the new directors would have been simple. The contract with the Alabama Power Company could have been renewed, effortlessly the government would have been assured of revenues, the fiefdom of the private power companies would have been secure, and the impact on the area would have been negligible. All this would have been easy, but it was exactly the kind of arrangement the Act of Congress did not permit. Options before the Board did not include abandonment of TVA's charter. The power program of TVA had to pioneer. In August, a statement of policy was issued. In October, preliminary rate schedules, wholesale and resale, were announced, and the first contract, with the city of Tupelo in Mississippi, was signed. The contract not only established the wholesale rates and the conditions under which TVA would sell power to local systems of distribution, it set out the basic retail rates and the terms under which the distributor agreed to supply electricity to consumers.

There was nothing new about the sale to municipalities of power generated at federal projects. The "preference" provisions of the TVA statute, which gave priority to nonprofit agencies of distribution, were based on those in the Reclamation acts, where they had long been used. But TVA power contracts were something more than sales agreements. They were the means by which the Board had determined to achieve the goals of the statute and to make electricity available to consumers at the lowest possible rates. They illustrated the application of the low rate–high use theory of marketing and, at the same time, demonstrated to the people of the region exactly what was meant by the decentralized administration of a federal program. There had been a good deal of talk about that characteristic of the new agency, but it was talk of more interest to political scientists than to the average citizen.

Academic observers understood that it was a stunning change in federal practice for the power of decision to be close to the problems to be considered, and to them the location of TVA headquarters in the Valley was itself impressive evidence of a new approach. They recognized that the thrust went further. Throughout the statute, there were references to cooperation with local institutions. The power program was the first to illustrate a method precisely. TVA would remain primarily a wholesaler of electricity, serving directly only a few large industries and certain installations of the federal government. With the exception of temporary service while local organizations were in process of creation, the energy provided by the federal agency would reach the consumer through locally owned and managed distribution systems, which by contract would accept an important share of responsibility for achievement of the objectives entrusted to the corporation by Congress. As it happened, the power program was the first major TVA activity to reach the people in their homes, and on their farms. It was one benefit they had to fight to obtain, and in the years ahead to protect from assault.

They fought—and in a variety of ways. In 1933, there was no program of rural electrification in the region. At hearings before congressional committees, representatives of the power companies then serving the area had testified that most of the farmers were too poor to be prospective customers. That expert opinion was disregarded when Congress directed TVA to manage its power facilities "primarily . . . for the benefit . . . of domestic and rural consumers." The farmers themselves were skeptical in the beginning, but when TVA started the construction of rural lines, and when the newly organized Alcorn County Cooperative in Mississippi actually received service in June, 1934, they began to believe that electricity was really coming down the road.

The organization of cooperatives spread, and soon the private power companies realized that farm electrification could no longer be postponed. Their response was immediate. Here and there over the region, and sometimes in the dead of night, company crews appeared to set poles along country lanes in the hope that they could claim as their own at least the most desirable of the once-rejected territory. They were not welcomed. The farmers had been spurned too long. With their wives, they came out with shotguns to bar the passage of the workmen or to uproot the poles as fast as they were placed along the roadside. It was an effective dissent. The objective was simple—the protesters wanted to choose their electricity supplier—and tranquility returned when it was attained. In fact, the revolt against the "spite lines" added a certain gusto, and tales of derring-do provided a little laughter at the meetings held in homes and farmyards, in churches and town halls, as more cooperative associations were organized to distribute the electricity the farmers proposed to purchase from TVA.

To visitors in TVA's first years, progress in river control offered the most compelling evidence of achievement. After Norris came Wheeler, called Dam No. 3 in the plan of the Corps of Engineers, located about fifteen miles up the Tennessee from Wilson. As in the case of Norris, final designs for the structure were completed by the Bureau of Reclamation. Pickwick Landing, fifty-six miles below Wilson, came next—the first dam to be designed by TVA's new staff. Others followed in a steady sequence, as the attack on stubborn unemployment expedited control of a willful river. Construction of huge dams is always dramatic, and thousands of the Valley's workmen found employment at every project. River control claimed widespread public attention, but to the people who lived in the country nothing could rival the excitement of rural electrification. They could watch the progress of lines under construction. In delight, whole families ran to the yard as the crews approached. As soon as lines were energized, houses wired, and light bulbs purchased at the country store, electricity was there to be used. The future had arrived. To the farmers of the area in the early years electricity *was* TVA. A roadside sign reflected the total identification—"Farm for sale. Have TVA."

Demanding as both were, however, river control and power utilization were not the only programs claiming priority in the Board's attention in the first few months. On July 1, only a fortnight after the first Board meeting, before a single bulldozer turned the earth at the site of Norris Dam or one consumer had used power supplied by TVA, the idle chemical plants at Muscle Shoals were turned over to the new Board. The directors had to decide how they should be utilized to "improve and cheapen" the production of fertilizer as the Act directed. To many representatives of the South in Congress, this was the heart of the whole development. It was vital to the regional program, for the depleted land resource was one of the major problems of the Valley. Agricultural scientists had long recognized that phosphate was a desperate need of the soil of the area, and Harcourt A. Morgan, now a director of TVA, had been one of their leading spokesmen. Their judgment was accepted and embodied in the decision by TVA to begin its fertilizer operations by renovating existing facilities and adding new equipment to produce a highly concentrated phosphatic fertilizer.

Phosphate was not a new plant food, but was usually received by farmers in small amounts as one element in their purchase of mixed fertilizer. Nitrogen was what the farmers wanted. Every year they needed more to stimulate the weary and rebelling land. The major crops the Valley farmers planted—cotton, corn, and tobacco—left no cover to shield the ground when the harvest was over. Without protection against the pounding rains of winter, the soil was washed away. Every year more worn out acreage was abandoned and chasms of erosion scarred the countryside. To improve the quality and to lower the cost of the kinds of fertilizer farmers were accustomed to using would have done little to save the land and improve the prospects of agriculture in the Tennessee Valley. The vicious cycle of soil abuse had to be broken. Farmers had to learn how to use a new kind of plant food and, with its help, change their farm management to make a living from soil-conserving rather than fertility-depleting practices. Agronomists were convinced that an adequate supply of phosphate would permit the process of rehabilitation to begin, but the findings of scientists had to be brought from the laboratory and the test plot to be applied on the area's farms.

A test-demonstration program was developed to accomplish the transfer of knowledge. It began in the spring of 1935 when TVA had completed preliminary experiments and produced a sufficient quantity of triple superphosphate to undertake large-scale testing. The new product, with some 47 per cent of plant food in every ton, was almost three times as concentrated as the superphosphate then available from commercial sources. Increasing the proportion of plant food was, of course, one way of reducing the cost of fertilizer to the farmer, for he bought it by the ton, paying freight and handling charges on worthless filler that accounted for much of the weight. In the 1930's, it was more than likely that he carried the bags on his back to the fields, burdened with material not worth his sweat and toil. The increase in concentration would be a great advance, the new material a boon, but only if the farmers used it. The problem was to demonstrate the value of the product in actual farming operations. This the new program undertook to do.

The question of day-to-day supervision of test demonstrations was settled when, after negotiating a memorandum of understanding with the Department of Agriculture and the Land Grant colleges of the Valley states, the directors announced that the program would be offered to the farmers through the existing institution committed to the improvement of agriculture, the Extension Service. In Section 5 of the Act, the Board had been authorized "to arrange with farmers and farm organizations for large-scale practical use of the new forms of fertilizer," to cooperate with

"National, State, district or county experimental stations or demonstration farms" and to donate or sell the products of the plant
"to be fairly and equitably distributed through the agency of
county demonstration agents, agricultural colleges, or otherwise as
the board may direct . . ."

Although TVA's determination to work through familiar agencies
was generally endorsed, this decision was not universally approved.
"Otherwise" gave the Board an option, and it was urged to exercise it to create an entirely new organization to work with farmers.
To many friends of TVA, the county agent system was part of
a discredited "establishment." They distrusted its close association
with the American Farm Bureau Federation, which had opposed
the creation of TVA, and would willingly have promoted its ob-
literation and the substitution of a new and more forward-looking
agency in the Valley. Unhappily for the success of their arguments,
few of the critics were qualified to determine just what methods
would be most successful in persuading the farmers of the area
to change their life-long habits, to use a new kind of fertilizer, to
plant unfamiliar crops and risk their meager incomes by adopting
a different pattern of land use and farm management. That was
the job confronting TVA, and despite adverse comments and contrary advice, the Board was steadfast in its commitment. It was
the county agent who explained the program to the farmers who
joined together to participate and selected from the volunteers
among their number those who would serve as test demonstrators.

In the early years, TVA provided the fertilizer without charge,
the farmer or the association to which he belonged paid the freight
and handling costs. For his part, the demonstrator agreed to follow
a land-management plan developed with the help of the county
agent and approved by TVA, to keep books and to let his farm
be used as a classroom by his neighbors. He ventured boldly as he
took his hilly acres out of the accustomed cash crops and planted
legumes, but he proved what the experts had been preaching—
that with phosphate provided by TVA, and using the lime abundantly available in the region, legumes would flourish and take
from the air at no cost to deliver free to the soil the nitrogen the
farmer had been buying by the ton. Without phosphate, legumes
and grasses would not flourish. With the new fertilizer pastures
could be established. Protected from the winter rains, the soil

would be kept out of the river. And, with electricity to provide refrigeration, livestock could be introduced into farm management
to make the land-conserving acres pay their way.

The water and the land were primary obligations of the new
agency, and programs to enhance their value were initiated
promptly, but there were other resources, other problems and
opportunities. The timber asset of the Valley was a concern of the
Board in the summer of 1933. The need for tree planting, for
better fire protection, and improved forest management was tremendous and could not be ignored by an agency committed to a
total effort in resource development. Some 14 million acres, more
than half of the Valley's land area, were wooded, over 80 per cent
in private ownership, about half in small holdings. More than
245,000 landowners controlled the long exploited and greatly depleted woodlands. The message of the President to Congress had
mentioned afforestation as an objective of the agency whose creation he recommended. The preamble of the Act listed reforestation
as a purpose,* but except for the Section 23 invitation to make
recommendations with respect to "the proper method of reforestation" there was no reference to tree planting in the statute
itself. There was however the useful word "otherwise" in paragraph
c of Section 5 which directed TVA to cooperate with landowners
to prevent soil erosion by the use of fertilizers and "otherwise."
Forestation was an accepted way of preventing erosion. It could
be undertaken, but how it should be accomplished presented difficulties.

At a meeting on July 30, the Board employed a Chief Forester.
With his arrival activities began. An inventory of the resource was
initiated, nurseries were established to provide forest tree seedlings,
and conferences with state and federal agencies were arranged to
make certain that TVA activities would not duplicate but supplement existing programs. The prospects for progress were not encouraging for there was little public interest in the Valley's woods.
In the seven states of which the Tennessee Valley is a part, there
were only thirty-six foresters employed by public agencies in 1933
and the combined annual forestry budgets totaled less than half
a million dollars. The people were resigned to the forest fires,

---

* Afforestation is the planting of trees on land not previously wooded.
Reforestation is the planting of trees to restock forest areas.

which damaged 10 per cent of wooded lands in many years and, in some, as much as 15 per cent. There was slight concern about reforestation. To TVA's Chief Forester, it appeared that direct federal action was required, and in March 1934, as part of an outline of goals proposed, he recommended the purchase of some 7 million acres then in private ownership. Under his plan, most of the acreage would become national forest areas to be maintained by the Forest Service of the Department of Agriculture, with half a million acres to be retained by TVA and administered "as a demonstration of scientific forest management and an experiment in the development of forest supported communities."

From the point of view of forest growth and land improvement, this was a bold and stimulating concept. It was warmly endorsed by the professional foresters consulted by the staff. TVA files reveal that in April of 1934 and again in January of 1935 Chairman Arthur E. Morgan reported the proposal to the Secretary of Agriculture, Henry A. Wallace, but there is no record of a reply from Wallace, nor of accelerated purchases by the Forest Service. Within TVA, there was a good deal of opposition to the plan, which involved a complex system of land use classification. To an organization already dedicated to working with the people and their local institutions, and to reliance on education and persuasion for accomplishment, the direct approach advanced by the foresters was uncongenial. The purchase plan was never carried out nor were suggestions that TVA should seek legislation giving it authority to regulate the practices adopted by the owners of private forest lands. The foresters kept hoping for action on the master plan, but in the meantime there was plenty for them to do. Various kinds of research leading toward woodland improvement were undertaken. The "surveys, studies, experiments, and demonstrations" authorized by the statute were begun. Plans for the enhancement of the forest lands TVA itself would own as part of its reservoir properties went forward. TVA nurseries were producing high-quality seedlings for the program of reforestation. The problem was to get them planted on privately owned lands.

No other major program faced the same difficulties. There was vigorous citizen interest in the case of power, and with considerable enthusiasm new local agencies were organized to assume responsibility for bringing electricity to the people. To test the role

of new fertilizers in improving agriculture an existing organization
—the county agent system—was at hand. To promote the objectives of the forestry program, neither pioneering excitement nor
familiar vehicle was available. As a whole, landowners were indifferent, and perhaps the task of devising methods to enlist their
cooperation would have been beyond achievement except for the
fortunate circumstance that more than a score of camps of the
Civilian Conservation Corps (CCC) were established in the area.
Enrollment in the Corps was open to young men between the
ages of eighteen and twenty-five who were unemployed and whose
families were eligible for relief. The Labor Department was in
charge of selection of recruits. The Army managed the camps, and
various government agencies planned and supervised the work to
be undertaken by groups assigned to them. TVA developed a
variety of measures of erosion control to be promoted by young
men from the camps. They learned how to build check dams, they
became skilled in terracing, and they planted seedlings. They
planted on TVA-owned land, and on privately owned acreage
where the landowner would accept responsibility for maintenance.
It was a modest start, and at first the interest of the people was
slight, but a landscape change began, and the reforestation of the
Valley was under way.

Public interest grew slowly, but it grew. Every year, more trees
were planted by farmers themselves. Requisitions for seedlings
from TVA nurseries steadily increased. Along with reforestation,
an intensive campaign to improve the fire protection programs of
the states and to increase their support by citizens was undertaken. Demonstrations of forest management were developed, of
selective cutting, and wood utilization. In the forestry program,
representatives of TVA dealt more directly with those who managed the resource than in any other major activity. Agronomists
from TVA approved the plans adopted by demonstration farmers,
attended meetings and made visits to inspect, advise, and report,
but constant supervision was the responsibility of the county agent
aided by a special assistant whose salary was paid by TVA. Rate
analysts and power managers conferred with those in charge of
local distribution systems but did not attempt to handle the problems of individual consumers of electricity. TVA foresters, however, worked with the landowners themselves, illustrating the

diversity that is the essence of decentralization as surely as uniformity is the hallmark of centralization. In the Tennessee Valley, different problems were approached in contrasting ways. The first Board of TVA was not committed to conformity nor fearful of innovation.

Some activities were visible, inspiring wonder in the area. By thousands, citizens came to watch construction of the massive dams rising to control the rivers and to gape at nimble crews erecting transmission towers and stringing lines. Boys planting trees and farmers fertilizing fields could be seen from country roads, but there were others whose contribution to the general program was hidden from view. Scientists were working in quiet laboratories, engineers at drafting tables, economists in cluttered offices, all promoting the same objective—the use of the resources of the region to enhance the well-being of the people. That was the goal laid down in the Act. As obstacles to progress were identified and solutions were advanced, the variety of undertakings increased.

When it became clear that the market offered nothing suitable, under a cooperative arrangement with one of the state universities, new machinery was developed, specifically adapted for use on the Valley's small and hilly farms. Electric hay-drying equipment was perfected to improve the quality and encourage an increase in forage crops. Community freezers were designed and installed at crossroad stores so that farmers not yet served with electricity could enjoy modern food storage. One corporation was established to finance the purchase of low-cost electric appliances by consumers, and another was created to supervise the distribution of a grant to cooperatives from the Federal Emergency Relief Administration. Studies and investigations proceeded. A plan for the unified development of the whole river system was submitted to Congress in 1936. The first of three reports on regional freight rates followed when specialists in the field determined that the existing structure was one factor limiting the progress of the South and helping to maintain its raw materials economy. Mapping of the Valley had begun, a soil survey and land-use study were under way, the inventory of the timber resource was continuing. A survey of the recreational asset of the watershed was undertaken, and areas on Norris Lake were developed to demonstrate how the shoreland could be used by the people for their enjoyment.

All these activities met with approbation, and, when TVA announced that there would be no billboards on the highway it constructed between the outskirts of Knoxville and Norris Dam, the decision was acclaimed. In some quarters, the road was described as the first rural freeway in the United States, a model for the nation. As river control projects were completed, the beauty of the multipurpose dams was widely praised, with recognition of the unusual and effective marriage of the talents of architects and engineers. The work of the landscape specialists who were planning and planting to enhance the appearance of the areas adjacent to the structures was noted, but they did not receive their most cherished accolade until a decade later. Then a writer from abroad soberly reported that TVA had been singularly fortunate because it was able to locate its major projects in handsome parks!

Local papers commented approvingly on the compassion with which TVA was engaged in the removal of graves from reservoir areas. The story of the transfer of an eternal flame excited romantic interest—and the assistance provided in the relocation of families required to leave old homes was described in sympathetic detail. The agency's concern about fish and wildlife quieted some of the doubts of conservationists inclined to fear the consequences of the system of water control that would change a river into a series of lakes. There was wide approval of TVA's acceptance of responsibility to reduce the incidence of malaria, a long-time threat in some areas along the river, and its early studies of water pollution were welcomed as evidence of the beginning of federal interest in water quality as well as water control. The village of Norris with its winding tree-lined streets and its electrically heated homes was described as the first "new town" in America, and became a kind of mecca for community planners. Designs of the simple houses were sold for fifty cents in an effort to share with the region the talents of the gifted architects employed by TVA. Visitors came to see the new tree nurseries and inspect the planted areas. Farm organizations that had opposed TVA in the beginning endorsed the test demonstration program. Experts in personnel administration arrived to study and to praise the merit system developed by TVA. Labor organizations hailed the union-management agreements and the apprentice program.

Euphoria was extensive, but even in the first five years, as in the years to follow, the power program was under attack. In an atmosphere otherwise felicitous, there controversy was sustained. The private power companies never gave up. They had fought enactment of the TVA statute and the predecessor Norris bills. They continued their opposition in Congress, in the press, and in the courts. It was a total effort.

When TVA first announced its power policy in August, 1933, it emphasized its intention to purchase the properties of private companies rather than to build competing facilities. To carry out this commitment, negotiations were undertaken with a view to the acquisition of certain properties belonging to subsidiaries of the Commonwealth & Southern Corporation. TVA would acquire the facilities relating to power generation and transmission, and concurrently municipalities desiring to receive power from TVA for resale to their consumers would purchase the distribution systems. A contract to accomplish the transfers was signed in January, 1934, but the municipalities were frustrated in their attempts to purchase the local properties and in September of that year an improbably vigilant stockholder named Ashwander *"et al."* moved to enjoin the Alabama Power Company from performance. With this action (*Ashwander v. Tennessee Valley Authority*), the first of two major constitutional cases began.

There had been other challenges. Earlier, in June, 1934, certain coal companies had filed a bill of complaint, and another was presented by a group of ice companies, each claiming that their businesses would be adversely affected by the activities of TVA. In all, over a period of less than five years, more than forty cases questioned the constitutionality of the TVA Act, but it was the Ashwander case that provided the headlines and absorbed the attention of the staff. In the U.S. District Court in Birmingham where the case was first tried, the decision was against TVA. The judge was reversed by the Circuit Court of Appeals, however, and on February 17, 1936, that court's decision was sustained by the Supreme Court of the United States.

The validity of TVA's disposal of power from Wilson Dam was affirmed, but the Court did not pass on all issues of the complaint and the power companies resolved to try again. Three months later, in May, 1936, eighteen neighboring companies discovered a community of interest and joined to file another bill. Their allegations were many. In general, they contended that TVA was entering into a vast program of power development while falsely claiming that its river control projects served the purposes of navigation and flood abatement. A preliminary injunction was granted in the Federal District Court in Knoxville in December, 1936. It was later dissolved by the Circuit Court of Appeals, and on January 3, 1938, a three-judge district court to which the case had been returned for trial held that the river control system under construction was in fact designed and operated with primary emphasis on navigation and flood control, and that it provided a system which could fully serve all three purposes (*Tennessee Electric Power Company v. Tennessee Valley Authority 21*). It was a victory for TVA, from which, not unexpectedly, the power companies appealed to the Supreme Court of the United States.

Clearly, development of the power program had been impeded by the years of litigation, although it is true that there had been dropouts during the progress of the "eighteen-company" case, and some purchases of facilities from a few of the companies had been negotiated. Rural electrification had gone forward because that involved no agreement with private companies. The litigation had been costly in time and money. It reduced the revenues the government might have received, and postponed the benefits that would have been realized by consumers. There were other results. Probably the utilities had failed to realize how greatly the injunctions would increase interest and support in the region. Just as in rural areas where there had been no electric service the "spite lines" made farmers more determined than ever to organize cooperatives to purchase power from TVA, so the efforts of the utilities to keep the cities captive through litigation only increased the pressure for change. By the end of 1938, eighty towns and cities had acted to purchase power from TVA when it could be made available, all but a score in citizen referenda.

There were other side effects. These two cases provided an intensive education for the staff of TVA. Most of the agency's attorneys were young and all were well trained. They were eager, and they found themselves involved in basic constitutional issues. They were forced to learn the complexities of the TVA statute, to test its flexibility, to understand its history and the congressional purposes it embodied. They had to prove that the goals of the statute were being promoted, and engineers were summoned from drafting rooms to describe to the court how dams were designed to achieve the objectives of the Act, their colleagues to tell how streamflow was controlled to advance its purposes. They had to report exactly what standards governed their decisions as the water was released from one reservoir and restrained at another. The trials were demanding, they were perilous, but as day by day the press reported proceedings the people of the region and the employees of TVA learned just what Congress intended TVA to do and be, and how effectively management was discharging its responsibilities. A resolute and knowledgeable staff resulted, a region fired with enthusiasm and faith.

TVA's annual report for the fiscal year ending June 30, 1938, was submitted on December 31 of that year. It presented a record of solid achievement. It led off with a discussion of river control, and reported the precise location of the 198 gauges then installed to record the water's flow. Construction progress was reported in detail. By this time, three multipurpose dams had been completed, Norris, Wheeler, and Pickwick Landing. Four more dams were under way in June, 1938, and the 9-foot navigation channel ordered by the statute was approaching realization.

More than 4,600 miles of rural lines had been energized by the end of fiscal 1938, and over 1,400 miles of high voltage transmission lines were in use. In spite of obstacles, forty distributors, municipalities, and rural cooperatives, were already receiving power from TVA, and electricity consumption in homes and on farms was growing as the low rate–high use policies were applied. In Tupelo, TVA's first municipal customer, annual domestic use had climbed to an average of over 2,000 kwh, more than twice the then national average of 802 kwh for consuming households, and almost four times the 588 kwh reported for the municipally owned system prior to its association with TVA. Already, the demonstration of the new pricing policy was effective. Its influence was spreading. Rate reductions on neighboring private power systems had lowered the average cost of electricity to their consumers from 5.77 cents to 2.9 cents per kwh. In response, use had more than doubled, from an annual average of 612 to 1,358 kwh, and the companies were prospering.

New kinds of fertilizer were being produced, phosphate lands and mineral rights had been acquired. More than 23,000 farmers in the Tennessee Valley were participating in the test-demonstration program by the summer of 1938 and twelve states outside the Valley were cooperating. According to the report, more than 61 million seedlings from TVA nurseries had been planted in the watershed and 645 landowners had joined the tree planting effort for the first time that year.

Some 13,000 men and women were employed by TVA on June 30, 1938. To fill technical, scientific, and management positions recruitment was on a nationwide basis, and from the country's most respected institutions of learning, graduates were arriving to apply their skills to the programs under way. For the labor force, varying in size with the demands of construction but usually about 60 per cent of total employment, recruitment was restricted to the region. Ph.D's and grade-school dropouts were working together for a common goal, to promote "the proper use, conservation, and development of the natural resources" of the Tennessee Valley. To a degree denied most agencies of government, objectives were clear and commanded allegiance.

The range of activities described in TVA's report for fiscal 1938 is impressive. But the document stands mute on the subject that dominated the news in the spring of 1938. There was grave trouble within the organization. For more than a year, steady progress in resource development had received little notice. In public attention, even litigation had taken second place to evidence of controversy on the Board of TVA. Arthur E. Morgan, the Chairman, had made public statements that appeared to question the veracity of his colleagues, to challenge their probity, and suggest malfeasance in office on the part of his fellow directors. His charges captured the headlines. On March 22, after a hearing in his White House office, the President of the United States had responded to the crisis by removing the Chairman from the position to which he had appointed him in 1933.

The association of the three men chosen to head the new agency was over. It ended in anger and distrust, in charges of impropriety and hints of corruption, but the decisions of the first Board had left an indelible mark on the corporation and on the region. The first half decade of its life had started TVA on the path it has pursued for almost forty years.

III

Three Men on a Board

Although the action of the President was rooted in Arthur Morgan's statements impugning the integrity of his associates, Harcourt Morgan and David Lilienthal, and his failure to observe acceptable administrative procedures, the removal of the Board Chairman was in fact the direct result of his contumacious conduct. He was, by dictionary definition, guilty of "obstinately resisting authority." During the several sessions of an extraordinary hearing in the office of the President, Arthur Morgan had refused to document or to withdraw "the grave and libelous" charges he had leveled against his colleagues over a period of many months. He denied any obligation to respond to the inquiries of the Chief Executive. He not only rejected the suggestion that he should resign, he challenged the right of the President to remove him. The President had no alternative. When he forwarded a transcript of the hearing and related material to the Congress, Roosevelt wrote in part:

> I call the attention of the Congress to the fact that on the evidence presented I was obliged to find that—(a) Arthur E. Morgan publicly made grave and libelous charges of dishonesty and want of integrity against his fellow directors, and when called upon to sustain them repeatedly refused to do so.
>
> (b) On the face of the record charges of the other directors that Arthur E. Morgan has obstructed the work of the Tennessee Valley

40

Authority were substantiated by proof, were not refuted and therefore must be accepted as true.

(c) Arthur E. Morgan was contumacious in refusing to give the
Chief Executive the facts, if any, upon which he based his charges
of malfeasance against his fellow directors, and in refusing to respond to questions of the Chief Executive relating to charges of
obstruction made against him by his fellow directors.

The record ultimately revealed that the Chairman's disenchant-
ment with his fellow directors was an early consequence of their
association, and that in the spring of 1936 he had unsuccessfully
tried to prevent the reappointment of Lilienthal, but it was not
until December of that year that he began his unhappy efforts to
destroy public confidence in his colleagues, the majority of the
Board, in the process risking the life of the agency he headed.
He made speeches, he wrote letters and articles for publication.
His charges were vague and generally undocumented, on occasions
only insinuations and innuendoes, but their purpose was clear.
With increasing vigor, Chairman Morgan was questioning the integrity of his associates.

He began with reasonable caution and somewhat obscurely,
first in a speech before the American Economic Association on
December 30, 1936. That was followed shortly by an article in the
New York Times of January 17, 1937. On April 26 came a speech
to the National Rivers and Harbors Congress, in August an article
in the Saturday Evening Post, in September a piece in the Atlantic
Monthly. All discussed TVA with particular emphasis on the
power program. All appeared while the agency was involved in
critical litigation. Many referred to negotiations between TVA and
private companies. They were encyclicals, gravely discussing those
standards of honesty and fairness which the author advanced as
his personal contribution to consideration of power problems, by
implication suggesting that they were not shared by his colleagues.
In an apparent effort to establish an atmosphere of even-handed
justice, some of the abuses of the private power companies might
be enumerated and then: "On the other hand, there are public
ownership advocates, sometimes open advocates, but sometimes
men who do not disclose their real purpose, who see nothing
to the power issue but a dramatic public battle which will mark
them as heroes." In the Atlantic Monthly article, after a lengthy

presentation of what he believed to be an appropriate relation between public and private power enterprises, Morgan wrote:

> The writer is a minority member of the Board of Directors of the Tennessee Valley Authority of which he is the Chairman. In important respects he differs from what he judges to be the actual power policy of his associates. This statement therefore reflects his personal views, and not the working policy of the TVA on the power issue. Neither does it undertake to criticize in detail what the writer believes to be the improprieties of that policy.

Improprieties undefined are teasing stimulants to a climate of distrust, and if a Board member who makes public witness to his devotion to honesty and fairness declares himself to be a minority, the standards of the majority inevitably become suspect.

Early in the sequence of statements, the Chairman referred to the relations between TVA and the private power companies —"what is primarily needed on both sides is common honesty and openness." Then he only hinted that honesty was lacking on the side on which he served, but as his confidence expanded his aspersions grew more specific and personal. Shortly before the meeting with the President, he wrote to a member of the House of Representatives, the late Maury Maverick of Texas, in a letter dated February 14, 1938, and published in the *New York Times* of March 7, reporting of his associates: "There is a practice of evasion, intrigue, and sharp strategy with remarkable skill and the malevolent habit of avoiding direct responsibility which makes Machiavelli seem open and candid."

By then, Harcourt Morgan and Lilienthal had taken steps to counterattack. In January, 1938, they had addressed a memorandum to the President stating that Chairman Morgan had been "guilty of actions which were not permissible in the conduct of his office." As the President pointed out in his communication to Congress, their charges were not made public by the directors. They were released by the White House. Unlike the Chairman, Harcourt Morgan and Lilienthal did not question the motives or integrity of their colleague. Their allegations did however illustrate the gulf between the majority and the Chairman, and as Arthur Morgan's accusations continued, the President concluded that the situation was of sufficient gravity to demand his official and public intervention.

The meeting held in the President's office on March 11, 1938, is probably unparalleled in the history of federal administration. All three Board members had been summoned. The President opened proceedings by stating:

> This conference is for the purpose of giving a hearing on grave charges which members of the Board of the Tennessee Valley have directed at each other. As Chief Executive, I cannot ignore charges of this character concerning an executive agency of the government. I have a responsibility to determine whether or not the facts bear them out and thereupon to take such action as may seem appropriate.

Roosevelt outlined the procedure he intended to follow:

> In these questions I shall first give to Chairman Morgan an opportunity to state facts supporting the charge he has made. As I finish with each charge I shall give the other directors an opportunity to reply. When Chairman Morgan has finished all of his charges I shall then follow the same procedure with Dr. Harcourt Morgan and Mr. Lilienthal with respect to the charges they have made, giving Chairman Morgan an opportunity in the same way to answer each of them.

Before describing the order of business, the President had turned to Arthur Morgan saying, "the time has come when, on your charges, it is necessary that I ask you to produce what is called a bill of particulars."

Stenographers were present and transcripts of the hearings were made available promptly and without correction to newsmen crowded in the anteroom, turning page after page to discover the response of Arthur Morgan to the President's request that he now produce his "evidence of dishonesty or malfeasance on the part of your colleagues." They read the Chairman's reply. He began by complaining that he had earlier and unsuccessfully "endeavored to secure the President's adequate consideration of grave conditions within the TVA" and concluded "I am of the opinion that this meeting is not, and in the nature of the case cannot be, an effective or useful fact-finding occasion." He declined to present evidence in support of his charges.

Despite the Chairman's refusal to participate, the inquiry went forward. The President endeavored to follow the procedure he had laid down, and reading from Arthur Morgan's published statements he asked the two directors for their replies to the accusations against them. To those charges that were sufficiently specific to permit an answer, responses were made in considerable detail, and supporting documents were offered in evidence. When the President had concluded his presentation of Arthur Morgan's charges, and the Chairman had again refused to offer any facts in support of his accusations, Roosevelt proceeded to examine the charges of the other directors.

Taking one by one their January catalogue of examples of his impermissible conduct, Harcourt Morgan and Lilienthal described how on two occasions the Chairman had interfered in the conduct of important litigation. In the "eighteen-company" case he had undertaken a series of personal conferences with prospective witnesses, and accused TVA attorneys of unethical conduct in their preparation of the case. In the opinion of his fellow directors, he had added dangerously to the strain under which the legal staff was laboring at a time when TVA's life was at stake. In another instance, they recounted how the Chairman had conveyed his lack of confidence in the agency presentation to the Commission hearing evidence in a condemnation proceeding and had insisted on appearing as a witness without conference with TVA counsel, an action that had led the majority of the Board to issue a public statement of protest and a defense of the lawyer involved. He had, his fellow directors alleged, intervened in delicate negotiations entrusted to others, conferred privately with TVA's adversaries, and attacked his colleagues publicly. As Chairman he had failed to carry out the decisions of the Board. All these well-documented incidents were, the majority contended, examples of the "actions . . . not permissible in the conduct of his office" that they had reported.

During every session of the inquiry (on March 11, 18, and 21), the President repeatedly urged Arthur Morgan to produce the evidence on which his charges against his colleagues had been based, emphasizing to his "old friend" the consequences of his obduracy. Failing to accomplish the presentation of supporting facts, at the final session the President said, "I feel myself under the painful duty of requesting Arthur E. Morgan at once publicly to withdraw the charges that he has made impugning the honesty, good faith, integrity and motives of his fellow directors . . . I make this request of him. If he cannot accede, it is his duty to resign." And later, "Chairman Morgan, I must tell you frankly, in the light of the record, that only two courses appear open—either your removal or your suspension as a member of the Board of the Tennessee Valley Authority."

To this, Chairman Morgan responded, "It is my judgment that my resignation at this time would not be in the public interest. Therefore, I do not tender my resignation. I also wish to say that I challenge the suggestion and deny the right and the power to remove or to suspend me."

So the White House inquiry ended on March 21. The following day, the President wrote to Arthur Morgan, advising him that "I feel obliged to remove, and do hereby remove, you as member and Chairman of the Board of the Tennessee Valley Authority." On March 23, in a special message, he informed Congress of his action, and outlined the basis of his decision. An opinion from the Acting Attorney General, Robert H. Jackson, advising the President of his authority to remove a director of the TVA, and a transcript of the hearing were attached.

In the judgment of the President, transmitted to Congress, "Arthur E. Morgan's whole attitude toward this inquiry in itself gives credence to the charge . . . that he is temperamentally unfitted to exercise a divided authority." If this soft impeachment is accurate, the circumstances attending the organization of TVA probably intensified the temperamental bias. Even before Congress had concluded action on the legislation creating the new agency, the President had selected Arthur Morgan for appointment to its Board, and indicated that he would be designated Chairman. Morgan had conferred with members of Congress during the final stages of enactment of the statute and the President had used him as a kind of talent scout in his search for the other directors. He had, in fact, recommended the appointments of his colleagues. His name was the first to be submitted to the Senate. He was the first to be confirmed, and at the beginning of TVA's life he clearly assumed leadership.

During the interval between his selection and the appointment of his associates, the Chairman had developed a number of proposals to submit to his colleagues and he had chosen persons for employment, subject to later ratification by his colleagues. At the first

Board meeting, at his suggestion his fellow directors gave him the additional title of General Manager, and it was clear that he expected to assume the executive responsibilities usually associated with the designation until a permanent general manager could be chosen. In any case, he would act until the other directors could devote full time to their new jobs. To begin his service with TVA, Harcourt Morgan had obtained a year's leave of absence from the University of Tennessee and he was obliged to give some time to assisting his successor in the presidency of that institution. Lilienthal had to make arrangements to move his family from Madison, Wisconsin, to Knoxville. Chairman Morgan, however, dedicated all his considerable energy to the task of getting the new agency under way.

The minutes of the early Board meetings reflect the wide range of his interests and the zeal with which he approached the task. On July 30, 1933, he presented twenty-two items as an "outline of elements" to be included in the activities of TVA. They ranged from such obvious responsibilities as commencement of construction of Cove Creek Dam (earlier that month named Norris) to the proposal that a commission be appointed "to study the proper function of the real estate man in organized society." The outline included recommendations that "a study of the succession of authority as a guide in our relations to organizing cooperatives" be undertaken, and the development of a "general social and economic plan" initiated.

Most of the items listed were related to the major responsibilities of TVA and were reasonable activities to consider, but the volume of suggestions and the velocity of their presentation were too much for Harcourt Morgan to endure. In the course of the congressional investigation that followed the Presidential inquiry, he testified that after the meeting of July 30 he had gone to his colleague David Lilienthal and stated that if conditions could not be corrected he would not be able to continue to serve on the Board. As a result, Lilienthal had joined with him in proposing that administrative responsibility for major programs be divided among the three Board members. Arthur Morgan, the only engineer on the Board, would be responsible for construction and as Chairman for the "integration of the parts of the program into a unified whole." Harcourt Morgan would be in charge of fertilizer development and agricultural activities; the power program, transportation, and legal matters were assigned to Lilienthal, who for a time also held the title of General Counsel. The talents of each one would be devoted to matters related to his background of training and experience.

All three directors regarded the division of responsibilities as a temporary measure. It proved to have serious disadvantages. Preoccupied with direct administrative tasks, the directors had too little time to function as a Board, and recommendations came to the Board from a member already committed to the proposal in question. It was not a good arrangement, but it was probably an essential make-shift in the beginning. It did ensure that the directors knew program details, and because of this initial immersion in the day-to-day problems of management it is likely that they were equipped more effectively to aid and judge the staff in the future than would otherwise have been the case. At the time, the Chairman appeared to accept the arrangement with good grace, although his hostility toward his associates may have begun at this early date. It is not unreasonable to regard their failure to ratify the proposals he offered and the resulting division of responsibility as the beginning of discord, for in his later testimony before the Joint Congressional Committee, Arthur Morgan revealed the resentment he experienced at the arrangement. At any rate and for whatever reasons, by the spring of 1936 the Chairman had determined that his relationship with Lilienthal was intolerable, and he endeavored to prevent the reappointment of his junior colleague.

The term of a TVA Board member is nine years, but to avoid the simultaneous termination of the services of all three directors and to provide future continuity, the initial appointments were for three, six, and nine years respectively. The Chairman was given the nine-year appointment, Harcourt Morgan the six-year tenure, and Lilienthal three. As the time approached for Lilienthal's term to expire, Chairman Morgan expressed his opposition to his colleague's reappointment to Senator Norris and the President, but despite their belief that the action would result in the Chairman's resignation, Lilienthal was reappointed and his selection confirmed by the Senate. At that date there was only a little public knowledge of the degree to which harmony on the Board was lacking and no understanding at all of the depth of the Chairman's distrust of his associates. Differences of opinion with respect to power policies were generally supposed to account for such difficulties as were recognized. Those differences were substantial. Perhaps they were basic to the whole controversy, but other issues were in conflict. There were divergent views with respect to forestry, the Chairman apparently sympathetic to the proposal for federal acquisition and regulation to which his colleagues were indifferent or opposed, and in fact the most publicized evidence of dissension involved a question of land condemnation, having no relation at all to power.

At the White House hearing, the President himself described one incident illustrating the Chairman's lack of confidence in his fellow directors. He told how Arthur Morgan had come to him earlier to complain about the administrative organization of TVA. The Chairman did not like the division of responsibility among members of the Board. The odd thing about this complaint is that the other two directors agreed. On May 22, 1936, only four days after Lilienthal's new term began, and almost two years before the White House hearing, the position of General Manager had been created. An Acting General Manager had been appointed with instructions to develop a scheme of organization, which would end the existing arrangement. A year later, the plan he submitted was approved and the word "Acting" was removed from his title. The troublesome system was abandoned, but harmony was not achieved, for Chairman Morgan did not approve of the General Manager selected. One of his proposals to the President had included the suggestion that he be permitted to "nominate" the General Manager and that decisions of the Board in policy matters must be unanimous to be effective. He did not trust his colleagues, the majority.

Public interest in administrative problems is limited, and the only questions fully discussed at the Presidential hearing were those raised by the majority of the Board. They related to administration. The two directors had documented their charges of Chairman Morgan's "impermissible" conduct, but his more intriguing accusations against them, suggesting malfeasance and corruption, were still enveloped in mystery when the sessions were adjourned and the Chairman removed.

At the White House sessions, Arthur Morgan had indicated
that he would testify only before a congressional committee. For
some time he had been demanding an investigation of TVA. By
this time, friend and foe agreed that an inquiry was essential, and
even before the White House sessions began, several resolutions
providing for an investigation had been introduced in Congress.
On April 4, 1938, a resolution creating a special Joint Committee to investigate TVA was approved. Five members from the
Senate and five from the House were selected for membership.
A distinguished lawyer, the late Francis Biddle of Philadelphia,
was engaged as chief counsel. A chief engineer was employed, a
secretary, an auditor, and a considerable staff. The nation awaited
revelation of the scandals promised by Arthur Morgan's attacks
in the press, with interest heightened by his refusal to disclose
his evidence to the President. On the Senate floor, the late Styles
Bridges, of New Hampshire, indicated the enticing expectations
when he announced that corruption "worse than Teapot Dome"
would be revealed. On May 25, the hearings opened in Washington. The caucus room in the Senate Office Building was jammed.
Former Chairman Morgan was the first witness.

Early in his statement, he recited his indictment. He said:

I have not charged that any director of the TVA has taken bribes
or stolen money nor have I charged that any director has profited
financially through any transaction of the Authority.

There are other and more subtle forms of failure to meet a public
trust which are no less a menace to good government.

My charges relate to the execution of public duty and responsibility by the majority of the Board. This has not been open, candid,
fair, and straight-forward, and hence it has not been honest administration of a great public trust.

To a good many observers, the former Chairman's statement
was disappointing. It was discouraging to opponents of TVA
to discover that the talents of the Committee and its staff were to
be employed in an investigation of such "subtle forms of failure"
as a lack of openness and candor. Sensation-seekers were still more
disgruntled when Morgan proceeded to the first item in a section
of his statement entitled "False and Misrepresentative Reports and
Statements." It seems that on September 14, 1936, Lilienthal had
used the homely phrase "starting from scratch" in a memorandum

to the President reporting on the progress of the power activities of TVA. Arthur Morgan contended that the words were misleading in introducing a discussion of revenues because TVA had not started "from scratch." The government had for some years sold power generated at Wilson Dam to the Alabama Power Company, which owned the only transmission line to the property.

Morgan ignored the fact that the memorandum was addressed to President Roosevelt, who was well aware of the situation. Privately and publicly, the President had deplored the once captive state of the hydro plant, and when the Committee of Conference submitted the question to him, he had insisted that the right of the government to build transmission lines be clearly stated in the Act. He would not have been misled by the introductory cliché, and the memorandum could not convict Lilienthal of the duplicity of which he stood accused. After the first day's hearing, discouraged newsmen faced the fact that revelations of scandal appeared unlikely. They could abstain from further attendance, but the Committee had to continue. It had the duty of investigating every one of Arthur Morgan's charges and those of his colleagues, every aspect of TVA's administration, and was obliged to report to Congress. For over a period of more than six months the inquiry went on, and the Committee report of almost 300 pages, not including minority views, is testimony to the diligence with which every topic was pursued.

At the end, the majority of the Committee concluded that Arthur Morgan's charges were groundless, adding, "Mr. Lilienthal and Dr. H. A. Morgan acted with forebearance and dignity during the severe strain to which they were subjected, and with due consideration for proper administrative discretion. This cannot be said of Dr. A. E. Morgan."

No one reading the record of the Presidential inquiry and the Joint Committee investigation can escape a sense of mystery. It is not hard to understand why Arthur Morgan may have regarded his fellow directors as subordinates and resented both their assumption of authority in the areas assigned to them and the public attention they received. It is not surprising to discover that men of great ability do not always like each other, nor work together in comfort. Jealousy is an endowment more widely shared than acknowledged, and differences of opinion are predictable. They are in fact desirable, for out of the tension of conflicting judgments wisdom often emerges. That is one of the virtues of a three-man directorate, and the record of TVA's first five years provides considerable evidence to demonstrate its worth. What is difficult to comprehend is the Chairman's apparent conviction that when his colleagues' opinions differed from his own it was proof of moral infirmity, sufficiently grave to justify public attacks upon them.

During the months when his aspersions against his fellow directors had been published from coast to coast, others had become convinced of the lonely rectitude he claimed—not surprisingly, for the Chairman's national reputation was more substantial than that of either of the other two. As a water control engineer, he was widely known. As an innovator in the field of education, he was respected. Because he talked and wrote so extensively about fair dealing, it was assumed that he was fair to his colleagues. That assumption gave the Chairman an advantage. But after months of the investigation he sought, it was clear that some charges of dishonesty were based on his imperfect appraisal of motives underlying reasonable differences of opinion, a few were the result of misunderstanding, and others appeared to be the consequence of erratic imagination or inconstant memory. Two charges he withdrew after listening to the evidence, although no information had been developed which was not available to him when he made the accusations. He stated that he had never meant to indicate that his colleagues were dishonest in the usual sense of the word. Yet during all the months when his charges were so interpreted there had been no explanation from him, no repudiation of the common understanding. So far as the public record stands, there was no word of regret or atonement.

Arthur Morgan brought suit to recover his position and his salary, but the action of the President was sustained by the courts, and the three men who had shared such great expectations in June, 1933, were never to meet together again. In spite of discord and strife, their accomplishments were impressive. A multipurpose program of resource development had been inaugurated. A force account construction program was a success. The principles of collective bargaining in a public agency had been accepted and were understood. An independent personnel system based on merit was working. Relations with other federal agencies and with more than fifty agencies of state and local governments had been established. The statute creating TVA had been defended successfully in the courts, and after an awkward beginning the function of the Board was clear. It was not to undertake the details of day-to-day management of the agency. The Board would make the decisions. It would give over-all supervision and provide leadership, but its determinations would be carried out by the staff. The directors had to accept responsibility for the conduct of every program and they were responsible for interpretation to the public. The pattern was established.

Together with the colleagues he attacked, the former Chairman had made a lasting contribution to the agency whose future he had placed in jeopardy. An excellent engineering staff had been assembled under his leadership, and a good many of his unacceptable proposals had stimulated decisions endorsing similar goals but employing methods more compatible with TVA's assignment. While establishing a code of conduct for real estate dealers and defining their "proper function in organized society" seemed to the majority of the Board an inappropriate responsibility for TVA to assume, the suggestion did call attention to a problem that had been sharply illustrated by the activities of speculators at the time the Ford offer was pending. The Chairman's concern may have hastened adoption of a no-price-trading policy for TVA's land acquisition, conferences with real estate boards in the area, and publicity designed to reduce the opportunity for speculators to profit.

A code of ethics for employees developed by Arthur Morgan was never officially presented to his colleagues but informally discussed, and because it assumed a right to intrude on the private lives of staff it was received with disfavor. Nevertheless, its consideration may have expedited the development of administrative codes and the inclusion of standards of official conduct that the agency had a right to demand. Long before such prohibitions were adopted by federal agencies generally, TVA forbade acceptance of gifts or favors from those with whom its employees dealt. Ideas are important even if they are not viable as administrative guides. Responses and reactions provide a basis for progress, and in TVA's first years the fertile imagination of the Chairman generated suggestions, which, with the measured responses of his fellow directors, created a climate hospitable to accomplishment.

A former member of TVA's legal staff, one who had suffered

Arthur Morgan's displeasure, summed it up when he said, "It was essential for the Chairman to be removed, but it was just as necessary for him to be appointed. The President was right both times."

When the disharmony among the directors became evident a good many people concluded that the concept of a full-time Board itself was on trial. It is true that such an arrangement presents difficulties—there were to be abrasive periods in TVA's later history—but it is equally true that no administrative device is free from problems. There is no way to manage large public enterprises with constant ease and invariable grace. Appointment of a single administrator is no guarantee of wise leadership nor internal harmony, nor is there much evidence to recommend a part-time Board. If judgment is based on a survey of the achievements of TVA's first years, the three-man Board merits high praise, and in succeeding years the triumvirate was to work effectively. One lesson was clear from the experience of the first half decade. Majority rule must prevail, and the allegiance of the staff must be to the Board as a whole, never to a single member. In later years, that well-established principle was to be a safeguard against schism.

The intervention of the President saved TVA, and provided a footnote for the specialists in public administration who write about the relationship of the Chief Executive to those independent agencies of government, including corporations, which are responsible to him directly. Generally, the experts tend to disparage such instrumentalities, holding that their existence involves an excessive burden on the President, demanding too much of his time and attention. Usually, they propose consolidation of independent agencies in existing departments or new ones to be created. This is a curious remedy. It is difficult to understand how the burdens of the Chief Executive would be lightened and his time conserved if problems requiring his attention were presented by an official at least one degree removed from the issues rather than by those immediately responsible. The critics tend to ignore the real remedy for the situation they deplore. The burdens on the President are not diminished by developing new channels for the referral of problems to him, but by discovering ways to settle questions where they arise. The TVA statute was designed to do just that and with the exception of the first few years, the agency has not required a great deal of Presidential attention.

It was natural that President Roosevelt should have devoted considerable time to TVA. After all, it was his dream. The agency was in its formative years, and the activities it was initiating related to problems then prominent in public attention. The record discloses a good many conferences between him and members of the TVA Board. Some of them were inspired by the President's desire to learn from TVA experience. Others were caused by the intervention of self-appointed mediators in the conflict with private power companies. Many of them resulted from Arthur Morgan's charges. Their number was sharply reduced when tranquility on the Board was achieved, when TVA procedures became reasonably well established, and when, with the conclusion of litigation and the later purchase of utility properties, some major disputes were settled. None of President Roosevelt's successors has had the same deep interest in TVA, and there have been relatively few occasions for conferences between the chief executive and the Board in recent years, but, with the single exception of periods during the Administration of President Dwight D. Eisenhower, relations between the agency and the White House have been cordial and undemanding throughout the life of TVA.

While some critics believe that independent agencies should be abolished because they may demand too much of the President's attention, others advance a contrary claim. They suggest that the Executive has too little control over their operations. There is scant merit in either contention. It is true that TVA is not responsive to the quadrennial elections in the way that many federal agencies are, with leadership changes inevitable when a new Administration is installed. By statute and tradition, it is somewhat isolated from the political scene. The TVA Board, which is low in the pecking order of the federal bureaucracy, is nonpartisan, not bipartisan, and the staggered terms of its members give continuity through Administration changes. Nevertheless, any President has great influence and genuine control over the agency. The statute is clear. The President nominates the directors and designates the Chairman, and with those acts the fate of the organization is ultimately determined.* Every year, the President's decision with re-

* President Roosevelt made eight appointments to the Board, but only four individuals were selected. By reappointment, he filled the vacancies as they arose. President Truman appointed three members, President Eisenhower four, President Kennedy two, President Johnson one, and President Nixon reappointed the Chairman initially appointed by President Kennedy, and has made one new appointment.

spect to the appropriations he will request of Congress establishes priorities in all programs supported by monies from the Treasury, and the Administration's approval or disapproval of legislation affecting TVA directly or indirectly is always influential and frequently decisive. These are important and routine channels of control. They exist whether the President in office is interested in TVA, indifferent or disapproving, and members of the White House and Executive Office staffs will make certain that every one is used to express their understanding of his position. If a President believes in TVA, his concern can be a vital stimulant to the agency and an endorsement to the public. Adversaries soon discover if he is hostile and TVA, without the shield of executive approval, is open to attack.

Every President has influenced the course of TVA's progress but in almost forty years there have been only two instances of interventions by a chief executive to accomplish objectives contrary to the judgment of the agency, and in neither case was the action effective. In an episode discussed in Chapter VI, President Eisenhower used his authority to order another independent body, the Atomic Energy Commission, to enter into a contract considered adverse to the interests of TVA and an invasion of its responsibility. Later, in 1961, President Kennedy, at the request of a senator, addressed a letter to the Board that was made public and widely interpreted as urging the location of a steam generating plant at a site known to have been recommended by the legislator. In the first example, the contract was cancelled before it became operative. In the second, TVA did not construe the letter as a directive. Respectfully, the arguments presented were rebutted, and, without protest from the President, the plant was located where the Board determined it should be placed to provide electricity to the consumers of the region at the "lowest possible rates" as the Act directs. That was the end of the matter. The removal of Arthur E. Morgan from the Board of TVA remains the only example of effective intervention by a President beyond conventional and routine requirements. It was a burden to the Chief Executive, but Franklin Roosevelt had to act to fulfill his obligation as head of the government of which TVA is a part.

IV

An Investigation: TVA Seen Whole

When the three directors appeared before the Chief Executive at the White House, the sessions were limited in objective. Early in the inquiry the President identified the scope of the proceeding. He said, "I am not concerned at this hearing with the pros and cons of any particular policy that the TVA Board has or has not adopted . . . It is an inquiry into charges of personal and official misconduct."

The investigation by the Joint Committee was broader. It, too, had been prompted by Arthur Morgan's accusations and all his charges would be considered, but the resolution creating the Committee went further. It included a general directive to make a "full and complete investigation" of TVA, with subsections from "a" through "s" listing specific questions for exploration. The wide range of the Committee's probings caused more than a hundred persons to take their turn in the witness chair. Representatives of private utility companies appeared, and of the fertilizer industry. Landowners and labor organizations were heard. Fourteen of TVA's twenty-one department heads were examined, and written statements for the record were submitted by another five. Fourteen printed volumes with a total of over 6,000 pages record the sessions. The Committee Report, with minority views and exhibits, provides two more volumes, and still another contains engineering reports and related materials.

During two days in Washington, the opening statements of the former Chairman and the two directors were presented. Charges and countercharges were offered, accusations and responses began, to be continued over the months of inquiry. Then the Committee moved to the Tennessee Valley where it inspected TVA projects before resuming hearings on July 18, 1938. The sessions in Knoxville opened with a change of pace. Harcourt A. Morgan, who had been designated Board Chairman by the President after Arthur E. Morgan's removal, was the first witness. For the moment ignoring the dissension recorded at the introductory meetings in Washington, he offered the Committee a quiet lecture on what would today be described as ecology. As a basis for their understanding of the functions of TVA, he outlined the relation of land and water:

> In the rains and the water is vast energy—energy which can destroy by erosion and by flood, or which can be captured and used as sustenance for plants and animals as well as for water power . . .
> These facts of nature—land and water—are not separable. The unwise use of the land by the destruction of its crop and forest cover hastens destruction of that soil by the water falling from above. Just one inch of rainfall on one acre of land weighs about 113 tons. Multiply that by averages of 40 or 50 inches per year and consider that that rain is falling upon millions of sloping, tilled acres, and we can gain some conception of the vast forces of nature with which we are concerned. When the water falling upon the land runs off over the land, rather than through it, the severity and suddenness of floods along the main stream are increased. And the erratic flow prevents the normal use of that stream for navigation and commerce.

The new Chairman described the topography of the watershed of the Tennessee. From the east, where forested mountains tower more than 6,000 feet, it ranges downward to Paducah, Kentucky, its western extremity, only a little more than 300 feet above sea level. He summarized the Valley's major resource problems, the floods to which it was subject and the 7 million acres of eroded farm land that denied the people a living and frustrated their hopes for the future. He emphasized that selection of the Tennessee

Valley for an experiment in unified resource development was "providential because no region presents in bolder relief the maladjustments of these fundamentals [land and water] and I might add the potential promise for human welfare which an adjustment of those fundamentals will produce."

He outlined what TVA proposed to do about the conditions he had described and to the seven Committee members present—two from Ohio, one each from Pennsylvania, New York, North Dakota, New Jersey and Texas—he gently stressed the national significance of the whole TVA program:

> . . . the unified attack upon these fundamental problems, if it might lay the basis for reversing the inevitable trend toward impoverishment in this southeastern region since the days of the War between the States, would rebound to the benefit of the entire nation.
>
> For I cannot believe that the gradual depletion of any section of the nation can be other than a cancerous growth which must affect adversely the entire national well-being. The loss of a national market and the growing burden of relief are obvious effects. But the real tragedy is a human one. It is the fact of degrading poverty in contrast to the potentiality of plenty.

Harcourt Morgan gave the Committee a review of the major problems of the watershed, a summary of TVA's purposes and programs. Before the investigation ended there would be further testimony on every subject raised in his general statement, but first Arthur Morgan took the stand again to elaborate on his charges against his former colleagues, providing in generous detail the evidence he had refused to submit to the President. He replied to the accusations of his impermissible conduct presented by his former associates, and the two directors responded to the complaints he made against them. For eighteen sessions, conflict between the Board members was the central theme. Then, for a respite, the Committee turned to an exploration of the administration of TVA.

Organization and Budget

The General Manager outlined the plan of organization adopted by the Board. The year was 1938, but with little modification his statement could be repeated today. At the time TVA's first General Manager spoke, the office he held had been established about two years. Its evolution had been described at the President's inquiry. In January, 1934, while direct administrative responsibilities were still divided between the three Board members a "Coordinator" had been selected, and in May, 1936, immediately after Lilienthal's reappointment, the Office of General Manager was established. The Coordinator was appointed Acting General Manager and instructed by the Board to prepare a plan of organization for the agency. In 1937, his plan was approved, and the basic arrangements have prevailed for almost forty years.

The organization chart submitted to the Committee by the General Manager was printed as an exhibit accompanying its report. (See Chart 1.) It reflected Harcourt Morgan's discussion of the relationship between land and water. Under the heading "Water Control in the River Channels," the responsibilities of the Office of the Chief Engineer were depicted. Three subordinate units, then called departments, were charged first with planning, then designing, and finally building the structures required to promote the purposes of the Act. "Water Control on the Land" recognized the activities related to achieving more productive use of the rainfall by the soil. It presented the functions of the Office of the Chief Conservation Engineer with three pendant boxes indicating the division of work among the Agricultural Relations, Forestry, and Chemical Engineering departments. A third Office, that of Chief Power Economist, was simply called Water Power Utilization, its responsibilities divided between a Planning and an Operations Department. Those were the major program divisions. They occupied the center of the chart.

At the left side, under what was described as a Management Service Council, the half dozen departments serving all programs were shown, Personnel, Finance, Legal, Materials, Land Acquisition, and Office Service. On the right a balancing Regional Planning Council was made up of five departments, Regional Planning Studies, Health and Safety, Commerce, Agricultural Industries, and Reservoir Properties.

All these activities were shown suspended from the Office of the General manager whose authority was derived by delegation from the Board, its primacy indicated by the use of larger type at the top of the presentation. Two of the General Manager's assistants

Chart 1

TENNESSEE VALLEY AUTHORITY
Organization as of 1937

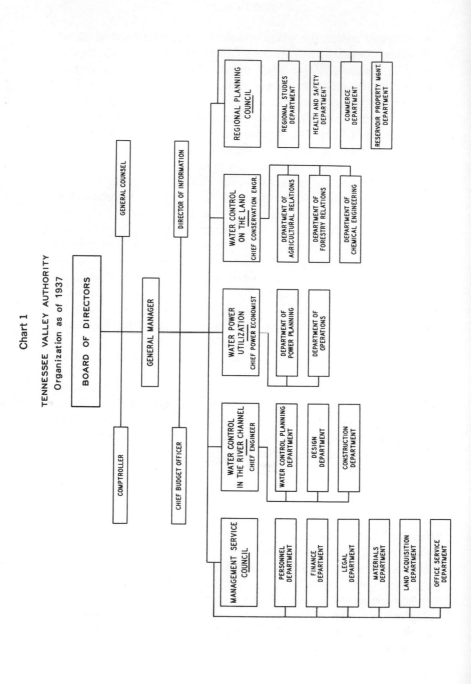

BOARD OF DIRECTORS

GENERAL COUNSEL

COMPTROLLER

GENERAL MANAGER

CHIEF BUDGET OFFICER

DIRECTOR OF INFORMATION

REGIONAL PLANNING COUNCIL
- REGIONAL STUDIES DEPARTMENT
- HEALTH AND SAFETY DEPARTMENT
- COMMERCE DEPARTMENT
- RESERVOIR PROPERTY MGNT DEPARTMENT

WATER CONTROL ON THE LAND
CHIEF CONSERVATION ENGR.
- DEPARTMENT OF AGRICULTURAL RELATIONS
- DEPARTMENT OF FORESTRY RELATIONS
- DEPARTMENT OF CHEMICAL ENGINEERING

WATER POWER UTILIZATION
CHIEF POWER ECONOMIST
- DEPARTMENT OF POWER PLANNING
- DEPARTMENT OF OPERATIONS

WATER CONTROL IN THE RIVER CHANNEL
CHIEF ENGINEER
- WATER CONTROL PLANNING DEPARTMENT
- DESIGN DEPARTMENT
- CONSTRUCTION DEPARTMENT

MANAGEMENT SERVICE COUNCIL
- PERSONNEL DEPARTMENT
- FINANCE DEPARTMENT
- LEGAL DEPARTMENT
- MATERIALS DEPARTMENT
- LAND ACQUISITION DEPARTMENT
- OFFICE SERVICE DEPARTMENT

were the Director of Information and the Chief Budget Officer, shown as directly responsible to him, and in addition to their administrative duties as heads of the Finance and Legal departments, the Comptroller and the General Counsel were directly responsible to the Board for their professional obligations, the disbursement of funds and rendering of legal opinions.

There have been reorganizations since that diagram was produced, and changes in nomenclature. The Management Service and Regional Planning Councils have disappeared. The word "Department" is no longer used. "Division" is preferred. Although the title "Office" has been retained to indicate major program segments, subordinate units under divisions have had a variety of appellations. They are not always shown on charts, but within TVA they usually have been called branches or sections. To avoid confusion with traditional government usage, the word "Bureau" has never been employed. Bureaus, units in the old-line agencies of the federal government, are often created by statute and their duties defined by Congress, not by the department in which they are lodged. That is not true of TVA. The structure of its organization is determined by the Board responding to Section 3 of the Act requiring the directors to provide a system "to fix responsibility and promote efficiency." It changes as the emphasis of programs change. Bulletins defining the responsibilities of each office or division are revised as new activities are undertaken or completed projects laid aside. The squares, the circles, and lines of organization charts move as consolidations or partitions of responsibility seem to be desirable, but the plan of communication is the same, and that is what such charts reveal.

The present-day organization chart (see Chart 2) shows that the decision-making process in TVA has been perfected and adjusted but not altered. To the General Manager, the Board still delegates responsibility for day-to-day administration. Recommendations and reports from division or office heads come to the Board through him. He prepares the agenda for Board meetings and provides the three members with the supporting material required for their decision. He arranges informal meetings of Board and staff for discussion of problems and opportunities seen to be developing, and to report progress on programs under way. That is the way it was in 1938. It is the way it is today.

Chart 2

ORGANIZATION OF THE TENNESSEE VALLEY AUTHORITY

NOVEMBER 12, 1970

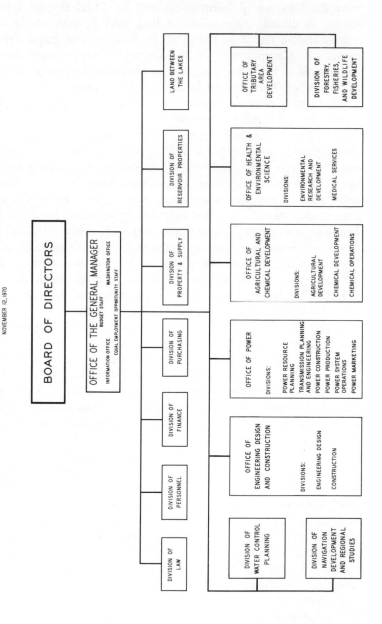

Then as now, preparation of the annual budget was a function lodged in the Office of the General Manager, and the Chief Budget Officer was named one of his assistants. Like all federal agencies financed wholly or in part by appropriations from the Treasury, TVA must begin to develop its requests for funds more than a year in advance of the time when the money can become available. In early summer, each division supported by appropriations must decide how much money will be required in the fiscal year beginning July 1 of the following year and ending June 30 twelve months later. Conferences begin in small units, at Chattanooga, Muscle Shoals, and Knoxville, where major administrative offices are located. When the head of the Office or Division has completed his study of the recommendations of his staff, his conclusions are submitted to the Budget Office and to the General Manager. The estimates are scrutinized. The examination is not confined to the future plans reflected in the request proposed. It includes a survey of the way current funds are being used, the record of the past. There are informal conferences with the directors. Out of this sifting process a budget for the agency is prepared and in early autumn submitted to the Board by the General Manager with a recommendation for adoption. Spirited discussions between Board and staff usually result as the proposals are reviewed, and finally the Board approves an appropriation request to submit for consideration by the Office of Management and Budget (until 1970 the Bureau of the Budget) established in the Executive Office of the President.

Some time in the autumn, hearings are held before the Budget examiners in Washington. The inquiry involves not only the activities supported by appropriations, but the expenditures estimated to be made from TVA proceeds, principally the income from power and fertilizer sales. Section 26 of the TVA Act permits the Board to use these proceeds "in the operation of dams and reservoirs, in conducting its business in generating, transmitting, and distributing electric energy and in manufacturing, selling, and distributing fertilizer and fertilizer ingredients." Although the statute lists together all those activities eligible to be supported by proceeds, from the beginning power earnings have been devoted to power purposes alone, and the income from fertilizer sales has been applied to the costs of operating the plants that produce the materials. No action by the Office of Management and Budget or Congress is required with respect to the use of proceeds, but reports and estimates are provided for the information of the Administration, Congress, and the public at the same time and in the same document that presents TVA's request for the appropriation of funds from the Treasury.

The examination by the staff of the Office of Management and Budget is extensive, and when a figure for TVA's appropriation request is finally established it is included in what is called "the President's" budget. This is the amount presented to Congress for its consideration. It may not approach the sum requested, but it is the figure that must be supported and defended by TVA witnesses before the Appropriations Committees of the House and Senate. That is the rule.

This procedure appeared to be reasonably familiar to members of the Investigating Committee. With the exception of the presentation of estimates reflecting the proposed use of proceeds, offered to Congress for information but not requiring action, it was no different from the practice followed by federal agencies generally. TVA's Chief Budget Officer described in great detail the way in which the funds were allocated within TVA and their use reported and checked during the fiscal year. One incident illustrating internal procedures captured the attention of the investigators. It appeared that the head of the Department of Chemical Engineering realized the necessity of acquiring additional phosphate lands to supply the plant he managed at Muscle Shoals, and in fiscal year 1937 an opportunity to purchase some exceptionally desirable properties unexpectedly emerged. At the time that the estimates for the year had been prepared, the possibility of the acquisition had not been foreseen. To meet the situation the department head presented a recommendation for the purchase and a request for a budget adjustment to the Chief Budget Officer and through him to the General Manager and the Board. To accomplish the transaction, he proposed to shift funds intended for other purposes within his program. The Board approved, and it was possible for the change to be made and the acquisition to be accomplished because Congress has traditionally provided a lump sum rather than an item-by-item appropriation for TVA. This was apparently a surprise to the probing members of the Committee, although it had resulted in a level of economy and efficiency that would have been otherwise impossible.

The lump sum appropriation is a particularly important device for promoting economy in a river control program where construction of several projects may be under way in any fiscal year. When the request for funds is presented, estimates indicate the amount expected to be spent for each one, but weather is no respecter of fiscal years nor of budget estimates, and weather affects construction schedules, sometimes slowing progress severely. There may be other obstacles to achievement. Delay in delivery of materials may postpone expenditures on some projects. At the same time, unanticipated opportunities to expedite completion of others may appear. Under the method by which Congress made funds available to TVA, it was possible for work to be accelerated at sites where favorable conditions prevailed when it was delayed elsewhere. More than estimated might be spent at one project in a given fiscal year, less at another, but efficient schedules could be maintained and total costs reduced. Detailed reports of current use of funds are submitted as part of the budget document every year. Changes from estimates presented earlier are disclosed and justified, responsibility is accepted.

Under an item-by-item system of appropriating funds, procedures would be a good deal more rigid. Unless authorization for fund transfers had been included in the appropriation bill, money that could not be spent on the specific project or activity for which it had been appropriated could not be spent at all. Changed circumstances could not be recognized. If more funds than provided were required because of exceptional conditions, a supplemental amount would have to be sought, and every step in procedure repeated—a necessity not encouraging prudent estimates, but prompting inflated requests with a built-in escalation for security, and in the end less pressure for economy in expenditures.

The advantages of the lump-sum procedure were familiar to TVA. Without it, the flexibility embodied in the basic Act would be restricted, the intent of the legislation frustrated. At times, its benefits suffer infringement. On occasion, committee reports go into detail with respect to the recommended allocation of funds, sometimes limitations are written into appropriation bills, but on the whole and over the years the advantages of a lump-sum appropriation have been available to TVA just as they were described to the Investigating Committee in 1938. Vital to the success of the construction program, the method provided a means of economy and a prod to efficiency for activities other than streamflow control. It encouraged both prudence and innovation. It was of considerable interest to some members of the Committee, however, and their curiosity was stimulated because acquisition of the phosphate lands had been achieved by the flexibility it provided. The purchase had been the subject of some local gossip, an expression of disapproval by the General Accounting Office, and an insinuation of irregularity (withdrawn during the course of the hearing) by Arthur Morgan. Harcourt Morgan was questioned about it at length, and Harry Curtis, then head of the Chemical Engineering Department, later a member of the Board of TVA, recited the circumstances prompting his recommendation. The General Manager testified on the matter as well as the Chief Budget Officer, the General Counsel, the head of the Land Acquisition Department, and TVA's Chief Geologist. Copies of correspondence and memoranda were submitted by TVA, reports of geologic explorations and of appraisers. The files presented for Committee examination were enormous.

Because the GAO report had referred to rumors that the transaction had been accompanied by bribery, graft, and fraud, with intimations that TVA's representatives might have been "incompetent, criminally negligent, or worse," the Committee referred the matter for investigation by the Department of Justice. The Criminal Division of that department and the Federal Bureau of Investigation made a thorough study of the charges and reported to the Committee, "We are of the opinion that the rumors pointing to criminality on the part of the Tennessee Valley Authority officials are unfounded and fictitional [sic] in character." The Joint Committee probed further. To review the technical question involved, that is the value of the mineral deposits acquired by TVA, the services of an interdepartmental committee made up of qualified specialists from the departments of Agriculture and the Interior were made available. That group found TVA investigations were proper, its prospecting methods in accordance with good engineering practice, the prices paid not unduly high, and the material of suitable quality for its use. When the inquiry was over, the Committee Report pointed out that the suggestion of fraud by GAO representatives "was made solely on the basis of superficial examinations, rumor, and hearsay," adding tartly: "The Committee has commented elsewhere on the tendency of the General Accounting Office investigators to question transactions on which they are not qualified to pass." The amount of money involved in the transaction was something over half a million dollars, small today, but in the course of the Committee's exploration a method had been surveyed, an advantage illustrated, and the operations of the chemical plant described.

LAND ACQUISITION—BY PURCHASE OR CONDEMNATION

The purchase of mineral deposits was a special case but TVA's general land buying procedures were something of an innovation. The head of the Land Acquisition Department described how the no-trading policy worked. In the purchase of reservoir properties, for example, he told how, after the engineering staff had determined the "taking line," the work of acquisition was turned over to the division of which he was in charge. First, a field appraiser inspected the property. Then his recommendation was reviewed by a committee of three and when agreement upon price had been reached it was submitted to the landowner. The TVA employees authorized to make the offer were not empowered to negotiate. If the proposal proved to be unacceptable to the owner, condemnation procedures were initiated. And under the TVA Act those were different from the conventional government arrangements.

The Department of Justice handles condemnation cases for most federal agencies. The TVA statute* provided that the corporation itself could institute such actions and set up a special procedure to follow. Proceedings were to be undertaken in the U.S. district court having jurisdiction over the area where the property was located, and the court was directed to appoint three commissioners "who shall be disinterested persons and who shall take and subscribe an oath that they do not own any lands, or interest or easement in any lands, which it may be desirable for the United States to acquire in the furtherance of said project, and such commis-

---

* Amended in 1968 with respect to these provisions, the changes described in Chapter XI.

sioners shall not be selected from the locality wherein the land sought to be condemned lies." The commissioners were authorized to hold hearings, receive evidence, and "to take such appropriate steps as may be proper for the determination of . . . value." Their report was filed in the court and their judgment was final unless appeals were taken by either side within twenty days. Appeals were heard by three federal district judges unless the parties stipulated that a lesser number might act. Further recourse to the Court of Appeals was authorized.

The statutory provisions had been carefully drafted. They were intended to correct some of the abuses alleged to arise from reliance on the jury system to determine land values. The procedure was working well in the Tennessee Valley, but there was little evidence that the Committee was deeply interested in appraising the unusual provisions. They were concerned primarily with the handling of one proceeding that had prompted Arthur Morgan to make statements widely interpreted as accusations of misconduct on the part of his colleagues. This was the Berry marble case, now long forgotten but a *cause célèbre* at the time. The *New York Times* of March 4, 1938, for example, carried a statement issued by the Chairman on the previous day in which he proclaimed his mission "to fight for certain decencies and proprieties in public life which are more important to good government than any particular government program." He cited the Berry marble claims as an instance of the necessity for his crusade. In his letter to Representative Maury Maverick, published in the *Times* two days later, Morgan stated, "The Berry marble claims, in my opinion, were an effort at a deliberate, barefaced steal. . . . The public and the Congress do not yet know the extent to which that was improperly handled."

For sixteen days, the Committee heard evidence relating to the Berry case. Eighteen witnesses were called. Some 1,000 pages record their testimony. In brief summary of this lengthy record, it appears that between January and July of 1932, prior to the creation of TVA, certain mineral and marble leases in the Clinch River valley were acquired by a group, including the late George Berry. At the time of the Committee hearings, he was a Senator from Tennessee and had previously been an official of the National Recovery Administration, but he did not hold public office when the leases were obtained.

The leaseholders put a value of several million dollars on the properties and claimed substantial damages because construction of Norris Dam had flooded some of the lands involved, and created access problems if other portions were to be developed. TVA geologists believed the holdings were not suitable for commercial operations and their judgment was supported by others called in as expert consultants. There were conferences between the two parties. The leaseholders were stubborn, but at one point an agreement was reached to submit the question of value to the Director of the Bureau of Mines. The "conciliator," as the Director was called in the proposed arrangement, would have no power to bind either party, he could not testify, nor could his report be used in commission or court proceedings. TVA witnesses before the Committee testified that they had expected his judgment to support the agency position and believed it might convince the claimants of the lack of merit in their claims.

Chairman Morgan opposed the agreement. He was influenced by the fact that although there was at the time no actual evidence of fraud, there were fairly widespread suspicions that the leases had been obtained, not for the purpose of producing marble for the market but in expectation that a dam on the Clinch River would ultimately be constructed by the government and that a damage claim might then be supported. It was a reasonable supposition. Such a project had been included in the plans of the U.S. Army Engineers and in the vetoed Norris bills. Arthur Morgan believed that TVA should not deal with the Berry group as long as there was a question of its ethical standards, a reminder of the position taken by him in July, 1933, when he proposed to his colleagues a study of the "proper function of the real estate man in organized society," to be followed by the development of a policy defining a code of ethics and a refusal by TVA to deal with those who would not subscribe to its terms.

As Chairman, Morgan forwarded to the Secretary of the Interior the Board's request for the services of the Director of the Bureau of Mines, but at the same time he revealed his own opposition to the proposal and the Secretary not unreasonably found it prudent to reply that the Director had commitments that would prevent him from undertaking the assignment. With the failure of this proposed arrangement, TVA proceeded to condemnation. The petition was filed on May 13, 1937, almost a year before the Presidential inquiry, and months before the series of statements by the Chairman that appeared to suggest collusion by his colleagues in the "barefaced steal." On March 3, 1938, the Condemnation Commission had filed its report, finding that the leases were without value and the claimants not entitled to an award, a judgment that was appealed.

The Berry case had assumed major importance in the press, and despite the favorable decision of the Condemnation Commission, it was the Committee's responsibility to consider whatever evidence Arthur Morgan was prepared to offer in support of his suggestions of dereliction on the part of the Board majority. As it turned out, he had no proof of malfeasance to offer. He had been opposed to the so-called conciliation agreement, which had been recommended by TVA's attorneys. That was well known. The proposed arrangement was unusual, but the eminence of the person selected to act as conciliator and the limited nature of his responsibility was a guarantee that no chicanery was involved and that the interest of the government was protected. Testimony before the Investigating Committee made clear that the Chairman's distrust was not limited to his disapproval of the agreement and that it was not allayed when the proposal was abandoned and condemnation proceedings initiated. It was, in fact, extended to the TVA attorney in charge of the case, as the other directors had testified at the White House hearing. They had described to the President how on the last day of the trial Morgan had advised the Condemnation Commission that in his judgment the case had not been adequately presented and, refusing to discuss his testimony with TVA's attorney, he had appeared to recite his suspicions of the Berry group, and his differences with his fellow directors.

Morgan's testimony was unnecessary. Evidence of bad faith on the part of the leaseholders had been discovered shortly before proceedings began and introduced by TVA's attorney, a circumstance of which the Chairman should have been aware. In rendering its decision some months later, the Commission made no reference to the issue of fraud, but held on the question of value that there was no merit in the contention of the leaseholders. Arthur Morgan listened to the testimony before the Joint Committee. He heard the sworn statements of certain subordinate staff members who by confidential reports to him had encouraged his doubts of the man who supervised them and in the end he rose in the hearing room to withdraw the accusation he had made against the TVA attorney, Evans Dunn. He said:

> . . . I have criticized his conduct in the preparation and trial of the condemnation case. When this criticism was made I had what I could not but believe was clear proof of its accuracy in every detail. His associates had talked with me. I had been told flatly that Mr. Dunn was not willing to push or even go on with the search for evidence of bad faith. I had made careful inquiry as to the reliability of those who had talked with me. In the light of this careful inquiry, my position as to the inadequate preparation of the case seemed fully justified . . .
>
> In justice both to Mr. Dunn and to myself, I must say that statements of witnesses before this committee have differed in very important respects from what they told me prior to my making any criticism. Not only that, but certain statements made to me do not appear in the testimony at all, and I must assume that these men have come to the conclusion that they misstated or overstated to me the facts with respect to the preparation and the conduct of the trial. I want the committee to know that I have been very much impressed with Mr. Dunn's testimony here . . . The case was won. I think Mr. Dunn ought to have the credit due him free from criticism. On his own testimony before this committee and also on the principle that all's well that ends well, I ask the committee to strike from the record any criticism that I have made of Mr. Dunn.

For his statement the former Chairman was warmly commended by members of the Joint Committee and its counsel, although the Committee Report later pointed out:

> When Dr. Morgan made his charges in 1938, he could have ascertained the circumstances that, when brought out before this committee, led him to withdraw his charges. His action in publishing these unfounded accusations, and failing to clarify his position when it was subjected to an interpretation much more unfavorable to the Authority than he intended, indicates a lack of sober consideration, and was unwarranted and improper.

The interpretation to which the Committee referred was illustrated by an account carried in at least two newspapers, the Chicago *Journal of Commerce* and the New York *Herald-Tribune*.

Both reported "Bluntly, Dr. Morgan charged that only his inter-vention had prevented the consummation of an agreement whereby his two colleagues would have permitted Senator George L. Berry, Democrat, of Tennessee to 'exploit,' 'hold up,' and 'defraud' the government." Until the hearings before the Joint Committee, there had been no correction of such conclusions although the former Chairman then testified that he had not intended to indicate that his colleagues were willing that the claimants should be paid more than the economic value of the claim. He was disturbed, he testi-fied, by an impression of what he described as a certain "tender-ness" toward the claimants, an attitude vehemently denied by the Board majority.

The conduct of the Berry case had been the basis of some of the gravest charges against Harcourt Morgan and David Lilienthal, and the Chairman's interference in the proceeding was one of the examples of impermissible conduct described by his colleagues at the White House hearing. It was one of the most time-consuming subjects reviewed by the Committee, but other charges were ex-plored with equal care. Testimony was heard on every allegation of the two directors, and on the formidable array of examples the former Chairman had amassed to illustrate his general theme of lack of integrity on the part of the other two directors. Detailed replies and lengthy rebuttals were presented. Under oath, individ-uals involved recited their stories. Recollections were compared with records. Conflicts were reconciled. Much was tedious and disappointing to headline-seekers, but as witness after witness was sworn in the federal court room in Knoxville the facts emerged. Ambition and malice were uncovered, gossip and rumor revealed. Dignity, decency, and honor were disclosed. Because of the total catharsis, there was little rancor when the examinations were over, and it was largely due to the extensive hearings conducted by the Joint Committee that the organization emerged unscathed by the dissension on its Board. There were no lingering doubts and un-certainties when the investigation was completed. There was noth-ing to wonder about any more. It was all in the record.

When the Committee reported in April, 1939, its general com-ment on the former Chairman's charges was brief. It read: "The Committee is of the opinion that Dr. A. E. Morgan's charges of dishonesty are without foundation; are not supported by the evidence; and, made without adequate consideration of the available facts, are unfair and unwarranted."

The hours of testimony behind that moderate statement had disposed of the conflict. Only a few members of the staff resigned when the inquiry was ended and the work of the agency went forward with no interruption. There was no disposition to deny the former Chairman credit for his part in the inauguration of TVA programs. There was new respect for the Board majority, and a wider understanding of activities and procedures, for to respond to Arthur Morgan's charges his former colleagues were obliged to describe the specific steps by which decisions had been reached—in the process revealing problems, principles, and achievements.

RATES, ALLOCATION, AND OTHER QUESTIONS

In the lengthy sessions, power questions were explored. The rates established were subject to critical examination. Independent experts summoned by the Committee were heard as well as witnesses from TVA. Negotiations with utilities were reviewed and the conduct of litigation. A good deal of time was devoted to an inquiry into the various methods proposed to allocate the common costs of multipurpose structures between flood control and power and navigation, the primary purposes for which they were built. In the 1970's, a reader of the record finds it difficult to realize how absorbing those questions were in 1938.

The issues have been settled. The rates charged for power have long since proved their viability. Adjusted from time to time over the years, they have from the beginning achieved the goals set out in the statute. Electricity use in homes and on farms has been increased, and production costs have been covered by the proceeds derived from power sales. The problems associated with the allocation of common costs are not remembered now. Briefly this was their background. When multipurpose dams are built some portion of the investment serves only a single purpose. Locks, for example, are needed only for navigation, generating facilities are installed for power use alone. Some investment is made specifically for flood control and would not be required for power production or navigation. When the investment related to each of these specific purposes is subtracted from the total and charged to the use it promotes, there remains a balance that serves all three. This portion of the investment, the common costs, is subject to allocation between the major uses, and Section 14 of the TVA Act required the Board to make a determination which, when approved by the President, would be final.

A number of theories were studied by TVA. Several different formulas were presented to the Joint Committee by the private utilities and by consultants. Today, depending on the reader, the discussion of allocation theories and practices are arcane or boring or both. Only the experts care. Interest in 1938 was lively, based on concern about the proportion of the common investment in multipurpose projects that would be charged to power. TVA's opponents wanted power's share to be high in the hope that its rates might have to be raised. In fact, witnesses representing the private power companies even proposed that the total investment in multipurpose dams should be charged to power, and that in this area alone the consumers of electricity should pay for navigation and flood control, while elsewhere the costs of those public improvements were borne by taxpayers. The suggestion was as unacceptable to the Joint Committee as to TVA.

When TVA's first allocation report was submitted, 25 per cent of the common costs of Wilson, Norris, and Wheeler dams was assigned to flood control, 35 per cent to navigation, and 40 per cent to power. Adding the direct costs incurred to serve each purpose, flood control was charged with 20 per cent of the total investment in the three projects, navigation 28 per cent, and 52 per cent was to be borne by power. The allocation had been made according to the respected "alternative justifiable expenditure" theory. The Joint Committee's engineers reported that the figures adopted were "within reasonable limits of what a group of impartial engineers and economists would determine." Some years later, the allocation was reviewed with approval by the Federal Power Commission, and the same theory has been applied to subsequent allocations of the common costs of the multipurpose system. The question is rarely mentioned now. Little investment in river control projects has been made to provide power in recent years, and in relation to the total power investment the portion subject to allocation is small. Its ratio diminishes every year as investment in coal-fired or nuclear-powered plants, transmission lines, and substations soars. All their costs are charged to power, there is no element of judgment, no reliance on theory, no temptation to argue.*

As time has muted the strident conflicts of the 1930's, it has given new significance to testimony on matters not then enjoying much public attention. For when challenges to propriety or probity were laid aside, when exploration of controversial issues was suspended the relentless examination continued. Congress had directed an investigation "full and complete." Every program was described. Members of the staff of TVA took turns in the witness chair. The kinds and tons of fertilizer produced and distributed, the number of states and farmers participating were recorded. Forestry problems and river control operations were outlined. Purchasing and auditing procedures were discussed. The personnel system was reviewed. Nothing was ignored. To begin his testimony, each department head described the activities for which he was responsible and summarized accomplishments to date. Out of their accounts an impressive record of cooperation with other agencies emerged. It was clear that established instrumentalities of the federal government had been generous in their assistance to the new agency and that TVA in turn was diligent in developing cooperative relationships with state and local governments.

RELATIONS WITH OTHER AGENCIES

The Army Engineers' proposal for the development of the Tennessee River system had been inherited by TVA, as well as preliminary plans for the first two dams that the new agency would construct. While the Bureau of Reclamation in Denver made final designs for Norris and Wheeler Dams, the Civil Service Commission assisted in conducting the first examination for Trades and Labor employees, and specialists from the Public Health Service conferred with the staff of TVA about measures to reduce malaria.

---

* The total investment in completed TVA multipurpose dams at June 30, 1971, was in round numbers $962 million. Of that amount $478.3 million was charged to power, and of this only $175.5 million was the allocated portion of common costs. The balance of the total power investment in completed plant of over $3 billion was made up of investment in single-purpose dams, steam production facilities, and other electric plant.

The Coast and Geodetic Survey and the U.S. Geological Survey cooperated in the mapping of the Valley, the Bureau of Chemistry and Soils in a survey of its land, the Weather Bureau in a study of rainfall and streamflow, the rates of evaporation and siltation. The U.S. Bureau of Fisheries participated in an inquiry to determine the future for fish in the changing river, and the Biological Survey in plans for improving the environment for wildlife. To aid in construction of facilities to demonstrate use of the new recreation asset, the National Park Service and the Forest Service provided labor from the CCC camps assigned to them. The experiment stations of the states tested the fertilizers produced by TVA and the Extension Service supervised the large-scale demonstration of their use on farms. There were others. Congress had contemplated that the help of established agencies would be required. In section 5(i) of the Act it had authorized the Board "To request the assistance and advice of any officer, agent, or employee of any executive department or of any independent office of the United States to enable the Corporation the better to carry out its power successfully."

The network of relationships with other federal agencies was equaled by the record of increasing cooperation with state and local governments. Agreements were expanding with every project, with highway departments, boards of education, and health officials. When the report of the Joint Committee was filed, thirty agreements with federal offices were noted, the same number with state governments, and at least one agreement in each of twenty counties.

The record of the hearings reveals occasional Committee impatience as TVA department heads submitted their lengthy and detailed reports, an impatience usually met with dogged determination to proceed on the part of the witness. Few accepted the frequent suggestion that the bulk of their statements might be filed "for the record." Most went on with their story. After the initial statement came questioning, not always gentle. It was an experience alien to the background of most of those who testified, their first encounter with one of the faces of accountability. There are many. The press had reported the sessions at the White House where the directors were held accountable to the President for their statements, and the transcripts were published. TVA had been brought to account in the courts, and members of the staff had participated. Before the Joint Committee they learned that in a public agency accountability has no boundaries. It is unlimited.

The investigation was a potentially destructive device for fact finding. It might have made the staff of TVA overcautious, fearful, and eager to avoid responsibility. That it did not is not only a tribute to the steadfast leadership of the majority of the Board and the competence with which the Committee proceeded, but to the caliber of the witnesses and the validity of the programs they were endeavoring to interpret. They believed in the objectives of the statute. They were stout in their defense of the work they were doing to advance them. Years later, in his account of the TVA investigation, included in his book *In Brief Authority,* Francis Biddle, the Joint Committee's chief counsel, wrote, "We found the sustained enthusiasm that goes only with work performed for an impersonal end. There was a strong community sense, and a profound conviction that the work was creative in human terms."

Of a later period, John Gunther in *The Story of TVA* wrote in 1951: "Never in the United States or abroad have I encountered anything more striking than the faith its men have in their work." They had that faith in 1938, and the hearings provided a matchless occasion for program review. The drafting and redrafting of the introductory statement, the consultation between staff members necessary in its preparation, the search of files, the copying and recopying, all these preceded the heart-stopping moment when the witness raised his right hand to be sworn. The attention of file clerks and stenographers, of technicians and administrators had been engaged. A self-examination without reservation preceded each appearance, and TVA emerged from the experience a stronger and more confident organization, aware of its obligation to report and willing to be judged on its record.

The objective of the inquiry was not to benefit TVA. It was to inform the Congress and the public, to investigate claims and charges, to appraise the work of half a decade. That was accomplished. The benefit to TVA itself was a byproduct. In January, 1939, the Joint Committee issued a preliminary statement, in April a complete report. With a minority dissenting and recommending the dismemberment of TVA, it was a general affirmation of approval. The administrative problems of TVA's early years were recited, the confusion of the initial land buying, the inadequacies of procedures for internal auditing. All had been freely admitted by TVA witnesses, and all had been corrected. No corruption had been uncovered, no gross mismanagement revealed. The hearings had disclosed that the exhilarating chaos of the beginning had been disciplined, and the new agency had assumed the character and shape that would mark it in the future. The Investigating Committee had spread the facts about every program on the record. TVA could be seen as a whole.

V

Of Wars and Politics

During the Joint Committee investigation, foresters and agronomists, geologists and chemical engineers had briefly held the stage. Navigation and flood control had been recognized as primary objectives of river control. But power was waiting in the wings to resume the role of star to which the public had assigned it. It moved back to the headlines in January, 1939, just a fortnight after the Committee hearings had been concluded when the Supreme Court announced its dismissal of the utilities' appeal in the eighteen-company case. With the Court's finding that the plaintiffs had no standing to sue, the power companies had lost their fight. They were ready now to sell their properties, for it was clear that the region was eager to move toward participation in a power system publicly owned and operated.

Negotiations had been halted while the constitutional case was pending. With the collapse of litigation they were resumed, and soon agreement between TVA, the Commonwealth & Southern Corporation, and various municipalities was achieved. TVA would purchase the facilities for power generation and transmission of certain subsidiaries, the municipalities would acquire the distribution systems. The private companies had failed in the courts, but their supporters in Congress had not surrendered. Vigorous opposition was registered when TVA sought an amendment of its statute to permit the issuance of bonds to finance the acquisition. The struggle was rigorous but brief. The legislation proposed was amended, but it was enacted in July, 1939, authorizing the issuance of bonds "not to exceed in the aggregate $61,500,000." The bonds were purchased by the Treasury, and in New York City on August 15 David Lilienthal handed a check for $44,728,300 to Wendell L. Willkie, then President of Commonwealth & Southern Corporation, in 1940 to be the Republican party's nominee for the Presidency. It was TVA's share of the total purchase price of $78,425,000 for the properties of the Tennessee Electric Power Company, the first and largest of the acquisitions made possible by the bond amendment. There had been a few purchases earlier, some came later, but with this major transaction specifically approved by Congress, the power program of TVA became a power system. Like other utilities, it would be a natural monopoly in the area it was to serve, solely responsible for meeting the expanding requirements of the consumers dependent on it for their supply of electricity.

An immediate problem associated with the utility purchase involved taxation, and Congress had to act once more. States and counties cannot levy taxes on properties of the federal government, but with the approval of Congress voluntary payments can be made. They are usually described as "tax replacements" or "in-lieu" payments. In the case of TVA, the provisions of the original Act were inadequate to meet the new situation as privately owned power facilities long on the tax rolls of state and local governments passed to public ownership. As soon as the Supreme Court's dismissal of the utilities' appeal in the eighteen-company case indicated that the purchase of private properties could be accomplished, a study of the problem was initiated. Experts on taxation were employed as consultants by TVA, and conferences with state and local authorities were undertaken. In July, 1939, even before the acquisition had been completed, the recommendations resulting from the inquiry were incorporated in bills introduced by Senator Norris and Representative (later Senator) John J. Sparkman of Alabama. When hearings were conducted by Senate and House committees in January and February, 1940, state and local officials appeared with representatives of TVA to advocate the proposal.

In spite of general approval, there was opposition from some who felt the TVA program as a whole would increase taxable wealth to a degree that would make unnecessary the replacement of the taxes formerly paid by private utilities. Harsher criticism came from those who wanted to burden power rates with larger in-lieu payments. There was hostility from others who were inclined to oppose any recommendation made by TVA—an animosity reflected in the somewhat unconventional progress of the legislation, for the provision became law as an uncomfortable section of a "Joint resolution making appropriations for work relief and relief, for the fiscal year ending June 30, 1941." The bill earlier introduced by Senator Norris had been passed by the Senate on April 30, only to be referred to the House Committee on Military Affairs, where the companion bill introduced by Representative Sparkman was languishing. The chairman of that committee, an implacable foe of TVA, had the measures buried and intended to keep them interred.

Fortunately for the region, Senator Norris was not only a high-minded statesman but a resourceful legislator. The Appropriations Committee of the Senate was persuaded to incorporate his in-lieu tax measure as an amendment to the pending Work Relief Appropriation Bill. In its new environment, the bill was adopted once more and when the House instructed its representatives on the conference committee to accept the Senate decision, approval was assured. The Committee on Military Affairs of the House could take small comfort in its control of the two bills it held captive. According to the language of legislative reports, they "died in committee," but the plan itself survived. With approval by the President, on June 26, 1940, the recommended provisions became law, and have remained unchanged for more than a quarter century. TVA sets aside 5 per cent of its gross power proceeds (exclusive of revenues derived from sales to the government itself) to be devoted to in-lieu tax payments to the states and counties of the area it supplies with power. The total is divided under a formula, based on plant location and power sales, laid down in the statute. In recent years, some dissatisfaction with the division of payments between states and counties has been expressed, and the methods used by states to share their payments with local governments are disputed, but the total sum to be divided has grown as TVA power capacity has expanded and use has climbed.*

With passage of the in-lieu tax amendment, the most pressing problems then before the agency were resolved. Major litigation had been concluded, and dissension on the Board was ended. In January, 1939, the Senate had confirmed the President's selection of former Senator James P. Pope of Idaho to be a director filling the vacancy created by the removal of Arthur Morgan. The bond amendment had been approved, the utility acquisition closed. The opinion of the condemnation commission in the Berry marble case had been sustained, and TVA had won that engagement.

The new decade might have inaugurated a period of relative tranquility, except that the war in Europe began to impinge on the serenity of domestic programs. The fall of France in the summer of 1940 accelerated preparations for defense in the United States. The National Defense Advisory Commission early directed attention to one serious deficiency in resources. The country's capacity for aluminum production was insufficient to meet the growing threat to security. Much of the metal then used in the United States came from the Tennessee Valley, where Alcoa, the major producer, had established plants long before TVA was created and had built dams on the tributary Little Tennessee to provide the energy required for processing. Since power is a limiting factor in aluminum production, the Commission requested a recommendation from TVA and a schedule of project construction to provide the increased energy essential to permit expansion.

A schedule was easy to develop. If adequate funds were made available, additional generating units could be installed at existing structures, the pace of construction on dams under way accelerated, projects planned but not yet started could be built, and a steam plant added to the system. In June, 1940, with a supporting letter of approval from E. R. Stettinius, Jr., chairman of the Advisory Commission, TVA requested the appropriation of the

* For example, TVA's in-lieu payments to states and counties amounted to $19.96 million in fiscal 1971. On their part the power distributors, now 160 municipalities and cooperatives, pay taxes or make in-lieu payments according to local law and custom. In fiscal 1971, they paid $25.3 million, making a total of over $45 million received by states and counties in taxes and in-lieu payments from the area's power suppliers.

necessary funds to begin. They were denied. Pressures for defense preparation did not lessen, however, and early in July it was determined that the request must be renewed—this time with a difference. The Defense Advisory Commission itself would ask that funds for power expansion be appropriated to TVA.

On July 9, 1940, its spokesmen appeared before a subcommittee of the House Appropriations Committee to urge the immediate appropriation of $25 million to permit TVA to begin construction of the increased power capacity that they had determined essential for national defense. The witnesses were men of stature in the business community—Stettinius of U.S. Steel, William S. Knudsen of General Motors, Gano Dunn, of J. G. White Engineering Corporation, and others, but that day they were not representing their private interests. They were testifying on behalf of the government they had come to serve in a time of crisis.

Stettinius called attention to their new role in his opening statement. Of Gano Dunn, adviser to the Commission on power matters, he said:

> In the lawsuit—this will amuse some of you—in the lawsuit which Wendell Willkie and the Commonwealth & Southern brought several years ago to test the constitutionality of the TVA Act, he hired Mr. Dunn's firm to represent him against the government. Mr. Dunn has previously been opposed to the government's policy of entering into competition with private utilities, but he now strongly is in favor of this request of TVA purely from the standpoint of the emergency at hand and the interest of the national defense.

Director Lilienthal and TVA's Chief Engineer, Theodore B. Parker, sat at the table with the major witnesses. Two TVA staff members, smothered in the charts and tabulations it was assumed might be required, were in the rear. Their material was not needed. Only a few inquiries were directed to Lilienthal. Parker answered technical questions, but the distinguished representatives of private enterprise made the case. They may not have believed in the "feasibility and wisdom" of the Act creating TVA, but they knew how desperately increased power capacity was needed and expressed their confidence that TVA could provide it. Without delay, the request was approved by the committee.

Favorable action followed in both houses of Congress. This

was the beginning, the first in a series of requests for funds to expand the capacity of the TVA power system. All were granted, only one was delayed. Aluminum production had to be increased. Other defense industries were being located in the area, then considered secure from attack. In 1940, its inland location, in a valley sheltered by mountains toward the sea, was considered protection enough. The most important of the new enterprises, which TVA staff dubbed the "mystery plant," was rising with its own new town at a place called Oak Ridge in Tennessee. Its purpose was then unknown, but TVA was advised that its demand for power would be enormous.

In the face of the growing national emergency, there was little opposition from traditional foes as power capacity was increased. At one time after the United States had entered the war, TVA had twelve projects under way and more than 42,000 men and women were at work, the largest employment figure ever recorded for the agency. The building of Fontana Dam, high in the mountains of North Carolina, revived the excitement of initiating Norris. The problems it presented were monumental. The site, formerly owned by the Aluminum Company of America, had been acquired by TVA after long negotiation. It was in a remote and mountainous area, something over sixty miles from Knoxville and about the same distance from Asheville, the nearest population centers. The dam had to be built in record time, not only for the addition to power capacity it would itself provide, but to accomplish the increases in downstream generation its streamflow regulation would make possible. The job was undertaken under wartime conditions, when labor was scarce, and gasoline was rationed.

A highway had to be constructed to bring in the heavy construction equipment. Because commuting was impossible, housing had to be provided, and as labor could not be spared to build all the houses on site, demountable structures were designed and ordered from factories outside the area. For a time, while the winding mountain road was still under construction, it supported a revealing traffic pattern. Bulldozers and trailers bearing houses were interspersed with buses and family cars carrying men to their new jobs, their wives and children to the homes that might be riding just ahead in the endless procession. While fathers checked in at the employment office, families watched workmen install the fully

The Tennessee Valley
as it was . . .

in 1933,
six million acres
of eroded land

Before rural electrification

President Franklin D. Roosevelt signing the Act establishing the Tennessee Valley Authority, May 18, 1933: The white-haired man with the string tie behind the President is the late Senator George W. Norris of Nebraska, seeing victory after his twelve-year battle to save Muscle Shoals for public operation. Next to him is Congressman (later Senator) Lister Hill of Alabama, sponsor of the TVA legislation in the House of Representatives.

President and Mrs. Franklin D. Roosevelt visit Norris Dam construction site, November, 1934. With them, behind the driver, is Arthur E. Morgan, Chairman of TVA's first Board of Directors.

Left:
The two Morgans, Arthur E. and, on the left, his colleague (no relative) on the three-man Board Harcourt A. Morgan, January 1, 1934

Right:
The third member of the Board, and later Chairman, David E. Lilienthal, in the Norris Dam powerhouse, 1936

Norris Dam under construction; below, Senator Norris, the only contemporary American for whom a TVA structure was ever named, at the dam, 1938

Under floodlights, work proceeds through the night on Fontana Dam, built in wartime in thirteen months instead of the three years projected. *Below:* workers leave Douglas Dam, another World War II project, at the end of a shift.

The coming of electricity:
A member of Congress
who spent his boyhood
on a Valley farm said
of the distribution
lines, "If my mother
were alive, you would have
a hard time convincing
her those lines are ugly.
She thought they were
beautiful. They
changed her life."

equipped houses. It took only a few hours. Then they moved in, and life at Fontana Village began.

Construction started on New Year's Day, 1942, less than a month after Pearl Harbor and the entrance of the United States into World War II. The dam was closed and the reservoir began to fill in November, 1944. Between those dates, men worked around the clock. Under floodlights through the night the great white structure rose, the tallest dam east of the Rockies, restraining the current of an improbable black river, the water stained with emissions from a paper plant upstream. The project had other distinctions. Unusual difficulties had to be surmounted, and exceptional measures were required to bring it in on schedule. Norris astonished experienced observers by providing Ping-pong tables as well as the study of fractions to occupy the workmen's leisure time. Fontana went further. An intricate public address system was developed to offer music, news, and entertainment during working hours. To startled men pouring concrete, a rousing speech by a visiting dignitary might come booming from the speakers, or the rhythm of a high school band enliven a change of shifts.

Fontana was a long way from city lights. No gasoline was available for the workmen to spend their off-duty hours far from the site. Jobs were plentiful elsewhere. The project manager was resourceful and imaginative, and somehow he kept construction going. Recreation for the whole family was provided, and the villages reached a population total of 6,000. A good library, good schools, and a well-equipped hospital helped to stabilize the labor force. Along with the cubic feet of earth moved every day, the manager once happily reported an average of one birth every twenty-four hours. There were garden clubs and PTA's at Fontana. One project involved high school students in a program of testing the soil around the dwellings in preparation for planting shrubs and flowers. TVA agronomists supervised the operation, and appropriate fertilizer was prescribed and supplied. Landscape specialists gave advice, seeds and plants were provided, and it was announced that prizes would be awarded in recognition of excellence in a home beautification program. A good deal of enthusiasm resulted, but when a visitor complimented the manager on his concern for enhancing the appearance of government property, the reply was a somewhat sheepish denial of aesthetic interest. "I'm just trying to reduce turnover," he said, "I know the wives and kids won't let these men leave until the seeds they planted flower, and some are mighty late bloomers."

Power requirements were not the only stimulant to production during the war years. For the chemical plant at Muscle Shoals, defense demands meant that it could serve the needs it was built to satisfy but was too late to meet in World War I. New facilities were added, old equipment put to work. Highly concentrated fertilizers were sent to England to maintain food production. Animal feed supplements were produced. Ammonium nitrate and phosphorus were made available for munitions, and calcium carbide for use in the manufacture of synthetic rubber. That was not all. Facilities developed to map the hills and hollows of the Valley began to serve the Army's needs as planes from theatres of war brought aerial photographs to Chattanooga. Pilots waited at the airport while the films were processed so that with no delay maps of proposed invasion routes could be flown from Tennessee to be used by commanders in the field.

The war years were years of pressure and achievement. It was a time when TVA's contribution to the nation was recognized and approved. But they were years when a second war had to be fought by the agency itself, when at great cost TVA defended its adherence to an inflexible standard of nonpolitical engineering. The controversy began in the summer of 1941 when mounting defense requirements prompted the President to forward to Congress a request for funds to enable TVA to begin construction of a dam, already named Douglas, on the French Broad River, a major tributary of the Tennessee.

For reasons not yet entirely clear, Senator Kenneth McKellar was determined that Douglas Dam should not be built. He was then not only the senior Senator from Tennessee but the ranking Democratic member of the Senate Committee on Appropriations, where his influence was potent. The Senator was not against dam construction. In fact, he proposed the substitution of four other projects for the recommended structure, two to be built by the U.S. Corps of Engineers on the Cumberland River system, two by TVA on other tributaries of the Tennessee. Congress accepted his judgment and funds were made available to TVA to start construction of one dam on the South Holston River and one on the

Watauga. These were good projects. They had been presented to the Office of Production Management (OPM), the successor agency to the Advisory Commission of the Council of National Defense, itself later succeeded by the War Production Board, in an inventory of available sites when it became clear that TVA would have to provide more energy. Unfortunately, the OPM was unable to make a prompt decision and TVA engineers had advised the Board and the Board in turn informed OPM and the Congress that the delay made it impossible to recommend these projects to meet the urgent needs. It would take more than a year longer to build the two dams, more critical materials and labor would be required, and the amount of power generated would be less. Only Douglas Dam would meet the specifications laid down.

Senator McKellar rejected every argument advanced. In December, Pearl Harbor raised estimates of power requirements once more, but he was adamant, and at a hearing before his subcommittee on December 11 he attacked TVA and officials of OPM for their continued efforts to obtain funds to build Douglas. His choler appeared to be inexhaustible, and his diligence in obstruction was unremitting. He was, however, confronting a President determined that war production should not be threatened by a power shortage. In his January address to Congress on the State of the Union, Roosevelt described the schedule of planes and tanks, anti-aircraft guns and merchant ships that must be maintained to equip the United States for war. Later, from the White House, he addressed a moving personal appeal to the Senator pointing out that the construction of Douglas Dam was essential to meet the goals he had established and the commitments he had made to the men who were going out to fight. The Senator surrendered. With withdrawal of his opposition, Congress provided funds for Douglas, and on January 30 the President signed the bill permitting work to begin.

Months had been lost because of the Senator's recalcitrance, and certain months are critical in the schedule of dam building in the Tennessee Valley. There, high water is expected only in winter and early spring when the runoff of the rainfall to the rivers is heavy. If there is urgency in power requirements, dam construction must be keyed to a closure date that permits a reservoir to fill promptly. The autumn months are generally dry, and a structure completed in summer is unlikely to provide power any sooner than one closed the following December. TVA had to make up the lost time. Construction of the "mystery plant," which turned out to be the atomic energy installation at Oak Ridge, then officially called the Manhattan Engineer District, was proceeding at a furious rate, and later announcements indicated that the availability of energy from TVA had been a compelling reason for location of the facility in the Tennessee Valley. To it and to other defense installations, power was vital. Not a day nor an hour could be lost.

Construction at the Douglas site could not begin until the President signed the bill, and arrangements were made with the White House to make certain that TVA was advised the moment his signature was affixed, no matter what the hour. First came the call from the President's secretary to the Washington office of TVA reporting "The bill has just been taken into the President's office. Stay on the line." Space flights and television have made split-second timing familiar to millions today, but this was 1942. It was no lunar orbit, but construction of a multipurpose dam was to begin, the nation was at war, and with the same sense that men's lives were at stake, TVA's Chief Engineer in Knoxville waited on a second line until the crucial message could be reported. When he heard the words "The President has signed the bill," he raised his hand. His assistant's telephone was connected with the access point where men and machines were waiting in queues for the signal to move. The word was "Go," and with the roar of machines and the shouts of men construction began while the Chief Engineer listened to the rest of the message. "The President says to tell you now it's up to TVA." Douglas Dam was completed in less than thirteen months, setting a world record for construction speed. It could trap the runoff from the rains of 1943. On time, its generators sent energy to the installations it was built to serve.

The dam was built. Power was available where and when it was needed. But the victory of technical integrity over political engineering was costly. It was years before Senator McKellar forgave, and he never forgot what he regarded as a humiliating defeat. He had weapons and he used them. The Senate, where he was powerful and experienced, was the arena he selected for confrontation. Out of the trauma of Douglas Dam came the "McKellar amendments," a series of proposed changes in the TVA Act, any one of which would have been fatal to the efficiency and probably the survival of the agency.

On March 10, 1942, only a little more than a month after Douglas Dam was started, McKellar's war against TVA began. It lasted more than six years. Over that period, his proposed amendments were introduced as separate bills and referred to the appropriate legislative committee. They were attached piecemeal as riders to the appropriation bills which he managed on the Senate floor. They were combined in one measure on which extensive hearings were held before the Senate Committee on Public Works. The conflict was fierce and protracted. There were hearings, there was extended debate, enlivened by parliamentary tangles, but none of the proposed changes in the TVA statute was enacted.

The key amendment would have denied TVA use of its proceeds. From the beginning, all the costs of operation and maintenance of the power system had been paid out of the proceeds derived from power sales. Proceeds of the chemical plant were used for operating costs too. Senator McKellar proposed a different system. He contended that all TVA proceeds should be paid into the Treasury as received and that the agency should rely upon the annual appropriations of Congress for its operating expenses, including those of the power system. On the floor of the Senate, he insisted that TVA should be run "like the Post Office." No power system, public or private, could exist under such a system, nor could a chemical plant. Even assuming that every President would recommend ample funds and that Congress would always be prompt and generous, operating expenses of a power system cannot be precisely determined two years in advance. Emergencies must be met.

There is no reason to believe that Senator McKellar wanted to destroy the TVA power system or to injure the agency as a whole, although that would have been the effect of his amendments. As ranking member and later Chairman of the Senate Appropriations Committee, he was doubtless certain that he could make sure that adequate funds would always be provided, and apparently he expected to hold his seat forever. He had worked hard and effectively in TVA's behalf. Without question, he intended to do so in the future. In his own fashion. The vitriolic campaign he waged made the investigation of the Joint Committee seem gentle, and the insinuations of Arthur Morgan paled in comparison with the frontal and personal assaults of the Senator. One of his amendments would have required the confirmation of every employee earning more than $4,500 a year, and a good many observers assumed that his quarrel with TVA was based on the fact that appointments to the agency were not made by courtesy of members of Congress. That explanation, oversimple and unconvincing, ignores the fact that for eight years Senator McKellar had supported every recommendation of TVA even though no appointments had been made under his patronage or due to the recommendation of any member of Congress. He knew that Section 6 of the TVA Act forbade it.

As a matter of fact, a good many members of Congress have found that provision of the Act a protection. Any politician knows the headaches that go with the power, or the reputation of ability, to influence employee selection. For every friend, a dozen enemies are made, and the luckless senator or representative is likely to discover that he has assumed a continuing responsibility for the welfare of his protégé, his working conditions, and his promotions. The relationship is frequently deplored, but as long as the system prevails, few members of Congress dare to waive their privileges. It is easier to complain about the quality of government service than to yield the opportunity to participate in appointment. In 1922, fifty years ago, some recognition of the problem was included in the report of a committee then considering legislation providing for operation of the facilities at Muscle Shoals. The committee said:

> To have the government undertake to engage in the manufacture of fertilizer ingredients, with political superintendents, foremen, and straw bosses is unthinkable, and to undertake such a scheme would be unspeakable folly.

Curiously the committee of that day saw no alternative to the "unspeakable folly," every member probably embracing the system whose results he scorned. In 1933 the TVA Act provided a remedy. It was simple. By the will of Congress itself, political considerations in appointment were outlawed.

What Senator McKellar wanted was not patronage but control. He wanted to influence the decisions of management. Up to the selection of the Douglas site, he had approved the projects for which funds were requested, and it probably came as a shock when a location he disapproved was not abandoned in response to his expressed displeasure. When the reservoir behind Douglas

Dam was filled, some fertile farm land would be flooded. Much of it was devoted to truck crops grown under contract to certain canning companies. Owners of the land were naturally opposed to construction of the dam and the canning companies were hostile. It seems probable that some, perhaps many, of the landowners and company representatives appealed to Senator McKellar, and that his promise to protect their interest was made because he never doubted he could effect a change. The substitution of four dams for one must have seemed to him a generous adjustment. It is unlikely that he ever believed that the two he proposed for immediate addition to the TVA system could not meet the urgent power needs. In his eyes, TVA was simply stubborn and ungrateful. That was precisely the point he made in a letter addressed to his colleagues on the Appropriations Committee on November 25, 1941. It was a general attack on the TVA position, replete with statements the agency disputed. After listing the dams which "I got the Congress" to approve, he added, "My thanks for these dams in this great emergency is a kick in the pants." The letter ends on a humble plea: "I earnestly hope that my colleagues on the Appropriations Committee will not also kick me in the pants . . ." They refrained from chastisement. Approval of funds for Douglas Dam did not come until later, and only when the Senator withdrew his opposition.

As the amendments to the TVA Act proposed by Senator McKellar were defeated in year after year of bitter controversy, the Tennessee Valley region, and even the nation, rallied in support of the agency. The area's press was vigorous and people saw the heartening spectacle of politicians speaking and voting on the floor of House and Senate and campaigning at home under the slogan, "Keep politics out of TVA." Politicians kept it out, for the Senator's effort to subject the agency to his will was defeated, not by TVA, but by his colleagues and his peers. Old friendships and alliances were shattered, but a principle of public management was upheld.

For Congress and the country, the controversy illuminated the strength of the nonpolitical standards of TVA, probably for the first time. It was not, however, the first such demonstration. As early as the autumn of 1933, when examinations were held throughout the region as TVA began to recruit a labor force, the people of the Valley learned that jobs would not be available through the customary political routes. The application forms distributed throughout the area then had the designation Form 10-TVA. The men who filled them out were eligible to take the examinations which tested their ability to follow written or oral instructions. The application was essential, but they needed no other introduction. Almost 39,000 "Form 10" men took the examination, not only creating registers from which TVA drew its workers but establishing awareness that the hiring policies of the new agency would not follow familiar patterns in recruitment for public works. That illustration of a principle was important, but the struggle over Douglas Dam went much further. It showed that projects would not be located and schedules designed to placate politicians. The impact within TVA was important. To many engineers it was a humbling experience to see members of the Board endure venomous personal attacks because they had accepted and defended the technical recommendations of the professional staff. To the organization as a whole, the controversy gave a heightened sense of responsibility, a renewed determination to be worthy of trust as a new breed of politicians pointed out that in the management of a public agency, no politics is good politics.

Resisting Senator McKellar not only resulted in years of controversy over provisions of the TVA Act, it demanded defense of the reputations of two Presidential appointees. In September, 1941, the President had designated David Lilienthal Chairman of the Board, succeeding Harcourt Morgan, who had been named Chairman when Arthur Morgan was removed but who was anxious to be relieved of the public responsibilities associated with the title. Lilienthal's term as Director would end in May, 1945, and in the face of Senator McKellar's displeasure, the President ignored tradition and although the nominee was "personally objectionable" to both senators from Tennessee (McKellar's junior colleague joining with him), Lilienthal was reappointed to the Board and his selection once more confirmed by the Senate. McKellar's boundless animosity continued, one defeat did not discourage him, and, when, in the autumn of 1946, President Truman selected Lilienthal to be Chairman of the new Atomic Energy Commission, the Senator fought confirmation of his appointment with enviable vigor and no mercy. At the same time, he also opposed the President's nomination of Gordon R. Clapp, formerly TVA's General Manager, to fill Lilienthal's unexpired term on the Board of TVA. Hearings on the two nominations were held before different committees, but concurrently, and with an agility belying his years, the Senator ran from one to the other presenting the witnesses he had assembled in opposition. Lilienthal's appointment was approved by the Committee to which it had been referred, but the Senator had reason to be jubilant when the Committee on Public Works recommended against Clapp's confirmation. His satisfaction was short-lived. The President and the nominee stood firm and the Senate approved both nominations over McKellar's objections.

When World War II had ended, work resumed on Watauga and South Holston, the dams the Senator had preferred over Douglas. Construction had been halted in 1942, only months after it began, when the War Production Board denied the critical materials required. The war years had not only increased the capacity of the TVA power system from a little less than a million kilowatts in prewar 1940 to something over 2.5 million in 1946, they had accelerated achievement of the major goals of water control. The primary navigation channel from Paducah to Knoxville was substantially completed by the autumn of 1945. In future years it would be improved, larger locks would be installed, and the channel would be extended to some tributaries, but the basic water highway had been created and the river was ready to take its place in the inland waterway system of the United States. From that date, too, great regional floods were reduced. The Tennessee no longer poured its waters through the Ohio to the lower Mississippi when the water crested on those rivers. Already, this was the most completely controlled river system in the United States. There was nothing like it anywhere.

At Muscle Shoals, the reduction of military requirements left enlarged capacity for fertilizer production. Even before World War II was over, the staff of chemists and engineers had turned their attention to a pioneering project to condition ammonium nitrate for use in agriculture and to the development of new kinds of plant food. The land of the Tennessee Valley, like the land in all the United States, had accepted the wartime burden of increased food production. Conservation practices had taken second place, tree planting had almost ceased. Those activities began again, to continue and to grow in the uneasy peace of the succeeding decades. Their resumption was expected, but the expansion of power capacity required in the postwar years defied the forecasts of the experts.

It had been widely predicted that, when defense demands were reduced, TVA would have an immense amount of capacity in excess of its requirements. Neighboring private companies were deeply concerned about the consequences of the abundance of supply expected on the public system. The experts who prophesied a surplus were wrong again, just as they had been wrong before. Consistently, they underestimated the growth of electricity consumption. They failed to measure the demand unsatisfied during the war when work was plentiful and wages were good but electric appliances were not available. As ranges, electric pumps, air conditioning systems, washing machines and dryers came on the market again, the use of electricity by domestic consumers soared, and it was clear there would be no idle capacity. Soon defense requirements, particularly those of the Atomic Energy Commission, rose to add their voracious demands. There was no question but that the power needs of the region were outstripping the ability of the river to supply. Water power had to be supplemented with steam generation. In January, 1948, the President's budget contained a request for funds to enable TVA to begin construction of a steam generating plant at a site on the Tennessee River near Johnsonville, Tennessee.

Opposition to power capacity increases had been reduced during war years. It had not disappeared, but its virulence was diminished. Because Watts Bar, the first steam plant built by TVA, was constructed to supply the requirements of defense it had been relatively immune to criticism. Johnsonville, proposed to meet the expanding demand of the region, and to satisfy normal load growth with a system of both hydro and steam capacity, was different. Opposition to its construction was vociferous. For a time, the attention of Congress and the public had been directed to the principles upon which TVA was founded, to its rigid adherence to a nonpolitical administration, and to those provisions of the Act which promoted good management. Now emphasis returned to power, and once more that program was attacked and defended on the floor in Senate and House.

TVA's authority to construct steam plants was challenged. Groups of supporting senators and members of the House met together for conference and for briefing in preparation for reply to the accusations. In debate, they could point out that thermal capacity had always been a part of the TVA system. A steam plant had been included in the properties at Muscle Shoals turned over to TVA by the Army in 1933. In the original Act, a provision authorized TVA to issue a limited amount of bonds to construct coal-burning plants as well as other facilities. With the approval of Congress, steam capacity had been purchased from private utilities in 1939, and in 1940 construction of the Watts Bar steam plant had begun. The project proposed did not represent a lawless innovation as the adversaries charged. In fact, TVA proponents on Capitol Hill took some sly satisfaction in emphasizing that certain members of Congress who had opposed dam building in the past and urged instead the construction of coal-burning plants by TVA were now among those claiming that the addition of steam capacity was not permissible under the statute or Constitution.

The issue, of course, was not the question of hydro versus steam. It was survival, and opponents grasped another chance to stop the TVA power system forever, for it was abundantly clear that water power alone could not supply the area's growing demand for electricity. Once more, conflict provided an occasion for a review of policies and rates and power system management. There were open attacks on the industrial growth of the TVA area. Ugly manifestations of sectionalism appeared. The questions raised were complex, debate was extended, and when the Eightieth Congress dispersed, its members hurrying home for the 1948 campaign, the appropriation had not been approved, and the future of the TVA power system was again in jeopardy.

Uncertainty was ended when the Eighty-first Congress convened and a resolute President Truman repeated his request for funds to begin Johnsonville. The lengthy debate of 1948 paid off, Congress granted the money, and in May, 1949, TVA began construction of its first peacetime steam plant. For its power system, this was the beginning of a new era.

VI

Some Very Difficult Years

Johnsonville was the first in a series of steam generating plants built by TVA after World War II. It was followed in rapid sequence by others: Widows Creek, Kingston, Colbert, John Sevier, Gallatin, and Shawnee, the latter built specifically to serve the facilities constructed by the Atomic Energy Commission (AEC) at Paducah in Kentucky. The war was over, but the threat of conflict was not ended. Defense as well as civilian power requirements continued to expand, and in the autumn of 1952 TVA submitted to the Bureau of the Budget a request for funds to begin construction of another steam plant to be located near the town of Fulton in Lauderdale County of Tennessee. Funds were also sought to add two units at plants then under construction, one at Kingston and one at John Sevier, both in east Tennessee. The capacity increases were approved and in January, 1953, the appropriation requests were transmitted to Congress in the budget proposed for fiscal 1954 by the outgoing Truman Administration.

As usual in such years of Administration change, Congress postponed action on the budget until the new President, Dwight D. Eisenhower, could present his proposed revisions. In 1953, the delay was prolonged with respect to the TVA appropriation, and when the recommendations of the Administration were received in May the position of the White House was clear. No funds were included

96

to start the new plant at Fulton. Only the additional units proposed for the John Sevier and Kingston plants were approved. Efforts to provide money for the Fulton plant by action in the House itself were probably doomed by Administration disapproval in any event, but failure was made doubly certain when, at a press conference on the morning of June 17, the day the House was to vote, the popular President referred to TVA as an example of what he had in mind when he had referred to the menace of "creeping socialism" in an earlier speech. In 1953, the phrase was a malediction.

The basis for President Eisenhower's distaste for TVA is unclear. His State of the Union Message, submitted to Congress on February 2, 1953, had contained one paragraph that seemed to endorse the principles on which TVA was based. Then he said:

> The best natural resources program for America will not result from exclusive dependence on Federal bureaucracy. It will involve a partnership of the states and local communities, private citizens and the Federal Government, all working together. This combined effort will advance the development of the great river valleys of our nation and the power that they can generate. Likewise, such a partnership can be effective in the expansion throughout the nation of upstream storage; the sound use of public lands; the wise conservation of minerals; and the sustained yield of our forests.

It was, however, soon apparent that the President's approval of partnerships did not extend to the TVA power system, although by that time there were 148 distribution systems, locally owned and managed, with a total investment of some $400 million, a reasonably impressive evidence of participation. On June 17, there was no possibility of misunderstanding the President's position. He was opposed to TVA. His press conference statement of that date indicates that he believed industries were deserting other areas to locate in the Tennessee Valley to take advantage of low cost power. He said, "So we get to this curious thing in the socialistic theory that we, all of us, provide cheap power, such cheap power for one region that . . . it can appeal and take away the industries from other sections of the country."

A check of the facts would have challenged his understanding on this point. The industrial growth of the TVA area was just beginning. It was then, and has been since, an addition to national strength, not a relocation. Nevertheless, the notion that industries were moving, particularly from New England to the Tennessee Valley, had wide currency for a time. It had been vigorously advanced in 1948, when the appropriation requested to begin construction of Johnsonville was pending. At that time, representatives of various business associations appeared before a subcommittee considering the question, and, although they testified with considerable fervor that industries from other areas were being "lured" to the Tennessee Valley, in response to questioning no witness could cite a single example. John F. Kennedy was then a member of the House and, persuaded of the emigration from his state, he spoke in opposition to the appropriation, taking a position he was to repudiate after further study. The facts were not difficult to obtain. A survey of the area using power supplied by TVA had revealed that only four small plants had moved to the region from other states between 1933 and 1948 and none had come from New England. Power costs were not a factor in any case, for not one was a large electricity user, not one a substantial employer.

In 1953, after the President's statement, TVA undertook another survey to determine whether the situation had changed. To respond to the general accusation with accuracy, the records of 148 power distributors had to be checked, since only a few industries, those using large amounts of power, twenty-five in number in 1953, were served by TVA directly. The inquiry disclosed that eight plants had moved to the region in the five years since the previous survey, making a total of twelve since 1933—an insignificant migration related to some 6,500 manufacturing establishments then located in the area. As before, not one of the eight was a substantial power user or a large employer. (It was estimated that no more than 650 jobs were involved in all.) Again none of the plants had come from New England. Those were the facts. Yet in the House of Representatives on June 16 a member from New York inserted in the Appendix of the *Congressional Record* a letter he had written to the Governor of Tennessee on June 11. In its lengthy text, he referred to "the hundreds of industries" that had moved from other parts of the country, especially New England, in order to take advantage of TVA's "subsidized power." Unlike others advancing similar complaints, he did cite an example, but unfortunately for his argument inquiry disclosed that the company he named, which had indeed moved from Massachusetts, had located in the Tennessee Valley in 1931, two years before TVA was born, and was operating in a community that did not receive power from TVA until 1939. The situation today is unchanged. It is true that textile plants have moved to the South from New England, but the TVA area was never their destination.

It is likely that President Eisenhower's discomfort about TVA sprang more from a subliminal preference for private rather than public enterprise than from any examination of industrial movements. In *The Ordeal of Power, A Political Memoir of the Eisenhower Years,* Emmett John Hughes recounts a scene at a Cabinet meeting on July 31, 1953, when the President referred to TVA, exclaiming: "By God, if ever we could do it, before we leave here, I'd like to see us sell the whole thing, but I suppose we can't go that far."

The TVA power system did present a problem to the Administration. In 1953, there were only two sources of capital for investment in the increased capacity the system required—the appropriation of funds by Congress and the use of the system's proceeds.* The latter were limited not only in size but in applicability. Since 1948, Congress had restricted their use. Proceeds were not available to start new projects, only to add units at existing plants. To maintain the efficiency and economy of the system, new projects were required. The proposed Fulton plant, for example, was to be located at a site selected because it would provide an efficient and economical source of power to serve the city of Memphis, TVA's largest municipal customer. The city's original twenty-year contract with TVA was due to expire in 1958. A new agreement could not be negotiated until additional capacity was assured. Before presenting its request for funds to begin construction of Fulton, TVA had conferred with municipal officials to discover whether the city might wish to build its own plant. There had been some dissatisfaction on the part of Memphis over certain contract provisions, but after consideration the city concluded that it wanted to remain a part of the TVA system, so the request for funds for the Fulton plant was submitted.

When Congress adjourned on August 3, 1953, money had been

* By June 30, 1971, earnings had provided $714,736,126 for investment in the power system.

made available to continue construction of power projects already under way and to add the requested new units at two of them. But no funds had been provided for Fulton. It was clear that a limit had been set on the investment the system's owner, the federal government, was willing to make in the capacity increases essential for regional growth. The threat to the future was grave, understood in Congress and the region. TVA was to be stopped. The spotlight was on power but other programs suffered, too. Even though the Administration did not recommend their elimination and had made only slight revisions in TVA's request, funds for programs presented under the heading "Resource Development"—activities such as mapping, forestry, agricultural and other research, economic surveys and development work in tributary watersheds —were stricken from the bill by the Appropriations Committee and the House in the general awareness that TVA was in disfavor and that this was a favorable time to achieve its extinction.

TVA was itself responsible for the budget arrangement that made these items a tempting target. Memory, unsupported by documents, suggests that the rubric introducing a variety of activities requiring smaller appropriations than power production, river control, or fertilizer development, was originally drafted to read "Other Programs in Resource Development." When it was shortened by an enterprising editor concerned with the limitations of space, it inadvertently and briefly contributed to the impression that power and fertilizer programs and river control were not examples of a total resource development effort, and that TVA's activities in the field were limited to the programs listed. That was misleading. TVA's entire appropriation is devoted to resource development, and the inept presentation almost cost the life of the unified program, for the Senate Appropriations Committee agreed with the action of the House, concurring in the elimination of every activity listed under "Resource Development" except forestry. Continuation of that program was approved.

By this time, TVA's work in forestry had made an impact on the region, and its success had justified the Board's indifference to the plan for acquisition and regulation proposed by the department in 1934. Although the recommendations of that first year remained in the archives of Board minutes as a policy statement until 1937, they had been ignored. In July, 1937, as part of the general reorganization then under way, the Board took note of the situation and adopted a new statement, observing of the 1934 document, "it appears that some of the statements of policy therein contained have never been adopted by the Board in practice, and that the aforesaid forest policy in many particulars does not represent the actual policy of the Board." The 1937 statement of forestry objectives emphasized the need for research, surveys, and investigations, and for cooperation with other agencies, and with landowners themselves to achieve erosion control, woodland improvement, fire prevention, reforestation, and improved utilization of forest products. Perhaps to mollify the Chief Forester, one sentence did authorize studies looking toward "recommendations for legislation relating to corrective forest conservation and programs for public forest land acquisition." No such recommendations were ever made, and the sentence disappeared in a revision of the policy declaration adopted in 1941.

By 1953, TVA nurseries had supplied more than 250 million seedlings for planting, with over 30,000 landowners cooperating in the program. Twenty-seven demonstrations of improved timber management were under way on large holdings, and 250 on farm woodlots. To arouse interest in the reduction of forest fires, films had been produced, and some 6,500 meetings had been organized in over 100 of the 125 Valley counties. The effort was bearing fruit. State and county fire-fighting budgets had been increased and the annual burn was going down. Over 5,000 people had attended fifty demonstrations of timber harvesting. Nearly 2,000 sawmill and timber operators had participated in conferences and attended demonstrations designed to encourage more efficient management. To provide fencing for the Valley's new pastures and a market for pine thinnings, a wood preservative had been developed and an inexpensive portable post peeler designed. The process of experimentation, education, and demonstration was accelerating. It was achieving results, and when word came to the Valley that the forestry program was in danger, a formidable array of supporters advanced on Washington. They told their story to members of the Senate Committee and when that body reported, funds to continue the forestry program were included in the bill.

The activities whose elimination was approved had no such clientele. Most of the staff involved did not deal directly with the people whose well-being their efforts promoted. Unless the decision were reversed, the work of scientists in laboratories would be terminated, the studies of technicians upon whose advice the Board relied for decision would be ended, water quality investigations would cease, aid to localities in the development of recreation would be stopped, and mapping of the Valley, vital to its development, would be halted. Men available to help state and local governments undertaking new responsibilities would be gone, and an innovative program to stimulate development in tributary watersheds would have to be abandoned. No citizen invasion of the capitol in support of these activities occurred, but a half-dozen senators, representing Alabama, Tennessee, and Kentucky, determined that they deserved advocates and defenders. They met together to organize a fight to overturn the committee decision and gain approval of all the programs rejected. They crammed on reports and memoranda. They sought replies to pending questions, and when they took the Senate floor, they saved the regional program.

They saved it by a detailed description of objectives, methods, and accomplishments. They spoke with precision and with passion, illuminating principles with illustrations and statistics. It was great debate. The opposition collapsed, the recommendation of the Appropriations Committee was rejected, the action of the House repudiated. When the differences between House and Senate had been adjusted in conference the programs had survived. Much more was at stake than the sum (some $2 million requested, $1.35 million finally allowed) needed to finance the activities for a single fiscal year. The concept of a decentralized administration of federal functions and a unified approach to development was the issue, and it triumphed. The victory received little public attention. The fact that, as anticipated, the Senate refused to add funds to commence construction of the Fulton plant was considered more newsworthy.

In the autumn of 1953, the Board appeared before the Bureau of the Budget to present its request for funds for fiscal 1955, the first hearing before a Bureau staff representing the Eisenhower Administration. Once more, an item to begin construction of the Fulton plant was included in TVA's proposals. In his presentation, TVA's Chairman Gordon R. Clapp emphasized the peculiar situation confronting this publicly owned power system and its consumers. At the time, more than 50 per cent of TVA's capacity was committed to meet the demands of defense installations, principally the plants of the Atomic Energy Commission at Oak Ridge, Tennessee, and Paducah, Kentucky—loads subject to sharp and unexpected increases. Because of this responsibility, the question of adequate capacity was more critical in the case of TVA than it would be for a system less vulnerable to the impact of national emergencies. As the Chairman pointed out, 1.3 million domestic consumers then relied upon TVA for their power supply, and it was unthinkable that they should be obliged to run a risk that electricity might be denied them because of the claims of defense when the danger could be avoided. Either additional capacity must be provided, or TVA should be relieved of some of its responsibility for supplying the power requirements of AEC facilities. This was Clapp's comment.

The second of these alternatives appealed to the examiners of the Bureau of the Budget, and the record, which was later disclosed, revealed that conferences between representatives of the Bureau and the Atomic Energy Commission began early in December. The initial effort was to find private power companies willing to build a facility to provide the energy then supplied by TVA's Shawnee plant, which, together with a plant built by a group of private companies organized as Electric Energy, Inc., furnished the power consumed by AEC's Paducah facilities. Shawnee capacity could then be devoted to serving general load growth on the TVA system. President Eisenhower's budget message, transmitted to the Congress in January, 1954, reflected this expectation. With respect to TVA it read in part:

> In order to provide, with appropriate operating reserves, for reasonable growth in industrial, municipal and co-operative power loads in the area through calendar year 1957, arrangements are being made to reduce, by the fall of 1957, existing commitments of the Tennessee Valley Authority to the Atomic Energy Commission by 500,000 to 600,000 kilowatts. This would release the equivalent amount of Tennessee Valley Authority generating capacity to meet increased load requirements of other consumers in the power system and at the same time eliminate the need for appropriating funds from the Treasury to finance additional generating units. In the event, however, that negotiations for furnishing these load require-

ments for the Atomic Energy Commission from other sources are not consummated as contemplated or new defense loads develop, the question of starting additional generating units by the Tennessee Valley Authority will be reconsidered.

This was the origin of the Dixon-Yates contract, which surfaced in 1954, one of the most extraordinary of the many assaults on the TVA power system and the first to be mounted by an Administration in office. It was the subject of extended debate in Congress, and of hearings before at least five different congressional committees. Before it vanished into history, it required in addition to the attention of the Bureau of the Budget, the consideration of the Atomic Energy Commission, the Securities and Exchange Commission, the Federal Power Commission, the General Accounting Office, the Internal Revenue Service, and the Federal Bureau of Investigation. The Court of Claims heard evidence. The Supreme Court of the United States was not spared. At one point, in August, 1954, the furor caused the President to order a full disclosure of every step leading to the decision to enter into a contract, and it appeared that, of all things, a representative of the Department of Agriculture had been present at one meeting. Candidates for Ph.D degrees have written dissertations on Dixon-Yates. It has been the subject of articles and books. The sinuous course of negotiations has been charted step by step. But at the time its origin was sheltered from view.

Perhaps no one except the few involved—representatives of the Bureau of the Budget, the AEC, and the private utilities—knew of the difficulties that immediately appeared in the search for an alternative source of power for the Atomic Energy facilities. The power companies were not interested in building another plant in the vicinity of Paducah for the sound reason that the concentration of capacity there would become unprofitable in the event of reduction in the AEC load. And it turned out that the AEC did not want to give up its contract with TVA. On January 14, a week before the President's budget message was presented, the agency had advised the Bureau of the Budget "if we purchased more power from private utilities in lieu of TVA power presently under firm contract . . . it would cost the AEC more per kw and would not be as certain a supply due to possible delays in construction and location of reserve power, etc." At this point, further exploration of the possibility of relieving TVA of its commitment to AEC must have appeared futile, even to those involved in the search. If there had been no other purpose to accomplish, conferences with TVA with respect to power supply would have been resumed. That was the procedure suggested by the President's message. There was, however, another objective.

As a matter of fact, the record shows that the effort to find another power supplier for AEC had been abandoned before the President's budget message was transmitted to Congress on January 21. It was concealed because a new and, to the foes of TVA, a very happy circumstance had developed. Private companies were unwilling to build a plant to supply additional energy to AEC at Paducah, but the inquiries made and the conferences involved provided an opportunity for the presentation of a proposal long cherished by certain companies neighboring to TVA, who were of course delighted to be assured that the new Administration was opposed to the addition of capacity to the TVA power system. They advised representatives of the Bureau of the Budget and AEC that they would be glad to meet the need. They would add capacity to their systems and sell the energy to TVA. To them the prospects must have been alluring, for if they could take over responsibility for power supply in the TVA area they could bring to an end the high use–low rate policy of the public system, which had been an irritant to them for years.

Officers of these companies reported, and correctly, that the Board of TVA had not welcomed such proposals. The response of the government representatives with whom they were then dealing was different. They were eager listeners. It was true, of course, that the Atomic Energy Commission had no responsibility for power supply in the TVA area, and no member of the staff of the Bureau of the Budget was entrusted with the obligation. That circumstance did not deter either agency, and together they proceeded to negotiate a contract with an entity invented for the occasion. It was called the Mississippi Valley Generating Company, a combination created by two private power systems the names of whose presidents, Edgar H. Dixon of Middle South Utilities and Eugene Yates of the Southern Company, provided the popular designation of the affair.

The arrangements were complex, but in brief the plan was this:

the combine would build a plant at West Memphis in Arkansas, across the Mississippi from Memphis in Tennessee, in the service area of a Middle South subsidiary; AEC would contract to purchase the energy produced, but not a single kilowatt-hour would be used by the buyer; it would be delivered to TVA over a transmission line to be built across the river, half by TVA and half by the generating company. According to the Administration's justification, this astonishing arrangement was legitimatized by what was described as the "replacement" theory. AEC would continue to receive power from TVA, and under its existing contracts. It would, however, "replace" that power by providing energy under a different contract from another location. The costs would be higher than those estimated for the Fulton plant, but neither AEC nor the Bureau was handicapped by commitment to the TVA statute that required power to be made available at the "lowest possible" rates. Costs were of no special concern to the prospective purchaser, AEC, for the Administration expected them to be borne by TVA.

When the proposal was disclosed to Congress, vigorous protests were registered. Friends of TVA were outraged. Acts of Congress had been ignored, the Board of TVA had been insulted, the wishes of the people of the region were denied. Some members of Congress not particularly concerned about TVA were incensed that AEC was acting as a broker to accomplish objectives that were none of its concern. There was enough doubt about the legality of the role assigned to AEC that the Administration felt obliged to seek an amendment to pending legislation in order to authorize the transaction under the remarkable replacement theory. Opposition to the amendment caused what is politely called "extended debate" in the Senate in the summer of 1954. From the Budget Bureau and from AEC came a stream of statements to be incorporated in speeches by members who were supporting the Administration's position. TVA's opponents conveyed the impression that without the proposed contract AEC's power supply would be in some way threatened, although the fact was that the agency's contracts with TVA were not involved at all. By repetition, great stress was laid upon the fact that Congress had refused to appropriate funds for the Fulton plant proposed by TVA, but it was never explained that Congress was responding to the recommendation of the Administration, which had eliminated the funds proposed by its predecessor for inclusion in the budget.

Late in July, debate on Dixon-Yates ended in the Senate with adoption of the amendment to the Atomic Energy Act designed to authorize AEC to enter into the contract. Interest did not subside, however. Charges of Presidential favoritism were made, and on August 21, 1954, the Bureau of the Budget and AEC carried out the order from the Chief Executive to make a full disclosure of all material related to the affair. Then it was clear how quickly the quest for an alternative source of power for AEC had turned into a scheme to make TVA dependent on its long-time adversaries. It was only then that TVA learned of the steps by which responsibility for power supply in the area it served had been shifted to one of its customers, AEC, and to the private companies with which AEC proposed to contract. Prior to that time, TVA's connection with the negotiations had been limited to an analysis of the additional costs to be borne by the government if the Dixon-Yates plant were substituted for Fulton. According to the calculations of TVA's staff, those extra costs would amount to somewhere between $7 and more than $8 million every year, a probable total of $200 million over the life calculated for the plant. Under pressure, the power companies submitted a revised proposal with the additional annual costs reduced, reaching a total of $3.6 million every year according to a Budget Bureau analysis, between $5 and $6 million according to TVA.

Publication of the record gave TVA and the public a good deal of information, but it did little to quiet opposition. Together with later testimony before Congressional committees, the account revealed that the proposed contract had had troubles within the Administration. Some members of the staff of the Bureau of the Budget had been unhappy about it. There was criticism from attorneys of the Federal Power Commission, to which the draft agreement had been referred for comment. The General Accounting Office had protested at one point and the contract had been modified to meet its objections. There had been opposition within the Atomic Energy Commission itself. Two of the five commissioners had written to the Director of the Budget to express their concern that the AEC was being involved "in a matter remote from its responsibilities." In their letter of April 16, 1954, Commissioners Henry D. Smyth and Eugene M. Zuckert pointed out:

> The proposal under discussion is an outgrowth of the response to the President's budget message, and your letter of December 24, 1953, requesting the AEC to explore the possibility of reducing existing commitments of the TVA to the Commission. In the course of that exploration, it was determined to be unwise to disturb the AEC arrangements with TVA, upon which our production schedules depend. Since that determination, the explorations have taken a different course.
>
> The present proposal would create a situation whereby the AEC would be contracting for power, not one kilowatt of which would be used in connection with Commission production activities. The creation of such a contractual relationship would place upon the Commission a continuing responsibility during the 25-year life of the contract for stewardship in respect to matters irrelevant to the mission of the Commission.

The letter ended, "Of course, if the President or the Congress directs the Commission to acccpt such a responsibility, we will endeavor to discharge it fully." A third Commission member, Thomas E. Murray, was not only opposed at this time, he was angered by the way the negotiations had been conducted. Thus, with a protesting majority, AEC Chairman Lewis L. Strauss, an enthusiastic advocate of the arrangement, had had to advise the President that it would be necessary for him to order the Dixon-Yates contract signed.

On June 16, 1954, more than a month before the legitimatizing amendment was adopted by Congress, that instruction was issued. In a letter to the Chairman of the AEC the Director of the Budget reported, "The President has asked me to instruct the Atomic Energy Commission to proceed with negotiations with the sponsors of the proposal made by Messrs. Dixon and Yates, with a view to signing a definitive contract on a basis generally within the terms of the proposal." On that same date he wrote to Harry A. Curtis, the senior member of the two-man Board of TVA (Chairman Clapp's term having expired on May 18), that "he [the President] has also requested that instructions be given the Tennessee Valley Authority and the Atomic Energy Commission to work out the necessary contractual, operational, and administrative arrangements between the two agencies." This letter, which also described TVA's obligation to assume certain costs connected with utilization of the power to be generated at the Dixon-Yates plant, was one of the few direct communications with the Board of TVA during the negotiations.

On July 2, Curtis replied, urging reconsideration of the whole question and pointing out TVA's unwillingness to assume responsibility for costs it could not control. When his letter was answered in August, there appeared to be some shift in emphasis and a prospect that AEC would bear a larger share of the costs. TVA then agreed to meet with AEC, but protested the earlier treatment of its representatives and the fact that it had never received a copy of the contract between AEC and the private companies, although its responsibilities were to be affected.

A meeting was postponed until the new Chairman of the TVA Board could take office on September 1. President Eisenhower had appointed a retiring general from the Corps of Engineers, Herbert D. Vogel, to the vacancy on the Board and designated him Chairman. Undoubtedly the Administration expected that approach to TVA would be more comfortable when he had been sworn in. Probably communication was more satisfactory, but the problems were complex and events moved slowly. There were conferences and hearings. In spite of debate throughout the country in the autumn of 1954, and turbulent hearings before the Joint Committee on Atomic Energy, the general opinion appeared to be that the Administration had won and that TVA could be forced to comply with the Executive decision. Although there was no agreement with TVA to accept the energy, the contract between AEC and Dixon-Yates had been signed, and preliminary work at the site had begun.

Indeed the sponsors of Dixon-Yates had always been confident of success. Their support within the Administration was too impressive to consider the possibility of defeat. In contemplation of victory there had been ground-breaking ceremonies in Arkansas in June, attended, according to the press, by an estimated crowd of seven thousand. A parade, with eleven state troopers assigned to preserve the order of march, speeches by the state's two senators, J. William Fulbright and John L. McClellan, and a barbecue enlivened the occasion and honored the climactic moment when

Edgar H. Dixon and Eugene Yates themselves turned the first earth with gilded shovels.

Troubles were in store for the contract's advocates, however. On February 18, 1955, Senator Lister Hill of Alabama took the floor of the Senate to advise his colleagues of his discovery that Adolph Wenzell, a vice president of the First Boston Corporation, a banking institution reported to be involved in the financing of the Dixon-Yates combine, had been employed as a consultant to the Bureau of the Budget during the period when the scheme was developed. To those who had always believed that the plan was part of a larger conspiracy to destroy TVA, this intelligence suggested that a plot would be revealed and the contract canceled. At the time, the Securities and Exchange Commission was considering the question of the financing proposed by the private companies, and the attorney for the State of Tennessee, which had intervened, called Wenzell as a witness. He frankly acknowledged his participation in negotiations. Alert reporters noted that his name had not appeared in the list of persons involved set out in the full disclosure ordered by the President in August, 1954, and requested an explanation. The initial suggestion that the name was inadvertently omitted from the report was generally found laughable, and later testimony attributing the elimination to a decision of the Bureau of the Budget seemed reasonable. The Antimonopoly Subcommittee of the Senate Judiciary Committee scheduled hearings, and witnesses from the Bureau of the Budget and other agencies appeared.

Reporters were avid, investigators were busy, politicians appraised the odds. Dixon-Yates was in trouble, but the Administration seemed determined to stick with the scheme. Then on June 23, 1955, the city of Memphis, the intended victim of the private power invasion, became the executioner of the plan. The municipality announced that it would build its own plant, and, on expiration of its current contract with TVA, would itself be responsible for supplying its consumers with electricity. The city refused to be forced into dependence on a brace of private companies, one of which it had rejected as a power supplier by a vote of more than 17-to-1 almost twenty years earlier.

Memphis had been ready to take the step for some time. It had delayed because it was reluctant to leave the TVA system, and there was always the hope that the Administration might change its position. It acted only when it was clear that whatever difficulties might be in store for Dixon-Yates the White House was adamant in its determination to deny funds for the Fulton project, or any other plant to be proposed by TVA. Time was running out. Construction had to begin. With the decision of Memphis, the Atomic Energy Commission was in the peculiar position of contracting to purchase power for which it had no use or market. Even before its construction, the Dixon-Yates plant was surplus. On July 11, 1955, with remarkable aplomb, the White House announced the cancellation of the contract.

Administration spokesmen indicated satisfaction at the outcome. The TVA power system had been fractured, and at least a beginning of demolition seemed to be accomplished. But that was only half a loaf; the fortunes of the private companies had not been advanced and they were not pleased. In fact, the companies claimed injury at the hands of their one-time associates. When their bill for over $3 million was presented, AEC, after a period of indecision, refused to pay, citing, among other circumstances, the fact that the activities of First Boston's Wenzell raised a question of conflict of interest. The companies resorted to the Court of Claims where their position was upheld, although the amount determined to be due was somewhat reduced. On appeal, the Supreme Court sustained the government's contention that the contract was invalid because of the conflict of interest involved in Wenzell's participation.

It was an odd outcome of a curious relationship. Wenzell and his talents had been welcomed by the Administration. His continued association with First Boston Corporation was never concealed from the government representatives with whom he dealt, nor were his conferences with the private power companies. On July 6, 1955, according to the *New York Times*, the President of the United States had responded to a reporter's inquiry by stating that he regarded Wenzell's activities as proper. But because of them the Mississippi Valley Generating Company, the Dixon-Yates apparatus, was, according to its calculation, out over $3 million. The amount may have been small in comparison with the dollars spent in litigation and in anti-TVA propaganda over the years, but its loss, the penalty of cooperation with an Administration hostile to TVA and friendly to them, must have been a bitter dose for the private companies to swallow.

For students of public administration, the Dixon-Yates affair is a fascinating study. It is a clear example of a President intervening to direct an independent agency, the Atomic Energy Commission, to undertake a responsibility unrelated to its assignment, which the agency itself would not have chosen to accept. It represents an invasion by one agency of the jurisdiction and responsibility of another. It also demonstrates how dependent a chief executive must be upon the information provided by his subordinates. In this case, the first record of the President's consideration of TVA matters is in an account of a conference with the man he had chosen to be Director of the Budget, Joseph Dodge, a banker from Detroit. According to Sherman Adams, No. 1 staff member at the White House, in his book *Firsthand Report,* Dodge called the President's attention "to a TVA request for funds to build a new steam generating plant at Fulton, Missouri, near Memphis, which in addition to meeting new demands within the region would reach out into new territory never before serviced by the TVA." The mind-stopping suggestion that the President was advised that TVA was considering construction of a plant at "Fulton, Missouri" would account for Adams's conclusion that TVA was reaching "out into new territory never before serviced by the TVA." Fulton, *Tennessee,* a community about thirty miles north of Memphis, was the proposed location, not Fulton, *Missouri,* almost 400 miles away, a municipality enjoying some national attention because a few years earlier Winston Churchill had delivered his famous "Iron Curtain" speech at Westminster College there.

The error may be due to careless editing of Adams's manuscript, but repeated references to the President's opposition to TVA's "expansion . . . into new territory" suggest that in fact the President may have been misled in this, as well as other matters. The notion that TVA was planning territorial expansion was as ill-founded as the conviction that it was responsible for the movement of industries from New England, and all accounts, including that of Robert J. Donovan in *Eisenhower—The Inside Story,* agree that such a fear was an important factor in the President's determination "to check further growth of the TVA." His major advisers on matters relating to TVA appeared to be Dodge and his successor as Budget Director, Rowland Hughes, and Lewis L. Strauss, then Chairman of the Atomic Energy Commission—none of whom had any acquaintance with the agency. Until his own appointees were in office, the President never discussed TVA affairs with any of its representatives.

Eisenhower may have regarded an encounter with Gordon Clapp, Chairman of the Board of TVA, as an avoidable embarrassment. Clapp had been associated with TVA since the summer of 1933. Before his appointment to the Board and designation as its Chairman in 1946, he had been General Manager, and prior to that Director of Personnel. The term to which he had been appointed when Lilienthal resigned was due to expire in May, 1954, and early in the new Administration his admirers were urging his reappointment. A delegation of senators and representatives from the TVA area visited the President to express their support and in March, 1954, a petition advocating Clapp's reappointment was delivered to the White House. Forty thousand signers were ignored. The President had made up his mind. According to Donovan, he said privately "that Clapp's approach to the whole power question in TVA was too doctrinaire and that he had to have someone who would look at facts objectively." It is not easy to understand precisely what the President meant. He had never met Chairman Clapp. Just as it is possible he was told that the plant TVA proposed to build was to be located in Missouri, and the evidence shows he was badly advised about the role of Adolph Wenzell, artlessly telling one press conference that "Mr. Wenzell was never called in or asked a single thing about the Dixon-Yates contract," so he may have been misinformed about Clapp's opinions. Yet it must be admitted that in the eyes of the President, TVA's Chairman would probably seem to be doctrinaire.

He had to be: In common with his fellow directors and the staff of TVA, the chairman was committed to the doctrine set forth in the statute. This was no ordinary power system. It was not only obliged to give preference to "states, counties, municipalities and cooperative organizations of citizens or farmers, not organized or doing business for profit," but, as has been noted earlier, the Board was "to make studies, experiments and determinations to promote the wider and better use of electric power for agricultural and domestic use" and to cooperate with others "in the application of electric power to the fuller and better balanced development of the resources of the region." The Act further declared that "the projects herein provided for shall be considered primarily as for the benefit of the people of the section as a whole and particularly the domestic and rural consumers," whose use of electricity was ordered to be encouraged by "the lowest possible rates." It was the solemn duty of all TVA Board members to carry out and defend those provisions. To protect the statute, it was necessary to understand its obligations, to argue and persuade, to reject easy answers—in a word to be "doctrinaire."

For TVA, cancellation of the Dixon-Yates contract reduced the threat of a major assault, for it seemed likely that it was to be the first of many such proposals. In June, 1954, the President of the Edison Electric Institute, an association of private power companies, had announced offers of neighboring private power companies to sell power to TVA in amounts that would make construction of capacity by the agency unnecessary, and one company had purchased a site on the Tennessee River not far from Chattanooga, like Memphis a major load center. Such a program would remove control of costs from TVA. The location, design, and construction of generating plants are important factors in the cost of power and therefore the rates at which it is sold. Transmission costs are significant, operating control is essential. No honest Board member could yield responsibility for decisions with respect to those matters. If the Dixon-Yates proposal had succeeded, it is probable that the other propositions would have been pushed. With its failure, interest in its imitators appeared to fade.

Dixon-Yates disappeared. Memphis began construction of a municipally owned plant. But the question of additional capacity for the TVA system was not settled, and demand was growing. Clearly, a new source of capital had to be sought, and, in the autumn of 1954, when the Dixon-Yates proposal was still active, TVA embarked on an intensive study of the legislation required to permit the agency to issue revenue bonds for investment in power facilities. This was not the first time such an inquiry had been undertaken. In 1948, after prolonged controversy had delayed appropriations to start construction of Johnsonville, the staff of TVA had been instructed by the Board to investigate all the alternatives to continued financing by appropriations. Suggestions of friends and foes were examined. Studies and conferences continued, but the problems were so many, and the difficulties so apparent, that no recommendation for change was submitted.

Bond financing was one alternative considered. To adopt it would require an amendment to the TVA Act, for the limited bonding authority of the original statute had been repealed when the bond amendment of 1939 was approved and the latter authorization had been exhausted with the acquisitions it made possible, and the bonds long since retired. President Eisenhower referred to the new exploration in his Budget message to Congress in January, 1955. He said:

> The Tennessee Valley Authority is giving immediate attention to the possibilities of financing further expansion of its power system by means other than federal appropriations. The Authority has been requested to complete its studies in time to permit consideration by the Congress at this session of any legislation that may be necessary. It is expected that the power needs for the system will be reexamined after the Congress has had an opportunity to consider legislation to provide for future financing.

In April, 1955, before the Dixon-Yates contract was canceled, the legislation proposed by TVA was made public, submitted to the Bureau of the Budget for Administration comment, and incorporated in bills introduced in Congress. In May, the Bureau's comments came in the form of a clutch of proposed amendments to the bills embodying the plan of TVA. The Dixon-Yates proposal had revealed the willingness of the Bureau to ignore the TVA statute, usurp the functions of the Board, and take over management of the power system. The amendments now offered by the Administration underscored the predilection. The purpose of the legislation was to permit TVA to issue revenue bonds to provide another source of capital for investment in power facilities. It would add to costs, but from the point of view of the agency there were some compensating advantages. The annual uncertainty associated with the appropriation process would be eliminated, and exposure of the system to the vagaries of politics would be terminated. It would give flexibility in timing. The most revealing of the many amendments proposed by the Bureau would have removed those advantages.

Although no funds were to be provided by the Treasury, the

Bureau proposed that the procedures of the appropriation process should be applied to the issuance of bonds and that, before TVA could approach the financial community, the approval of the Bureau and Congress had to be obtained. Nor was that all. Proceeds provided funds for investment in power facilities, and, although they could not be used to initiate construction of new projects, they were available to finance the addition of units at existing plants, to build transmission lines, and for other purposes. The Budget Bureau now proposed that expenditures from earnings be subject to appropriation procedures, too. It would put bond issuance under control of the Treasury even though the bonds were not to be guaranteed by the government. Taken as a whole, TVA and its friends believed that the Bureau's proposals were intolerable and that if they were adopted the life of the government owned system would be brief.

Fortunately, perhaps, the Administration's action in disapproving the Fulton plant and the Budget Bureau's role in connection with Dixon-Yates had given the friends of TVA an effective demonstration of the probable consequences of yielding control to the Bureau. It had refused to include the agency's request for funds for power capacity in the President's budget. It had rejected TVA's estimates and by the material it supplied for its forces in debate endeavored to undermine confidence in TVA's rates and management. There was not the slightest reason to expect its approval of new projects, even though financing was not to be provided by the Treasury. It was clear that when considering problems relating to the region's power supply, the counsel of private power and banking companies was preferred to that of TVA. Hostility was not a new position for certain ranking members of the Bureau staff to assume. It had been apparent for a long time, only slightly masked by the civility with which adversaries in the bureaucracy communicate. In earlier years, the Board of TVA had frequently been obliged to appeal to various Budget Directors the decisions of their subordinates. Now, for the first time, those to whom the independence guaranteed in the statute was abhorrent were able to seek their objective openly and in the name of the President.

For four years, the controversy over power financing raged. There were extended hearings before subcommittees of the Public Works Committees of House and Senate. There was debate in both houses, but at last, on August 9, 1959, a bill was signed. It was satisfactory to TVA. Amendments had been added in the course of its progress, but none was crippling, and responsibility for management of its power system remained with the Board of TVA. A ceiling of $750 million of bonds outstanding had been added,* as proposed by the Administration, not the unspecified amount recommended by TVA. The requirements for cash payments from power proceeds to the Treasury had been increased. Under the original TVA proposal, an annual dividend on the government's—that is, the owners'—investment of appropriated funds in power facilities would be paid into the Treasury. Although it was not a payment of interest, since the money was not a loan, its size would be determined every year by applying the government's current cost of money to the investment made from appropriated funds.

To this provision, drafted by TVA, Congress added a schedule for reduction of the appropriation investment in power facilities (then about $1.25 billion) until $1 billion had been repaid. The amounts of repayment were fixed; $10 million annually for five years; $15 million in each of the following five; and thereafter $20 million every year until the total was reached. This was the second time the amount of power proceeds to be paid by TVA into the Treasury of the United States had been determined by Congress. In the beginning, the Board was directed to pay into the Treasury six months after the end of each fiscal year all proceeds that it determined were not needed in its business. No sum was fixed as a requirement. Decision was left with the Board. In 1948, Congress devised a plan popularly called the "forty-year pay back," under which the agency was required to pay to the Treasury from proceeds amounts that, in forty years from the time a plant began operation, would equal the investment of appropriated funds in the project. That plan was succeeded by the present arrangement, adopted in 1959.†

* Lifted by acts of Congress to $1.75 billion in 1966, and to $5 billion in 1970.

† Through June 30, 1971, TVA had paid to the Treasury a total of $909 million from power proceeds, including $65,072,500 for the payment of interest on and the retirement of bonds held by the Treasury. Payments

Those were the major changes from the text of the bill as drafted and submitted by TVA. One additional amendment was successfully sought by private power companies. It was not included in the Administration's proposals. Its effect was to establish a boundary beyond which power from TVA would not be available to consumers. Exceptions were made in the case of a number of communities whose applications had been pending but could not be considered during the six-year siege when provision of increased capacity was in doubt. TVA contended that the limitation was not required, but did not urge extended opposition. The issue was not that important. For years, service areas had been reasonably stable. An area limitation would not interfere with TVA's ability to serve its present customers. Its only function was to give peace of mind to neighboring utilities, and unless tranquility were reflected in lessened service or higher rates it would be relatively harmless.

It is true that an area limitation was a regression from the spirit of the original Act, which offered any community "within transmission distance" the hope that power from TVA might be available to it, power produced at the lowest possible cost and sold at rates designed "to encourage use." Unquestionably, TVA's influence on the rates charged by neighboring companies might be diluted, but the limitation no longer presented the vital issues it had embodied in the beginning. A territorial boundary was one of the earliest indulgences sought by private companies from the Board. It had been a stumbling block in the way of early purchase plans. It was one of the questions on which Arthur Morgan differed from his colleagues, who had refused to accept a limitation, regarding it then as a clear rejection of a basic principle of the Act of Congress.

In a way, the anticlimactic quality of the companies' delayed achievement was a symbol of change. The protection they won was a shield against a threat no longer existing.

---

from chemical plant operations and miscellaneous receipts raised the total Treasury payments to almost $950 million. To the same date, some $2.5 billion had been appropriated by Congress to support all TVA activities. It has been used for flood control and navigation as well as power facilities, for research and experimentation in fertilizer production and use over the nation, for mapping, for investigations of water quality, activities in forestry and wildlife protection, for leadership in the development of recreation, and other statutory purposes.

VII

Quiet Work in the Valley

With passage of the revenue bond amendment in 1959, public attention to the power system began to diminish. The fight for survival had been won, and the private companies reduced their attacks.

There was no repetition of a general assault like the one advanced in the late '40's and continued for some years. That campaign was discussed at the convention of the Edison Electric Institute held in Atlantic City in 1950. Apparently the private utilities had employed a research organization to conduct a public opinion poll, and in 1949 the survey revealed that 63 per cent of the people interviewed not only approved of TVA but thought more such organizations would be a good thing for the country. Particularly unnerving to the power companies was the report that 45 per cent of their employees favored the government agency. A pamphlet prepared for utility executives by a New York advertising firm presented the conclusions of the inquiry with the comment:

This is a shocker.
Sixty-three percent of the people approve TVA. Are they Socialists? Liberals? Fuzzy thinkers? Low income folks?
Apparently not. In the upper income group, only 16 percent are against TVA. Republicans 17 percent. Among editors and educators, 7 percent disapprove. And among those whose answers to

other questions definitely place them in the "free enterprise" class, only 23 percent dislike TVA.

These are people who read and get around and think and supposedly recognize a fact when they see it. This chart gives very strong evidence that private industry's side of the TVA story has been buried in the rubble of bureaucratic propaganda.

Along with approval for TVA, the survey revealed that 60 per cent of those interviewed were against socialism. A recommendation resulted. "It is apparent that to link our fight to the TVA question would run us into a lot of opposition, most of it based on lack of knowledge. But to link our fight to socialism is something else again." As an apparent consequence, advertisements appeared throughout the country "linking" TVA to socialism, and in 1953 encouraging results were reported to the private companies. No doubt the Electric Companies Advertising Program (ECAP) was given credit for the erosion in approval of TVA it reported—from 67 per cent in 1947, 63 per cent in 1949, to 55 per cent in 1953— for it continued to be supported. According to *Printers Ink* something over $17 million was spent by ECAP for advertising between 1949 and 1960.* Much of that expenditure was directed against TVA, and guaranteed that the publicly owned system would not be ignored.

In the past decade, however, with controversy lessened, TVA power operations have been conducted in relative obscurity. There were headlines in 1955 when Memphis withdrew from the system to build its own facility, but seven years later, there was only local interest when the city again became a customer of TVA, which took over operation of the municipal plant under a lease with option to purchase. Whether the territorial limitation included in the bond authorization in 1959 did relieve the fears of neighboring companies and therefore reduce general hostility cannot be determined. It seems unlikely, for experienced managements must have known how little danger of substantial expansion existed. TVA's reliance on bond sales for funds for capital investment has probably proved to be a greater factor, removing, as it did, the obligation of utility lobbyists to organize annual campaigns against

* Revealed by statistics appearing in the issues of November 23, 1951; October 21, 1955; August 23, 1957; October 31, 1958; October 30, 1959; and September 9, 1960.

the appropriation of money for capacity increases. Perhaps, too, acceptance of TVA bonds by the financial community has invested the agency with an aura of expensive respectability.

A new source of funds was provided in 1959, but the policies of the TVA power system were not changed. It is still endeavoring to provide electricity "at the lowest possible rates" and to make certain that it is applied "to the fuller and better balanced development of the resources of the region" as the Act directs. It is managed by the same people for the same purposes, and capacity additions have continued. Two giant coal-burning plants, Paradise and Bull Run, have been built since the bond amendment was adopted, another is under construction, three nuclear power plants are under way; and plans for one more have been announced.

For almost thirty years, power held the center of the stage. TVA press releases, its publications, and the speeches of its directors made valiant but fruitless efforts to direct attention to other programs. Even a President tried. When, in January, 1940, President Roosevelt transmitted to Congress a TVA report on "The Recreational Development of the Tennessee River System" he began his message with this statement:

> So much publicity has been given by the press and in other ways to the power development feature of the work of the Tennessee Valley Authority that it is fair to assume that many of our citizens and even government officials hold a belief that the purpose of the act creating the Authority was primarily the development of electric power.

"It is perhaps time to call attention to this utter fallacy," he wrote, and after enumerating various objectives incorporated in the TVA statute the President continued: "In other words, it is time that people should understand that power development was only a part—and ultimately only a relatively small part—of a great social and economic experiment in one of our major watersheds."

The President's effort was unsuccessful. Within a few months, power capacity was being increased for national defense and for almost twenty years thereafter TVA's power system continued to receive major public attention, obscuring other achievements. The excitement and conflict it continued to generate fostered a curious school of criticism, one which did not oppose nor attempt to discredit power operations, but instead attacked the agency's performance in other areas, holding that TVA had become "only" a power system, and that its initial concept of total resource development had been abandoned. It was a reminder of the "eighteen-company" case, and the contention of the private companies that the projected system of water control served the requirements of power production alone. The new critics offered credentials, sometimes self-awarded, as conservationists, and while the general public can be forgiven, it is odd that specialists in the field failed to observe that even when dramatic battles over power were being won the slow process of resource development continued. In Washington, senators were debating about power and TVA witnesses were appearing before congressional committees to testify about electricity production and use. But in the Tennessee Valley, landowners were planting trees, farmers were experimenting with new kinds of fertilizer and changing their pattern of farm management to take advantage of technical advice, cattle were grazing on pastures where cotton used to grow, new parks and recreation areas were opening, and the battle against pollution was gaining support. This is resource development. As President Eisenhower had observed in his State of the Union address of 1953, it cannot be accomplished by the federal government alone. States and local agencies must be involved, citizens individually and in their private associations.

The people and their local institutions are involved in the Tennessee Valley, where a federal program continues to strive for achievement through a decentralized administration. Participation of citizens is wide, and local organizations are active. They share responsibility for power system operations, and for the development of recreation. They are engaged in fertilizer testing and in forestry improvement. Their role is basic in one program planned by TVA in the late 1930's, submerged during the war, revived in post-war years, and by the 1960's matured and flourishing—Tributary Area Development. Inauguration of the TAD program reflected TVA's conviction that for total regional growth intensive efforts would be required to develop the resources in many of the tributary valleys that make up the huge watershed, and that major responsibility must be assumed by the people who live there. Specific remedies for local problems had to be developed and applied.

The oldest such program now functioning began its work in the

Beech River watershed in western Tennessee in 1950. It was just getting under way when its future was endangered, for this was one of the activities selected for termination by the House and the Senate Committee when TVA's appropriation for fiscal year 1954 was pending and only rescued from sudden death by the vigor of its advocates on the floor of the Senate. Like most others, organization of the Beech River TAD was a response to recognition of a specific problem, in this case the intermittent flooding of farm lands along the river. When a group from the small watershed called on the Chairman of the Board of TVA, their request was modest. They wanted the river dredged and the channel cleared so that runoff from the rainfall would move more swiftly down the Beech to the Tennessee. Unfortunately, protection from flood damage was not that simple. The area drained by the tributary is characterized by some of the most highly erodible soil in the Tennessee Valley, and investigation made abundantly clear that dredging and channel clearing alone would be a waste of time and money. Flooding damage might be briefly reduced, but unless land use changes followed, silt would accumulate again—and promptly. The job would have to be repeated. The area had other problems discernible to specialists and technicians but to the general public not so apparent as persistent flood damage, and a counterproposal was offered. If the community would work with TVA to identify and reduce every obstacle to progress and to promote every opportunity for its advancement, a program of total resource development would be launched, a sort of mini-TVA, with enhancement of the whole environment as its purpose. The government of the state was consulted and its agencies invited to join.

From that small beginning in 1950, the program in Beech River has grown and TAD has spread to other tributary areas, sixteen in all, covering more than half the land area of the watershed of the Tennessee. There is no uniformity in organization and no formula limits participation. The problems are not identical and solutions are not alike. Methods differ but the objective is the same in every area and initial organization steps are similar. All the organizations are endeavoring to promote economic well-being and to make their communities pleasanter places to live in, and citizens ready to join in the undertaking are divided into work groups in the beginning. Bankers and businessmen, farmers, teachers, local officials, and housewives merge their diverse talents and select the particular area in which they want to work. A technician from TVA (and, if available, one from the state) is assigned to each work group. Foresters consult with those whose major interest is in the timber resource, agronomists with those dedicated to the improvement of agricultural practices. There may be a dozen work groups, as the basic resources—the water, the trees, and the soil—are studied, schools and people are surveyed. Each group explores its chosen area. That is the first step. As problems are uncovered and opportunities revealed, they are reported to the organization as a whole and as the resource inventory progresses, citizen education expands.

Resource inventories are common today. Often financed by federal agencies, many are conducted by professional services, with conclusions and recommendations carefully written and presented in impressive bindings. The Tributary Area Development surveys are different. The people themselves discover the facts, discuss the remedies, and settle the question of priorities. Technicians from TVA define the data to be collected, and a good deal of information already accumulated by the federal agency is made available at the start, but local citizens develop the inventories themselves. In the process, they discover that adverse conditions long accepted as inevitable can be changed, and opportunities ignored can be embraced. They learn how private decisions affect the public welfare.

In general, TAD programs are conducted in rural areas, and in every one active groups of landowners have justified redoubled efforts by TVA in the familiar fields of agriculture and forestry. In a few, the increased responsibility assumed by the local organizations has made feasible the construction of relatively small systems of water control to permit streamflow to contribute to expanding opportunity. As flood danger is reduced, a recreation resource is provided, and a better supply of water for municipal and industrial use is assured. The benefits these structures provide are largely local. They would not be realized nor would the investment of federal funds be justified without community acceptance of a share in the responsibility for planning and operation. This is the contrast between the development of the main stream of the Tennessee and its major tributaries and the control of streamflow in smaller rivers under the Tributary Area Development program.

Great dams like Norris and Fontana had to be built to accomplish regional objectives. Engineering factors determined their location, and the ability of adjacent communities to capture potential benefits was not an element in decision. Local benefits were expected to be small compared to the regional results achieved when Norris Dam was constructed, or when Fontana, Hiwassee, and Kentucky were completed. Then flood danger in the watershed would be reduced, and the waters of the Tennessee could be restrained from adding to damage along the lower Ohio and Mississippi. Goods from other areas could ride a modern river highway to markets in the Tennessee Valley and power could be supplied to the people of the region. Those advantages were far reaching. They were of national significance, and the projects were built to provide them. Fortunately, experience proved that waterfront cities and towns profited substantially, too, as new industries located along the channel, recreation developments added to community attractions, and a better municipal water supply became available. But these great multipurpose dams would have been constructed even if their potential local values were never realized.

That is the difference. The structures associated with Tributary Area Development would not be built unless the people of the area were prepared to guarantee their productivity, to undertake the responsibility of management, and to share in the costs. Beech River was the first such cooperative stream control project. By 1960, after ten years of work in the small valley, progress was apparent in the two counties of the watershed. New pastures and growing trees were holding the restless soil; silt in the watercourses was reduced. The appearance of Lexington, the largest town, was vastly improved. An attractive new courthouse surrounded by a nicely landscaped lawn symbolized the change, and the shrubbery, planted by the county judge himself, was a testimonial to citizen participation. Already the area had begun to share in the industrial growth of the region. New plants had located there, and an inventory disclosed that in the 10-year period 2,300 new jobs had become available in a valley whose total population was reported as 24,000 in the 1960 census. This evidence of growth was impressive, a resounding endorsement of the method, but investigation revealed that unless a more dependable supply of water could be provided a ceiling on progress must be acknowledged. Streamflow control could give it. A system of eight small dams was designed by TVA and the community organized to guarantee a return of benefits from the investment. Construction began in the autumn of 1962. In 1965, TVA completed the system, and the shoreland was turned over to the Beech River Watershed Development Authority (BRWDA) chartered by the state of Tennessee, for management.

From its experience on major waterways, TVA had learned something about the increased value accruing to land which becomes lakeshore property when reservoirs are filled. It had learned from its mistakes as well as its successes how to assure the greatest public benefits from the investment of public funds in projects for water control. Beginning with Norris Dam, the general practice had been to purchase a somewhat larger acreage than the land to be flooded. The amount varied, and there was no rule about it. To a considerable degree, it was determined by the willingness of landowners to sell and the desire of TVA to purchase whole farms rather than just the portion to be inundated, avoiding alternative costs such as severance damages and the highway relocation required if certain areas were to remain in private ownership. After a reservoir was filled, the shoreland was surveyed again, in an effort to determine its best use. Much was suitable for public recreation, a smaller amount for industrial location, and some for residential or commercial development.

Some areas were sold at auction. Of these a number became attractive residential communities, but a few were bought by irresponsible developers, who took their windfall profits, leaving behind poorly planned and shabbily built vacation facilities. There are not many, and where they exist, they are reminders of some of the pitfalls inherent in devotion to the principles of decentralization. TVA was eager to return to local control as much land as possible, and to do it promptly, but few jurisdictions had zoning regulations at the time, and there was no way the communities could make certain that the asset gained by the expenditure of public funds was prudently developed and in the public interest.

TVA learned, and after a few years land sales were halted until the situation could be reappraised.

Even before construction on Beech River had begun, the lessons drawn from experience on the first reservoirs had been applied at Melton Hill, a dam on the Clinch below Norris begun in 1960 and completed in 1963. The primary purpose of the Melton Hill project was to extend the navigation channel upstream, but it was apparent that development of the shoreline would add greatly to community assets. For the first time in connection with construction of its major river system, state and local authorities met with TVA to plan shoreland use in advance of construction. Industrial, recreational, and residential areas were identified and preparatory work done in advance of filling. Zoning regulations were adopted. Acceptance of responsibility by the people made certain that local benefits would be fully realized.

The methods developed in connection with the Melton Hill project were applied on Beech River. TVA followed its usual practice, purchasing the land to be flooded and the prospective shoreland in fee. Then its use was planned. A part would be sold for residential development. Some was suitable for public recreation. From the revenues it would receive from sales and fees the Beech River Watershed Development Authority contracted to repay to TVA a portion of the investment in construction. In addition to revenues from shorland development the BRWDA has other sources of income. The city of Lexington, Tennessee, pays for the water it draws from one of the new reservoirs. Experiments under way suggest that irrigation may permit some farmers to move to a more profitable kind of agriculture, and that the sale of water from the impoundments can add income to help cover the costs of management. Tax receipts from farms afforded flood relief should increase, and payments from the counties to the local authority should grow.

It is now seven years since the Beech River water control system was completed, twenty-two years since the developmental program was initiated. According to a survey undertaken in 1969, the severe erosion that afflicted the land in 1950 had been reduced by 85 per cent and demonstrations throughout the watershed were pushing its total elimination. There are other indications of progress. Jobs in manufacturing and commerce have continued to increase. Tax collections have expanded as incomes have grown, public services are improved, and the welfare rolls are lighter. A program of total development takes time. It requires patience and skill, and there are disappointments, but the over-all record in the watershed of Beech River is gratifying. The changes have come because the people were willing to raise their sights from the flood relief they sought in 1950, and work with their government in the general program under way today. They have come because TVA's commitment to resource development has been steadfast, and the energies of its Board and staff have been applied to quiet programs as well as to controversial issues.

In the Bear Creek watershed lying in northwest Alabama and including a little of northeast Mississippi, the problem first identified by the people was different from that at Beech River—a water shortage. There were flood problems at Bear Creek too. Land along some streams would be inundated in times of heavy runoff. But the major concern was water poverty, for in this valley, as in some other areas of the Tennessee River basin, the supply of ground water is limited, and streamflow control is essential to provide a stable source. For years, Bear Creek farmers wasted money in costly attempts at well-digging, and the combination of intermittent flooding and constant water scarcity had established a limit to growth. The dismal outlook frustrated public or private enterprise, until the Bear Creek Watershed Association was organized in 1961. Then change began.

The people were right in identifying a water shortage as a major problem, but it was only one of the many factors frustrating the productivity of this pleasant valley, denying its children the choice of remaining, forcing their emigration because there were no jobs at home. An intensive campaign to improve the area's considerable forest resource was initiated in the beginning of the Bear Creek program, and woodlands have been extended by the planting of some 24,000 acres of once eroded and idle land. Livestock improvement was adopted as an important agricultural objective, and well-managed feeder pig sales have demonstrated one method. Five years after the program began, TVA commenced construction of a system of streamflow control. When completed it will prevent flooding and guarantee a supply of water adequate to support sound growth. Those are its major purposes and at the same time it has demonstrated an innovation in design to avoid impairment of the habitat for fish and wildlife. The first of four reservoirs was filled in 1969. Schedules have had to be slowed and completion postponed because of priorities established for the federal budget, but work is under way and is now expected to be completed in 1975.

Not every TAD will have water control structures as part of its developmental effort. Beech River, Bear Creek, and the Elk River programs include them, and one other system has been designed for a location in middle Tennessee. In some areas, river development has already been accomplished. Others are on streams not susceptible to control. But all have agricultural and forest resources, the value of which can be enhanced in every small watershed.

Tributary areas have other problems and potentials in common. Their towns and small cities, which began municipal life as trading centers for surrounding farmlands, show the effects of decades of low income. To attract the industries that must be established if income is to be raised and a wider choice of jobs offered to young people, and to give residents a sense of pride and pleasure in their environment, improvement in the appearance of the towns is essential. To encourage it, TVA offered to help communities interested in what was not very originally called "Operation Townlift." The endeavor may be part of a general TAD program, or the individual and independent effort of a single community; in either case, counsel is provided whenever local sponsors request the service. TVA planners and architects visit the municipality to discover its problems and the desires of the people. After a preliminary survey, they present their ideas for improvement, with drawings, to the city fathers, who then decide what action to take.

To the surprise of everyone, this modest effort to encourage local concern was one of the few activities sponsored by the Tributary Area Development program that stimulated opposition. Not long after it was initiated, certain architects in the Valley protested that the government was competing unfairly with them by presenting preliminary plans and suggestions at no cost. They complained to TVA. They wrote letters to local newspapers and to members of Congress. Like all such attacks, this assault drew attention to an activity that was, in fact, relatively slight in scope. Applications from towns increased, and a worried member of Congress requested an explanation from the Chairman of the Board of TVA. He had to answer letters of inquiry and of protest. The Chairman's response was simple:

> Sir, if you take a fashion magazine home to your wife tonight, do you think you will be taking work away from dressmakers, or clothing stores? She will see a picture of how she might look with certain garments. It is up to you to get them for her. That is exactly what we are doing. We are showing municipal officials and community leaders what their towns might look like if they are willing to make the necessary investment.

As understanding increased, opposition was stilled, and private architects, planners, and builders began to get business because of the interest in municipal improvement generated by TVA.

Whether the initiating impulse is cosmetic improvement or the abatement of flooding, the area of activity inevitably widens. From paint up and clean up campaigns it spreads to highway beautification, from improved garbage collection to tree planting as local groups engage in the slow process of environmental change. Here and there the traditional town squares of southern villages are being restored, small downtown parks and better parking facilities are appearing, building codes are being revised, zoning schemes adopted. Today, there is a great deal more help available than when TVA began its intensive efforts to stimulate local action. Now a variety of federal agencies are ready to lend their assistance, and the citizen organizations guarantee effective use of many kinds of aid. There are grants and loans for sewage treatment plants, for urban renewal, for small business and other developments. Hospital construction is assisted. Educational efforts are funded by the federal government, and, by example, they stimulate the organization of training devices by others. Increasingly such programs have become a vital part of TAD.

As in all impoverished regions, and especially rural areas, the educational level has been low in much of the Tennessee Valley. In one small watershed, a survey conducted in 1960 by the Human Resources Work Group revealed that 75 per cent of the adult population had less than a high school education. In another, fewer than half had completed the eighth grade, and only 20 per cent had finished high school. In area after area, similar reports have been compiled. Until recent years, agriculture had been, throughout the Valley's history, the major source of employment. No academic achievements were considered necessary to work on farms, but the number of such jobs steadily diminished, and, for the Valley's wage earners to qualify for the opportunities in industry and commerce that improved at the same time, their educational level had to be raised. With help from TVA and other agencies, federal and state, and with the cooperation of local school systems, a web of adult training programs has been spread across the Valley by the TAD groups.

One of the first was organized in 1962 in the Yellow Creek watershed in northeast Mississippi, a low-income rural area. To avoid the all too frequent error of training men and women in skills for which there is no local demand, the Personnel Division of TVA first conducted a survey to determine precisely what employment opportunities existed in the few industries newly located in or near the small watershed and in the service establishments their initiation had encouraged. A demand for office skills was disclosed. There were openings for competent automobile mechanics and men qualified to do electric wiring. A need for licensed practical nurses was revealed. Local educational institutions developed training programs to meet the specific opportunities. By 1966, some 260 adults had been enrolled, and every year the program has expanded.

In 1964, the Elk River, Beech River, and the Clinch-Powell TAD's joined in a program financed by the Department of Labor, organized to train those considered the hard core of unemployables in their areas. A total of 272 trainees, all with less than a sixth-grade education, enrolled at seven centers in the basic education classes, the first phase of a two-part program. Instruction in reading, writing, spelling, and simple mathematics was followed by the second phase, on-the-job training for specific employment. Some 180 completed the course and were placed in permanent jobs. Today, they are producers and consumers, participating in community life, and a survey disclosed that more than half of the dropouts from the classes were enjoying improved circumstances as a result of the limited training they had received. It took more than the funds provided by the Labor Department's Office of Man-power, Automation, and Training, more than the skill of teachers knowledgeable about new instruction methods, more than the cooperation of local business in providing job training to achieve the considerable success. The whole community was involved. Car pools were organized to bring the students who lived in the country to the classrooms and to take them home—an important support for the program since adequate public transportation was not available and few of the trainees owned automobiles or had permits to drive. Attendance would have been meager and irregular without the volunteer taxi service that provided a value beyond transportation. The evidence of community concern it offered contributed to the growth of the trainees' dignity and pride, which in turn supported the acquisition of new skills.

In more than half of the sixteen areas organized under the TAD program, educational and job training programs have been undertaken or are under way. They vary in kind. Several associations have sponsored courses to prepare their adult students to receive the high school equivalent certificates necessary for many kinds of employment. Since 1960, more than 1,000 adults have received some kind of training in courses, academic or job-oriented or both, sponsored by the Tributary Area Development groups. And as the dropouts of prior years are given an opportunity to resume their schooling, groups of business men have organized to counsel and to aid the actual and potential dropouts of today, to prevent the human waste their lack of training would occasion if they do not remain in school or return for further education. The diverse programs are significant not only for the increased skills they make available to the communities and the enrichment of the students' lives, but for the evidence they offer of a new appreciation of the necessity to upgrade standards of education generally and, specifically, to prepare the youth of the region for opportunities newly revealed. Increased public awareness of the value of the timber resource and the employment its development will offer has resulted in the organization of pioneering courses in forest management and wood utilization. Vocational schools, technical institutes, and at least one university and one state college are now training students in the variety of skills related to the conservation and the use of the Valley's forests. Throughout the region, interest in improving schools and libraries is growing, as the TAD groups assume leadership for developing the human resources of the Valley.

Interest in training people is not new for TVA. From the beginning, much of its work has been in the field of adult education. About 2,000 employees have completed the apprentice training program developed by TVA and the Tennessee Valley Trades and Labor Council. Many of the former apprentices remain in the employment of TVA and rise to positions of responsibility, but others have applied their skills to the jobs offered by the Valley's new industries. The test demonstration program has been an educational effort in which thousands of the Valley's farmers have participated, and demonstrations of tree planting, selective cutting, forest management, and sawmill operations have made technical and scientific knowledge available to those who control the Valley timber resource. In these programs the student body is composed of persons, usually self-employed, who want to improve their skills, raise their incomes, and conserve for the future the asset they manage. They are not designed to equip their clientele for the new jobs available in the changing region, as the training programs sponsored by the TAD's are trying to do.

The Tributary Area Development program is an outstanding example of TVA's efforts to stimulate and abet the assumption of local responsibility, but it is not the only one. Local flood studies provide another. When, by 1950, the major components of the regional flood control system had been completed, it was recognized that a good many flood problems remained. Some communities lay beyond reach of the existing system, on tributaries above the dams that protect the waterfront downstream. The severity and frequency of floods in these locations differed but it was estimated that about 150 small cities and towns lived with a damage potential limiting their progress to some degree. Few municipalities understood the exact extent of their danger. They simply knew that over the years floods had occurred, and with a curious kind of pride senior citizens would display to visitors the high water marks on old buildings. There were tales of past disasters but no knowledge of what might happen in the future. To meet the situation, TVA announced that at the request of any community in the Valley and with the approval of the planning commission of the state a study would be made and a report submitted disclosing the current flood danger.

More than 130 reports have been completed. They show, with maps and graphs, just how much of the community is exposed to possible damage by floods. With appreciation of the degree of risk, scores of towns have changed the direction of their growth. More than seventy communities have adopted zoning regulations as a result of the data presented, and in others the redirection of development has been accomplished voluntarily. Land subject to occasional flooding is not without value to the community. Parks and parking lots and playgrounds—areas easy to evacuate and to restore—can be located there, while homes and stores, hospitals, industries and office buildings are built on higher ground.

The steady increase of potential flood losses can be frustrated by zoning to prevent building in areas of danger, but reduction of the existing threat requires other remedies. Where the need is great enough and the citizens care enough to share in responsibility, TVA enters into cooperative projects. In Bristol, on the Tennessee-Virginia border, a small dam system has reduced flood danger and provided a recreation resource. Its construction was preceded by a contract between TVA and the cities to make certain that all benefits would be realized by the community, and here, as elsewhere, arrangements went further. It is rare that total protection can be provided to communities long settled on the river's banks. The frequency and severity of floods can be reduced by project construction, and when that is done TVA makes certain that the community understands precisely what damage potential remains, and that no false sense of security is fostered by the work accomplished. Enterprises likely to suffer some degree of loss from flooding at some time are informed. To reduce their vulnerability, ways of flood-proofing buildings are outlined. Plant reorganizations and equipment relocations are recommended, and little by little the community is involved in the effort to promote its security. The prevention of damage and enhancement of values require not only the efforts of local government but the cooperation of private citizens as well.

In general, but in different ways and at different paces, communities where local flood prevention projects have been undertaken have used them as take-off points for some version of

"Operation Townlift." The danger of flooding smothers public and private enterprise, and when it is removed or substantially reduced, initiative is released. At Coeburn, Virginia, a disastrous flood in 1963 brought a request for help. Almost five feet of water had rushed through the main business district, damaging 160 homes and forty business enterprises of the small town. To a community already experiencing the economic decline associated with reduced employment in coal mining, the flood was a final tribulation. Something had to be done. After a year spent in investigation and planning, enough chance of progress was disclosed to warrant inauguration of a flood-prevention project by TVA.

The community first adopted a land-use plan, zoning ordinances, and subdivision regulations. Then TVA cleared, enlarged, and improved about four miles of the channels of the three streams that flow through the town. On one, which courses through the business center, a major beautification effort was initiated. Arched footbridges were built, brick sidewalks laid, seats, planters, and shrubbery appeared, a paved and landscaped parking area was provided. Railroad tracks were screened by a redwood fence and trees, and the old and abandoned station was converted to serve as a town hall and community center. New street lighting was installed, new water and sewage systems built. "Operation Townlift" is under way, and reduction in potential flood damage has generated the vitality and faith that are illustrated by private investment in new buildings, new enterprises, and the creation of new jobs. The story is repeated in Oliver Springs in Tennessee where activities undertaken in response to the opportunity resulting from TVA's flood prevention program demonstrate the renaissance of community spirit apparent throughout the Tennessee Valley today. A municipal planning commission has been established, and with technical assistance from the state has developed a design for community growth. Zoning and subdivision regulations are now in force. New park and recreation areas have been provided, new street lights and signs installed. Two public housing projects and two residential subdivisions are under construction. Better police and fire protection have reduced insurance rates, and garbage collections in Oliver Springs have been improved.

Some flood problems are minor, and with improved land use in the area only channel clearing to relieve the effect of past abuse is required for substantial relief. Channel clearing removes nature's litter from the streams, the uprooted trees and tangled branches that prevent the swift passage of runoff from the land in times of heavy rainfall. At the same time, it reveals the incredible waste men have deposited in the creeks. Channel clearing was one of the major community efforts in an experimental program sponsored by TVA in one small watershed years ago, the forerunner of the sixteen TAD's now flourishing. There, TVA furnished the machinery and supervision, the men of the community volunteered their labor, the women of the town provided lunch, and in the spirit of a pioneering barn raising, the cleanup of the small river began. Two miles were cleared of obstruction. That experiment was not continued. As a TVA staff member on the job reported, "when the average age of the male population is around sixty, there is a limit to this kind of effort."

A more suitable working force was assembled by a TAD group in southwest Virginia. There, in 1966, boys from the Neighborhood Youth Corps cleared some sixteen miles of streams, and in the summer of 1967 a hundred of them removed obstructions in another forty-five miles. Like members of the Civilian Conservation Corps in the 1930's, the boys were recruited from low-income families, and like their predecessors they found useful employment and at the same time contributed to enhancement of the region's resources. Car bodies and tires, tin cans, furniture, bedsprings, and wash tubs came out of the channel, as well as trees and brush. When the obstacles were removed, the aesthetic value of the streams was increased and the intermittent flooding, which occurred after only moderate rainfall, was reduced, but as often happens, the solution of one problem presented another. Something had to be done with the trash.

Waste disposal is a problem common to most rural areas in the Tennessee Valley where, for generations, garbage, and refuse have been dumped on roadsides and in streams, just as cities once discharged raw sewage to the rivers. Techniques for treating municipal sewage involve no change in the habits of the people, only the investment of public funds. To substitute organized community handling of waste for individual disposal requires not only money but a change in life-long habits. That change is coming. There is a new acceptance of responsibility by the people, and a new determination to clean up the streams and roadsides. Eyesores to which generations had been accustomed are now identified and rejected. When the Bear Creek watershed group undertook to beautify a 12-mile stretch of scenic highway in the summer of 1969, they discovered that before the planting of rosebushes could begin, ten truckloads of litter had to be collected and removed. TVA technicians have responded by developing and recommending to the TAD groups a solid waste–management program. It involves the systematic collection of waste and its disposal in a central sanitary landfill, the most satisfactory solution presently available. Counties within the watershed are adopting the plans, and requests for information are received from areas remote from the scene of demonstration.

Under TAD auspices, in late 1970, Anderson County in Tennessee demonstrated a way to remove a special kind of waste—the abandoned automobiles that deface the countryside in the Tennessee Valley as elsewhere. TVA developed and leased equipment to the county, which organized the pickups, using workers trained by the community group. The derelict cars were hauled to a commercial salvage yard, stripped and flattened, then shipped to a nearby processing center to be melted for use in steel reinforcing bars. From this pioneering demonstration, contagion has spread to other areas. Three hundred citizens came to a meeting to plan a campaign in one county. More than fifteen hundred cars were picked up in another, and in one northern-Alabama area a preliminary inventory revealed more than four thousand abandoned vehicles ready for collection. In some counties, rural mail carriers and school children have been provided with maps and trained to help the collectors by identifying the location of derelicts. With experience, methods of work are improving, and although in the early demonstrations the economic results of recycling were marginal, there is nothing marginal about the aesthetic improvement accomplished nor the determination of the people to accept responsibility for promoting it.

On the whole the results of trash collection efforts are encouraging, but even when there is general community support compliance is imperfect. A sign neatly lettered, "Stop Littering" was found abandoned by the road, and household waste repeatedly dumped on TVA property next to a sign forbidding the practice contained a child's essay, reading in part: "Litter is a very messy thing . . . I hate litter very much." Good intentions are not enough and habits are hard to break. There are moments of discouragement, but, throughout the watershed of the Tennessee, resolute people are banded together, determined to make their communities better places to live, and TVA is working with them.

Today geologists and agronomists, economists and foresters, engineers and architects, specialists in stream sanitation, in recreation and public health go from valley to valley, from group to group, providing the technical service and advice the people need to make their concern for their communities effective. Progress is uneven, but much accomplishment can be reported, and more is anticipated. The life style of a region does not change overnight. But it changes, slowly. The process begins with awareness and moves forward with the acceptance of responsibility. No one should underestimate the push toward the future, nor despair of success because beginnings are small. Small movements grow. They are important, for in the end the future of the great watershed of the Tennessee will be determined by the sum of progress in all its tributary valleys.

VIII

In Praise of a Statute

TVA's relationship with the TAD organizations is different from its association with power distributors, test-demonstrators, or forest owners, and the TAD's are not alike. The underlying purpose of every activity is the same—to develop the resources of the area for the benefit of the people—but the means employed are diverse. The lack of rigidity, the absence of formulae, and the encouragement to experiment rest on the Act creating TVA. Management has respected and used the provisions that gave freedom from traditional restrictions, but the Act was not formulated by the agency. It was written in Congress, and, although legislators rarely get sufficient praise and less frequently adequate blame, it is probably true that their decisions have more to do with the success or failure of administration in federal agencies than the skill of managers and technicians.

In the case of TVA, Congress provided conditions that encouraged achievement. When projects to advance its objectives were authorized in the basic Act, speed and economy were promoted, for the necessity of obtaining enabling legislation prior to initiation of each one was eliminated. Restraint in application of the item-by-item method of appropriating funds has resulted in savings and permitted TVA to respond to unexpected opportunities and adjust to changed conditions. When the resources of an area can be treated as a whole and not in fragments and the power to decide is close to the problems, action can be swift and sure. The total effect of these advantages has been pervasive, for the ability of the Board to make prompt decisions encourages enterprise within the staff. Suggestions can be considered at any time. They are, in every season. New ideas do not have to wait for presentation until the budget program for the following year is under consideration.

Some years ago a technician on TVA's small staff of recreation specialists was flying back to his office in Knoxville from Paducah in Kentucky. Below him was the outline of the shore of Kentucky Lake. Construction of Barkley Dam on the Cumberland River just a few miles north of TVA's Kentucky was under way, and to a knowledgeable eye it was clear that when the dam was finished and the reservoir was filled a peninsula would be created, a stretch of wooded land roughly eight miles wide and about forty miles long, lying between Kentucky and Barkley lakes, its coves and inlets providing more than 300 miles of shoreland. It occurred to the airborne observer that unless some kind of action were initiated promptly a remarkable opportunity for a great recreational development might be lost.

The next morning he voiced his concern to the head of the office in which he worked, then to the General Manager and with his endorsement to the Board, which authorized an immediate exploration of the possibilities. Few government employees have such easy access to those with the power to decide. Few can present their proposals directly to the head of the agency that employs them. That they can in TVA is one result of the location of headquarters in the region, not at the nation's capital. In the centralized agencies of government, it takes time for an idea to work its way from the "field," as offices outside Washington are described, to the site of decision, and there may never be a confrontation between the proposer and the deciders. If his suggestion is rejected, the former may always wonder whether it was adequately presented—a gnawing doubt that discourages future initiative. In TVA, he can be certain, for he participates in the presentation, and hearings for suggestions are easy to arrange. If the head of the division approves, and the General Manager can be persuaded of merit, the Board listens, and promptly.

In this case, the idea was warmly welcomed. Further investigation proved the soundness of the proposal. Officials of Kentucky and Tennessee, the two states in which the land was located, were enthusiastic. The Corps of Engineers, the builder of Barkley, was consulted, as were the Fish and Wildlife Service, which then operated a refuge in the area, and the National Park Service. Authorities in the field of recreation endorsed the plan, and when the preliminary survey was completed in June, 1961, the Board forwarded to the President a Section 22 report recommending the development of what was named "Land Between the Lakes" as a national recreation area.

The site was singularly well suited for such use. It was secluded and tranquil, but accessible to the population centers of mid-America and the Southeast. One calculation demonstrated that at least 75 million people lived within a single day's driving distance. About 75,000 of the total of some 170,000 acres were already in the hands of the federal government. TVA owned about 4,000 acres along Kentucky Lake, the Corps of Engineers almost 12,000 on Barkley reservoir. A National Wildlife Refuge encompassed nearly 59,000 acres, much of it acquired in the 1930's by the Resettlement Administration in an effort to encourage residents to move to areas with better prospects to make a living. They were not bright in Land Between the Lakes. The soil was poor. The cutover timber had little commercial value. There was no railroad. There were no factories. A century ago, the ridge had supported an iron industry. Ore came from the hills. Oak from the virgin forests was cut to feed the furnaces and pig iron was shipped away on river boats. With the discovery of richer veins elsewhere, prosperity was doomed, and except for its moonshine whiskey, which had a considerable reputation, the area was now almost wholly unproductive. Development as a recreation resource offered a matchless opportunity for it to contribute to regional and national assets.

President Kennedy referred the proposal for review to the Department of the Interior where the National Park Service is lodged. Almost two years later, on March 25, 1963, the Department advised the President of its approval and recommended that the project should be undertaken by TVA. The recommendation may have been based in part on recognition that the idea and the basic data came from TVA, but more importantly it responded to the need for celerity in action. Barkley Dam would soon be closed. The waters would rise, and the chance to accomplish shoreline improvement "in the dry" would be lost. That was not all. Developers were already moving in. Private investment would increase and costs would rise. Problems would multiply with every month's delay, and delay could not be avoided if the project were undertaken under the procedures available to the National Park Service. Enabling legislation would have to be adopted, and it was clear that projects earlier proposed and waiting for congressional authorization would have precedence. TVA could proceed promptly when money was provided, and the President approved the undertaking to be carried out as a demonstration under Section 22 of the Act. Money for the survey upon which the initial report to the President was based had been made available by internal budget adjustments. There was no delay, for there was no need to seek an appropriation. After delegation of the project to TVA, funds to purchase the land and develop the area were requested and included in TVA's annual appropriation allowance.

The idea of developing Land Between the Lakes and preliminary plans came from specialists of the Recreation Staff, but when responsibility was assigned, it became a project of TVA as a whole, not the enterprise of one division. Appraisers and buyers from the Land Branch moved in, along with engineers, architects, agronomists, and foresters. While specialists in recreation designed a variety of camping sites and engineers began construction, other staff members prepared to aid in relocation of the people whose homes would be purchased. There were some seven hundred permanent households in the area. Many of the residents were poor and aged, inexperienced in business transactions. Nearby towns were canvassed, an inventory of available property was developed, and the prospective buyers were escorted on as many inspection trips as required before their decisions on new locations were reached. They were helped in making arrangements for moving and adjusting to new surroundings. Not all residents needed or desired advice or assistance. Some knew exactly where they wanted to go, frequently to join children or relatives who had moved away. But more than four hundred did take advantage of the aid, which was offered to all, and after relocation many for the first time found themselves near community services, with access to medical attention and to neighbors, their housing and environment immeasurably improved.

Assurance of improved environment does not always relieve the heartbreak of forced removal, nor reduce reluctance to face new surroundings. The program of assistance cannot guarantee happiness, but it does confirm acceptance by the agency of responsibility to lessen the problems of change as much as possible. Beginning with Norris, the first structure it built, TVA has provided help in relocation. One of the amendments to its statute requested by TVA in 1935 and approved by Congress gave specific authority to venture in the then untried field of the population readjustment required by construction of federal projects.

Land Between the Lakes required a total agency effort. No division of TVA was without a share, and because of the energetic application of talents the peninsula belongs to the public today. In 1971 more than 1.5 million visitors enjoyed the facilities. Since the first camping area was opened in June, 1964, over 6 million visitors have been received at a variety of attractive areas. There is opportunity for hiking, for fishing, and for water sports. Bird watching attracts the nature lover, and there is hunting in season. A herd of buffalo once native to the land has been introduced to add to the variety of wildlife. Hundreds of children have enjoyed the Center for Conservation Education where teachers and pupils meet for classes in the woods. An old-fashioned farm shows youngsters from the city what life in the country used to be like, and a paved trail makes it possible for the crippled and elderly in wheelchairs to enjoy the woods. With the exception of the shoreland, the area had little natural beauty, consisting largely of cutover timber land and neglected farms. It had no dramatic phenomena, but foresters, landscape architects, and agronomists have worked together and now there are vistas and roadsides of considerable charm. Within Land Between the Lakes there are no commercial services of any kind. It is planned for campers. There are no hotels or motels, no bars or movies or stores. Those facilities are available across the lakes, and the development has stimulated growth in nearby communities at an even greater rate than estimated by TVA.

Land Between the Lakes was born because an idea was good and was welcomed, and because decision making in TVA is continuous and the channels of communication are always open. They were open in late 1960 when a member of the staff proposed a plan for current use of the phosphate reserve owned by TVA in Florida. Although the Florida phosphate used at the fertilizer plants is purchased from private suppliers, a reserve had been acquired to be mined if for any reason commercial sources failed to provide the public agency an economic source. The land was idle, and it occurred to the manager of TVA's chemical facilities that a portion of the acreage might offer site and opportunity for a unique experiment in forest fertilization. The Board agreed, and in a few weeks the Division of Forestry and the Office of Agricultural and Chemical Development launched a joint project. Both seedlings and fertilizers were available from TVA, and specialists in the disciplines affected were ready to proceed. No nonaggression pact had to be negotiated, no complex interdepartmental arrangements devised. Action did not have to wait the beginning of a new fiscal year.

Today, 400 acres are devoted to the most precise and controlled experiment in forest fertilization in the United States. Much of the remaining reserve has been sold, but the portion devoted to this special use has been retained. TVA has conducted experiments on existing timber stands and they will continue, but this one is different. An outdoor laboratory, it is without competition from other forest uses. Response to different kinds of fertilizer, to time and rate of application is tested. Records and measurements are exact. Representatives of lumber and fertilizer companies, state forestry officials, and experts in conservation visit the site. Public knowledge will be advanced by the experiments, a contribution TVA can make because management could see its jobs as a whole, and act without delay, and because members of the staff are encouraged to present new ideas and plans for consideration.

When any project is undertaken, various divisions work together as one, and it is not uncommon for separate offices to consult informally and to offer joint recommendations for consideration by the Board. That was the situation in the late 1950's when the

Manager of Power and the Director of Purchasing together presented a problem and a recommendation to the Board. For several years, prices on electrical equipment, particularly steam turbogenerators, had been rising. There are only a few manufacturers of such heavy electrical equipment in the United States, and the Power and Purchasing staff joined to report that in a 6-year period prices for turbogenerators had risen more than 53 per cent while the wholesale price index of all commodities had increased only a little over 5 per cent. The same companies that manufactured generators were making vacuum cleaners, ranges, refrigerators, irons, and toasters, and the prices of such household appliances were going down. Competition appeared to account for the difference. Small appliances are made by a number of manufacturers, and there is no captive market secure for the products of a few. With charts and tables, members of the staff supported their recommendation that bids to supply TVA's next steam generator should be invited from foreign suppliers. Already, TVA and others had purchased hydro units abroad; but no power system in the United States had purchased large steam units, of 500,000 kw, from European sources. The Board agreed that for a power system required by law to make energy available at the lowest possible rates the rising equipment prices were intolerable. Foreign bids were invited, and in February, 1959, an award for a half million kw unit was made to the Parsons Company of England.

All provisions of the Buy American Act and the related executive order had been observed and the percentage differential required to justify purchases abroad was more than met. Estimates of TVA's extra inspection costs were added to the bid before acceptance of the offer. Nevertheless, the Board's decision aroused the frantic opposition of two American giants, General Electric Company and Westinghouse Electric Corporation, whose rejected bids were some $6 million higher. They employed lawyers. They held press conferences to charge TVA with a lack of concern for national defense, domestic prosperity, and the welfare of labor. They managed to generate substantial political pressure urging reconsideration of the decision and cancellation of the award. Members of Congress made speeches. They wrote letters, demanded interviews, and stormed by telephone. The clamor came at an awkward time. The bond amendment was pending in Congress and advocates and friends complained with some heat and considerable justification that TVA had made their job harder. The Board stood firm under the besiegement and the tumult died. But there were consequences. Prices of domestic equipment tumbled down, at least for a time, and the award to a foreign supplier was the first in a sequence of events which contributed to the revelation that the manufacturers who had so self-righteously attacked TVA were themselves guilty of collusive bidding. There was in fact a conspiracy to keep prices high to others as well as TVA. The cost of generators was not, as the companies claimed, solely a result of the higher wage levels prevailing in the United States.

In response to the initial attacks of the companies, TVA had issued a careful statement outlining the situation that led to the decision to seek bids from foreign firms and the award to the English company. That was in February. The companies replied with vituperation. In May, in connection with a routine release announcing a number of contract awards, TVA called attention to the fact that, on several of the items, identical bids had been received from various suppliers. This was not the sudden appearance of a new repudiation of the principle of competition. It had been going on for a long time. Bids on TVA invitations have always been open to inspection but no public notice had been paid to the situation. Somehow, the comment in this particular government press release and others that followed received more attention than usually accorded "the rubble of bureaucratic propaganda" of which the power companies complained. A Knoxville newspaper carried a series of articles, which were widely reprinted. The Antimonopoly Subcommittee of the Senate Judiciary Committee responded with hearings. It is unlikely that TVA's obvious exasperation with identical bids would have attracted so much attention if it had not followed the widely publicized foreign purchase, and the resulting attacks by the manufacturers.

The Department of Justice took note. At the time, its antitrust attorneys were engaged in an investigation of the practices of electrical equipment manufacturers, and it occurred to those in charge that the records of a public agency concerned about costs and believing in competition might provide the evidence required to support a presentation to a grand jury. The files of TVA's Purchasing Division in Chattanooga were examined for clues and in

June, 1960, when a federal grand jury in Philadelphia returned indictments one paragraph read:

> At a meeting at the Barclay Hotel in New York City in about September 1957, representatives of defendant manufacturers met and discussed invitations for bids issued by Tennessee Valley Authority for a 500,000 kilowatt turbine-generator unit. It was agreed that General Electric Company would have "position". Thereafter General Electric Company bid approximately $16,112,000 and Westinghouse Electric Corporation bid approximately $16,225,000 to Tennessee Valley Authority. The contract was awarded to General Electric Company.

What had been uncovered was not identical but collusive bidding. Under an arrangement appropriately described as "phases of the moon," this corporate lunacy permitted each of the companies to have its turn as the low bidder. A number of companies were involved in the proceedings. All pleaded guilty or *nolo contendere,* and in February, 1961, a federal judge disclosed the penalties: jail sentences for a few executives, fines (totaling just under $2 million) for others and for twenty-nine companies. Damage claims were filed by more than one thousand purchasers, including TVA, which alone recovered some $8 million. According to the public statements and private assurances of officials of the major companies, a new era then began, to be characterized by higher ethical standards, more efficient organization, and lower costs.

There was a kind of poetic justice in the fact that specific bids on a certain turbogenerator in the autumn of 1957 were cited in the indictment, for those were the bids that proved to be the last straw for TVA. In sorrow and in anger, the contract was awarded to General Electric Company, but early in November the investigation of European sources was undertaken, and when in February, 1959, the contract for the next unit was awarded to the English company, the cycle of retribution started. TVA did not set out to help uncover a conspiracy, nor to fumigate the marketing policies of the equipment manufacturers. It was simply pursuing one of the objectives of the statute its Board and staff were obliged to promote, providing electricity to be sold at the lowest possible rates to the homes and farms of the area, the goal set out by Congress. Somewhat unexpectedly, benefits accrued not only to TVA, but to others.

Decisions like the one that resulted in the award to the Parsons Company are made by an agency where every division and all the staff share the same commitment, and where the Board has authority to match its responsibilities. The directors had the power to act, but without a genuine dedication to the obligations of the statute they might have found it difficult to endure the explosive hostility of these important industries as imperturbably as they did. That the agency as a whole was accustomed to attack probably fortified endurance. TVA had survived litigation and investigation. It had endured the opposition of Senator McKellar. It had lived through Dixon-Yates and was nearing the end of a bitter four-year struggle to amend the TVA Act in order that revenue bonds might provide a source of capital for investment in the power system. It was not about to surrender to the General Electric Company or the Westinghouse Corporation.

Congress devised a statute that has made TVA a singularly satisfactory place to work. Communication is easy, decisions are not delayed, experimentation is encouraged, and the total resource approach is an impressive educational device. The recommendations of specialists in every field are subject to the criticism of experts in other disciplines, and the specialists themselves are exposed to presentations and discussions relating to problems alien to them as technicians, but important to them as employees of TVA, as every project enlists the effort and support of the whole agency. When an engineer who had been in charge of one of TVA's most demanding war-time projects returned to visit his onetime colleagues he expressed his recollections this way. "I always felt that everyone was working with me." He was right, his project was everyone's, and his success an agency triumph, not his alone. Accomplishment is shared.

TVA works to increase the sense of common purpose that the Act permits. For several years, what was called the General Manager's tour took senior staff members—heads of divisions and offices, about twenty in number—to visit a variety of activities throughout the Valley. The annual tours were hard working seminars, lasting a week. In daylight hours, the group would be divided for inspection trips. Recreation areas and tree nurseries were surveyed; privately owned forests under management were explored; power plants, laboratories, test-demonstration farms, and demon-

The Tennessee Valley
as it has become . . .

Fontana Dam today

Where there had been no cattle, dairy cows graze

President John F. Kennedy at Muscle Shoals on
the thirtieth anniversary of TVA, May 18, 1963

Pickwick Dam
powerhouse

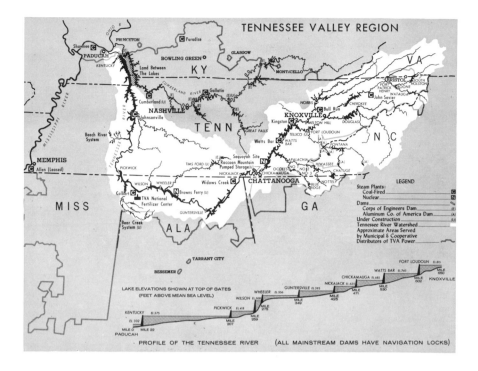

Visitors from abroad: His Majesty Sri Savana Vatthana, King of Laos, and Prime Minister of Laos Prince Souvanna Phouma, right, accompanied by TVA Chairman A. J. Wagner, second from right, visit the Knox County, Tennessee, test-demonstration farm of the Tom McKee family during a tour of the Valley in 1963.

Reforestation, before and after:
The owner of this land in
Buncombe County, North
Carolina, planted TVA-
produced pine and locust
seedlings in the late 1930's.
At right is his growing
woodland photographed
again less than
twenty years later.

Navigation, before and after:
The Tennessee River at Knoxville
before the completion of the Fort
Loudoun Dam sometimes looked
like this. Year-round navigation
was impossible. The photograph
at the left, taken near the
same spot, shows the
deep-water, all-year
channel as it is today.

Other TVA activities

Left: Orphan strip mine, Morgan County, Tennessee, reclaimed by TVA in a demonstration project begun in 1963—photographed in June, 1971, eight years after replanting. *Below:* Junk cars being collected for disposal by a vehicle built to TVA design, Asheville, North Carolina, 1971

Left: Visitors to a demonstration farm, Land Between the Lakes, 1968

Right: Adult education class, part of the Tributary Area Development program, Delano, Tennessee, 1968

Land Between the Lakes

Extending almost 40 miles, with over 3,300 miles of
shore line on Kentucky and Barkley lakes, Land Between
the Lakes offers unlimited opportunities for outdoor
recreation and conservation education. Camping,
fishing, boating, swimming, hunting, bird-watching, and
hiking, as the photos on the facing page show, are
among the many activities available in this area.
Even in winter, conservation and recreation
programs continue.

"If we are successful here . . ."

Fontana Lake

Fontana powerhouse

strations of strip-mine reclamation were visited. Every evening, the whole group met for reports and discussion, for questions and answers stimulated by the programs of the day. The tours intensified the sense of unity established as workers in many fields sat around the table at meetings of Board and staff. There engineers concerned primarily with construction costs and schedules listened while the recreation staff reported. Agronomists paid attention when problems of power system management were presented. Men to whom labor relations were assigned as a specific responsibility learned as experiments in forest genetics were described and the questions involved in litigation were analyzed. Experts in pollution control reported progress and advanced proposals. Horizons broadened and awareness of the multiplicity of factors affecting regional growth inevitably spread. Few problems are the exclusive concern of any discipline no matter where they occur, but, in the Tennessee Valley, dialogue between specialists is easy and swift, and common action can be immediate because responsibility is not divided. A single management has the power to decide.

When an obnoxious aquatic weed—water milfoil—invaded a secluded cove of one reservoir on the Tennessee it was a matter of immediate concern to recreation technicians, for by spreading it could make swimming and boating impossible, and destroy the value of many shoreline establishments. It could be ignored neither by power operations, because water intakes could be clogged by its accumulation, nor by specialists in public health, as it provided a breeding place for mosquitoes. Milfoil could, it was apparent, damage the whole river development. The infestation was spotted early, and action was immediate. The division then called Health and Safety* was directed to undertake a campaign of control and, if possible, eradication. That division could not do it alone. Water control engineers were involved as reservoir levels were manipulated to discourage survival of the weed. Scientists worked in their laboratories seeking remedies, which regrettably proved to be elusive. The Division of Reservoir Properties spread word of the menace and suggested measures of control to the proprietors of lakeshore establishments, to landowners along the reservoirs, and

* Now the Office of Health and Environmental Science.

to the users of TVA-owned land. The Information Office issued press releases. TVA as a whole was fighting milfoil, and a region-wide campaign of education was combined with the agency's spe-cific activities. The first infestation was identified in 1960. By the spring of 1969, some infected areas had been cleansed of the in-vasion, the spread of the plague had been limited, but the threat of growth of aquatic weeds is always there. Today TVA has the un-happy distinction of being the most knowledgeable agency in the United States with respect to water milfoil, but in spite of total effort, no certain cure has been discovered.

The Tennessee River is not the only waterway whose use has been jeopardized by this particular kind of vegetative pollution. In March, 1965, a serious situation on some of the eastern bays and rivers was recognized in the introduction of legislation to permit the Corps of Engineers to undertake a program of milfoil control. Authorization to proceed was included in the Rivers and Harbors bill adopted eight months later, in November of that year. The House Committee Report made clear that Congress was aware of the program already under way on the Tennessee River, and that the general responsibility given to the Corps was not intended to infringe on the activities of TVA, but to stimulate cooperation and the exchange of information between the two agencies. Information has increased, but optimism is restrained, for the problem is not solved and TVA is aware that the dumping of the contents of a single fishbowl can start a new milfoil colony.

It has discovered that waste from a discarded metal drum can kill millions of fish. In the summer of 1968, a fish kill on Boone Lake in northeastern Tennessee was reported. On a 13-mile stretch of the shore more than a half a million fish lay dead. TVA's Divi-sion of Forestry, Fish and Wildlife, with the cooperation of various divisions in TVA and state and other federal agencies, did the scientific detective work required to discover that a discarded metal drum, apparently empty but with a residue of a highly toxic mercury compound, was the lethal agent. Metal drums have long been used along the lakes as inexpensive devices to float docks and boathouses. Hundreds deteriorated beyond further use have floated free, and are derelicts along the shore. TVA has taken steps to bar the use of such drums in new structures and has set a deadline of 1972 for their replacement by safer means of support for existing facilities. It has sponsored a cleanup campaign to remove all those abandoned, but the danger is not over. Months after the first kill, more than 2 million fish were dead on another arm of the lake. There were indications that a similar toxic invasion was responsible, and until all old drums and similar devices are removed, the peril remains.

Today, research in water quality and efforts to protect and enhance it are widespread. In the 1930's they were modest, and TVA was the only federal agency undertaking a program of water control and at the same time engaging in studies of water quality and a campaign of public education to reduce pollution. Standards of water quality are rising along with standards of clean air, and one of the results of TVA's total approach is that the staff directly concerned with the specific problem advances environmental claims against TVA itself. In the past, internal pressures have been more insistent than public demands.

Some years ago when a visitor commented on the atmospheric stench from a nearby pulp mill a resident of one Valley town responded, "Lady, we don't mind it—we smell jobs," and in the 1930's nearby residents welcomed the plumes of smoke when TVA operations began at the chemical plant at Muscle Shoals. They furnished a dramatic symbol of productivity, of jobs available in a facility which had been clean and quiet for too long. No one complained that the emissions might be debilitating to vegetation in the neighborhood. When the plant was built in 1918, and when major additions were constructed in the 1930's and during World War II, the waste disposal facilities incorporated were considered advanced. They were, however, not good enough to meet present standards and at the insistence of technicians in TVA whose special concern was pollution reduction a program of improvement began some years ago. The air is cleaner today, and the Tennessee is spared the small amounts of plant food that, when discharged as waste to the river, nourished the aquatic weeds that finally broke the surface of the water, a sign that improved facilities were urgently required.

In 1949, when it commenced the unbroken series that has resulted in a system total of ten coal-burning generating plants* in opera-

* An additional plant, the Allen plant built by the city of Memphis, now operated by TVA, is capable of using coal or gas as fuel.

tion today, a good deal of attention was paid to avoidance of air pollution. As a general rule, plants were located away from population centers, and as the region turned to electric space heating and less coal was burned by householders the reduction in urban air pollution was widely hailed. Clearly, that represented a gain for the area, but as standards rose, the further reduction of pollution from the plants themselves became an urgent objective. Repeated tests by monitoring stations in helicopters and on the ground showed that additional investment had to be made to reduce atmospheric pollution. Taller chimney stacks to discharge emissions at higher altitudes and the installation of electrostatic precipitators have offered a measure of relief. Without the pressure of newly enacted legislation, over $50 million has been spent in the past few years to bring existing plants up to current standards in controlling fly ash alone, and it is estimated that an expenditure of twice that amount will be required to make certain that particle emissions are reduced at every plant operated by TVA.

In the case of the chemical plant, efficiency was promoted by the investment made for pollution abatement and the program of essential improvements extended to a general cosmetic effort unanticipated by the technicians who had insisted on more advanced methods of waste disposal. As a result the reservation is a pleasanter place to work, and higher production rates reflect the change. Except for the fact that the fly ash collected has been found to be a valuable constituent of concrete, the power plants, which were modern, well designed installations at the start, enjoyed no such fringe benefits. The investment in pollution reduction is being made in the interest of wider environmental concern. For TVA is not just a power system. It is devoted to total regional development, and in a unified program the pressures for balance are built in. They are constant and unremitting.

At the moment, pollution, a fashionable culprit, is blamed for every adverse development along the river, sometimes unfairly. The research that can assign guilt on occasion suggests exoneration. Mussel fishing is an old occupation along some stretches of the Tennessee. For years before TVA, the shells were a staple of the "pearl" button industry. After the war, that market was surrendered to zippers and plastics, and mussel shells were exported to Japan to be used in the production of cultured pearls. In 1950, over $1 million was realized from their sale. By 1956, the harvest had dropped and $350,000 was the total received from the sale of some 2,400 tons that year. For the region, this reduction in income was not significant, but it was catastrophic to the nomadic groups of the unskilled who had relied upon the harvest for their livelihood, and it reflected diminution of an asset that should be preserved. An investigation was launched, conducted by TVA's Fish and Wildlife Branch, in cooperation with the Bureau of Fisheries of the Department of Interior. The life cycle of the mussel was studied; the quality of streamflow was examined; the runoff from the land adjacent to the beds was tested. Gradually it appeared that production was not greatly threatened by pollution. The investigation indicates that it is primarily human error, over-harvesting, which jeopardizes the future. Regulations have been adopted by the states concerned, but the outcome is still in doubt, and study of the problem is continuing.

TVA's Manager of Power is in charge of a system reporting gross revenues of almost $600 million in fiscal 1971, and agency engineers are designing, building, or operating projects valued at some $6 billion. The Manager of Agricultural and Chemical Development is responsible for the production, distribution, and use of over 200,000 tons of plant food every year. There are others whose talents are dedicated to major enterprises. It is not bad for them to be reminded that TVA is concerned with the disappearance of a resource that at its best added only $1.24 million to regional income. It is a salutary experience for men engaged in massive construction programs to hear analyses of the effects of completed projects, to be reminded that the structures built by TVA are not goals but tools, whose contribution to progress in the area is the test of their worth. Their benefits must be measured in terms of new jobs, new houses, and new schools. As President Theodore Roosevelt phrased it in the Instrument quoted in Chapter I, the objective of resource development is "the making and maintenance of prosperous homes."

When technicians and specialists in different disciplines are aware of the overriding purpose to which every program must contribute, there emerges a sense of unity, of mutual forebearance and respect, which accounts in part for the high morale of the staff of TVA. In the statute, the purpose is repeatedly expressed:

every project and every program must be part of the total effort
to enhance the environment in which the people live, to promote
their well-being. The contribution of each activity is recognized,
whether it is large or small. A recent visitor to the Valley commented on what seemed to him an extraordinary atmosphere. He
told how he had been taken to see the Browns Ferry project under
construction by TVA in northern Alabama. When completed it will
be the largest nuclear power plant in the world. Its construction
has involved extraordinarily difficult engineering problems and the
structure is awesome although incomplete. According to the
visitor's report, within a few hours he was taken to see a collection
point for the deposit of abandoned automobiles and there watched
the operation of a machine developed by TVA which, with one
man at the controls, delivered derelicts on the way to their extinction. Next he saw a small town where, with a spirit fostered by
TVA's local flood control program, the community had accomplished a transformation of the business area. It was amazing
to the visitor that his guides were just as proud of the latter undertakings by the people of the area as they were of the majestic
and innovative structure being built by TVA itself. But he understood the point: The intent of the law was being carried out in
a variety of ways, and each one was equally respected.

On one occasion when amendments to the TVA Act were under
consideration, it was reported that a caller suggested to Senator
Norris that a major effort might be made to improve the statute,
to eliminate its verbosity and reduce its repetitions, to make it
shorter and neater, more precise and professional in draftsmanship.
The Senator is said to have smiled in sympathy for the critic. He
knew the Act bore the scars of its long journey through Congress,
but he was content when he said, "But everybody knew what we
meant." He was right. Successive boards and the staff of TVA
have known, members of Congress have realized, and the courts
have joined in understanding.

In 1946, a unanimous decision of the Supreme Court delivered
by the late Justice Hugo L. Black (*United States* ex rel. *Tennessee
Valley Authority* v. *Welch,* 372 U. S. 546) illustrated the accuracy
of the Senator's appraisal. The case involved a condemnation proceeding under which TVA had acquired certain privately owned
lands adjacent to Fontana reservoir. The acreage was promptly

turned over to the National Park Service for incorporation in the Great Smoky Mountains National Park, part of the solution of a difficult access problem arrived at after extended negotiation involving TVA, the state of North Carolina, the county in which the property was located, and the National Park Service. The agreement, welcomed by all the government agencies involved, was protested by a few landowners who contended that the transfer proved their property was not needed by TVA, and their opposition ultimately brought the arrangement before the Court. The Justice wrote:

> And we find not only that Congress authorized the Authority's action, but also that the TVA has proceeded in complete accord with the Congressional policy embodied in the Act. That Act does far more than authorize the TVA to build isolated dams. The broad responsibilities placed on the Authority relate to navigability, flood control, reforestation, marginal lands, and agricultural and industrial development of the whole Tennessee Valley . . . It [TVA] was particularly admonished to cooperate with other governmental agencies—federal, state, and local—specifically in relation to the problem of "readjustment of the population displaced by the construction of dams, the acquisition of reservoir areas, the protection of watersheds, the acquisitions of rights-of-way, and other necessary acquisitions of land, in order to effectuate the purposes of the Act." All of the Authority's actions in these respects were to be directed towards "development of the natural resources of the Tennessee River drainage basin and of such adjoining territory as may be related to or materially affected by the development consequent to this Act . . . all for the general purpose of fostering an orderly and proper physical, economic, and social development of said areas."

The Supreme Court knew what Congress meant, and TVA has not forgotten. The years of trial and conflict have fortified the sense of purpose the Act itself expressed, and, perhaps because TVA is different in major characteristics, its Board and staff have found the courage to be different in small ways. The agency has developed traditions. Unlike other branches of the federal government that build public works, TVA has never, with the single exception of Norris Dam, named its projects in honor of contemporary Americans. The present Chairman of the Board, Aubrey J. Wagner, explained the reason in correspondence with a friend who had written to suggest that a major structure be renamed to honor a supporter whose sudden death was a cause of general grief. He wrote, in part:

> Your letter of . . . has been difficult for me to answer, for memories intrude upon dictation, and I find myself recalling the sadly lengthening roster of those who have made great contributions to TVA and to whom we can no longer express our esteem and appreciation.
>
> In a way this illustrates one of the reasons why, with the exception you referred to, TVA has never named one of its projects in honor of a contemporary American. The present Board believes the policy is wise. We would be unwilling to select one person out of the many deserving recognition, or to choose one project from the system for such special distinction. We prefer to think that every program and every project is part of a whole development which, in its entirety, will forever honor every man and woman who has contributed to its strength and its vitality over the years.
>
> You are right, of course, that there is ample precedent for naming structures after public figures. In this respect, as well as others, TVA has chosen deliberately a different course from the one usually followed. As you know, a good many public works have physically engraved upon them the names of designers and builders as well as administrative officials. That is not true of structures built by TVA. Nowhere will you find the name of architect or engineer, or member of the Board. The inscriptions are impersonal and alike. They affirm that the projects were built by the "Tennessee Valley Authority" for "the people of the United States of America." From the beginning TVA has tried to substitute pride in total accomplishment for individual recognition as a source of satisfaction. This is why we do not follow the usual government practice of granting cash awards to individuals for suggestions. It is why, with the exception of technical or scientific presentations, TVA publications rarely mention the name of their authors. It is why the Board has steadfastly refused to recommend any member of the staff for special awards or recognition by others.* We have eschewed individual tributes, believing it is one way to demonstrate that every man who contributes to the limit of his capacities has a share in the agency's achievements and that all contributions, conspicuous or quiet, are equally respected.

Some years ago, an official group came to visit TVA to make an inspection of its operations. It was headed by a man unsympa-

* In 1963, G. O. Wessenauer, then TVA's Manager of Power, received one of the coveted Rockefeller Public Service Awards. His nomination was not submitted nor supported by the Board and the honor he received represented no exception to TVA policy.

thetic to the agency's objectives and its methods. At his insistent request, a car driven by a public safety officer was assigned for his use and when he left he offered the driver a generous gratuity. In Washington on his return, the visitor reported his bewilderment that the gift was refused, with courtesy, he said, but with firmness, and his astonishment when the driver added, "TVA employees don't take tips. We like to show folks what we are doing." To a skeptic it was incredible that pride in agency accomplishment might be a substitute for personal profit, but that is the case.

Since 1933, thousands of men and women who have worked for TVA have said "we" with satisfaction. They are proud to have a part in a great undertaking. Like the small boy who danced with glee on the overlook at Fontana and to the agonized embarrassment of his parent and the amusement of a group of tourists pointed to the dam and shouted "My daddy made it, my daddy made it," they identify. There are always exceptions. A few miss the personal acclaim that might be garnered elsewhere and leave TVA deploring the paucity of individual recognition. But not many. Most members of the staff are proud of the achievements of their colleagues, and find gratification in the changes they can see in the region. Engineers can look at long tows using the river channel their efforts created. In times of flood they can watch the rising waters held securely in the reservoirs by structures they designed and built, and know that the Valley is safe. Men who advise on recreation developments can see people enjoying the facilities they recommended. Seedlings stretching upward and pastures spreading wide give satisfaction to those who have labored for their growth. When Congress indicated that TVA headquarters should be in the region, proximity to problems and achievement was guaranteed. It is a constant stimulus to endeavor. When a visitor commiserated with a former Manager of Power because his salary was meager compared to the remuneration of officials of private companies he replied, "But I can get in my car at sundown and drive along one of the back country roads. I can look at the lighted barns, the bright kitchens, and through the windows I can often see the children at their lessons. Then I remember what this Valley was like when I came here in the thirties, and I wouldn't trade my job for any other in the world."

Successive boards have been effective in their administration of the TVA Act, but it was the Congress of the United States that fashioned a statute permitting TVA to develop those traditions which characterize it today. It was Congress that made it possible for management to conduct its operations so that each man and woman could feel a share in every achievement, and find satisfaction in enhancement of the lives of others. The legislative body deserves the credit.

IX

On Being Different

The management of TVA has treasured the statute it inherited, and successive boards have utilized its provisions with skill and acumen. Students of government have praised the administration its terms encourage, but neither effective application nor impartial approbation can diminish the pressure to obliterate or weaken the special characteristics written into the Act creating TVA. The push toward uniformity is insistent, and the qualities that distinguish TVA from other federal agencies are the ones in constant peril. The ability to maintain a nonpolitical and unified administration, to provide a responsible independence in management, and to make decisions in the region—directly or indirectly these basic characteristics of the statute are threatened every year.

Open assaults on individual programs can be openly resisted. When the private power companies challenged TVA in the courts, the agency could organize its defense, and when appropriations for needed capacity additions were opposed in Congress, friends and foes could muster their forces for debate and decision. When, in 1953, adversaries endeavored to deny the funds required for important activities, the intent to destroy was plain and could be defeated. Not all dangers are as clear. Skillful opponents have not limited their opposition to overt attacks. They have tried to destroy the programs they resist by amendments of the Act which would impair TVA's ability to conduct them effectively—a slow but certain way to ensure their failure and demise. Such devious efforts have first to be exposed and then defeated. Still other proposals are inadvertently destructive, and they are sometimes more difficult to repulse than those of hostile purpose. Advocates of centralization who urge uniformity as an end in itself and the sponsors of general reforms who are unaware of the impact of the measures they propose on an agency whose structure is different from others —these generate problems that are a constant if sometimes unintended danger. Bills are introduced in Congress, plans are developed in executive agencies, recommendations are offered by advisory groups and commissions that would fragment the charter of TVA, weaken the Board's authority and begin the liquidation of the nation's single experiment in the decentralized and unified administration of federal functions in resource development. From a variety of sources, impelled by a diversity of motives, deliberately or through inadvertance, the statute of TVA has been under siege throughout its life.

The General Accounting Office (GAO), headed by the Comptroller General of the United States, was the first of the central agencies to assert an infringement of the authority of the Board of TVA. Its intrusion was deliberate. The GAO is an arm of Congress, frequently described as its "watch dog" over executive agencies. There were many difficulties between the two organizations in the 1930's, but few were caused by the admittedly imperfect system of accounting used by TVA in the beginning. They arose because of disagreement as to function. The GAO was empowered to "settle and adjust" the accounts of traditional federal agencies. It passed on the legality of their expenditures. Something different had been proposed for TVA. Under the Act, the GAO was empowered to audit TVA's accounts, it could question its expenditures and report its findings, but the right to "settle and adjust" was lodged in the Board of TVA. There was considerable legislative history on the question of congressional intent, but TVA's interpretation of the statute was not accepted by the Comptroller General, and in the beginning, in an apparent effort to demonstrate the need for its control, GAO contributed to public misunderstanding of the new agency by challenging the legality of an almost endless list of actions. In the words of the Joint Committee, which was directed to investigate the situation, GAO sought to impose a "strait jacket of red tape" on TVA.

The issue was not settled until 1941 when an amendment to

the TVA Act clarified the relationship between the two agencies. Since that time, the GAO has audited TVA's accounts every year. It reports its "exceptions," its questions about specific actions, to TVA, which in turn provides a written explanation. If any items remain in dispute after conference between the staffs of the two agencies the Board of TVA must determine the issue by formal resolution and submit its justification to the GAO, which transmits its final report together with the comments of TVA to the Speaker of the House and the President of the Senate. During the years when the GAO was providing an indictment rather than an audit TVA had turned to a commercial enterprise for service, a practice resumed since adoption of the bond amendment of 1959, with cooperative arrangements between the private firm and GAO avoiding duplication of effort.

Relations between GAO and TVA have been amicable since adoption of the 1941 amendment. In its audit report for fiscal year 1945, for example, the GAO stated:

> In our opinion, TVA's accounts generally were well conceived, supervised, and maintained, and the Authority is to be commended as one of the foremost government corporations in the use of accounting in management, comparing quite favorably in this respect with well managed private corporations.

Two years later, when the head of its Corporate Accounting Division testified before a subcommittee of the House Committee on Appropriations, he went further. After commenting on the confusion of TVA's early accounting practices, he said, "Today . . . TVA probably has the finest accounting system in the entire government and probably one of the best accounting systems in the entire world." Then the climax: "There is no private enterprise in this country that has any better."

The motives of the General Accounting Office in coveting increased authority and ignoring the function of the Board of Directors in TVA's first years have never been clear. At the time, other government corporations appeared to be enjoying freedom from GAO control without apparent challenge. Whatever the purposes, they were frustrated, but when the Government Corporation Control Bill was introduced in 1945 it included provisions that threatened the hard-won legislation by which relations between TVA and the General Accounting Office had been settled four years earlier. The objective of the proposed legislation was to reduce the administrative chaos resulting from the proliferation of corporations created during the war and earlier to meet the needs of the Depression. In describing the situation to which the measure was related, one of the sponsors pointed out that there were then forty-four "main" government corporations, with subsidiaries bringing the total to 101. Some remedial legislation was desirable, but there is no record that the emergence of so many corporations caused any reexamination of traditional government procedures to discover why new agencies appeared to be needed, nor was there any effort to determine whether their achievements justified the administrative disorder that resulted. The Bureau of the Budget, the General Accounting Office, and the Treasury Department moved to bring the corporations under their control, and insofar as budgeting procedures were concerned, to make them conform to the practices followed by conventional government departments and bureaus.

The declaration of policy stated in the bill was "to bring Government corporations and their transactions and operations under annual scrutiny by the Congress." TVA was included although it already presented its appropriation requests for action by the Bureau of the Budget and Congress every year, and reported estimates of its intended expenditures of proceeds, at the same time disclosing records of the past and current fiscal years. It was accustomed to the "annual scrutiny." Every year, as required in its charter, it submitted a report to the President and Congress, a document printed for public distribution. Its accounts were audited annually. Under the proposed legislation, all corporations were required to make disclosures already made by TVA, including at least two, both part of TVA's early history, that were dead at the time the bill was introduced. The bill was that sweeping. There was no discrimination, no precision, and no escape.

On December 19, 1933, the President, under authority of the National Industrial Recovery Act, issued an executive order establishing a new government corporation, the Electric Home and Farm Authority (EHFA), to facilitate the purchase of low-cost electrical appliances by consumers. Its creation had been recommended by the Board of TVA, the members of which were named as directors of the new agency. EHFA functioned in the Tennessee Valley for less than two years. Then, its success having been demonstrated, TVA Board members resigned from its directorate and the corporation moved to Washington. Reorganized under the wing of the Reconstruction Finance Corporation, and under the laws of the District of Columbia, it was made nationwide in application and when the wartime shortage of critical materials and the consequent dearth of appliances occasioned its demise in 1943 it left an enviable record of accomplishment and a surplus for the Treasury. To meet another situation, the Tennessee Valley Associated Cooperatives (TVAC) was created by TVA's directors in 1934. As private citizens, and under the laws of Tennessee, they established an organization with a single function —to receive and distribute a grant of $300,000 from the Federal Emergency Relief Administration. The money was used to assist the organization of a number of cooperative organizations as part of the general effort to reduce the relief rolls in the region by aiding the economy of rural areas. Some of the cooperatives organized then are prospering today. These corporations, effective instruments devised to deal with special circumstances and of brief duration, no longer existed when the Government Corporation Control Bill proposed to bring them under the jurisdiction of the Bureau of the Budget as an essential step in providing an annual review of their activities by Congress.

The bill illustrates the problem of producing a single piece of legislation affecting dissimilar enterprises, a problem ignored by most draftsmen. TVA had been chartered by Congress itself. Many other corporations were not. TVA's activities were visible and open to constant review. Some corporations were not subject to routine inspection by Congress. But in the clumsy effort to make others subject to disciplines already familiar to TVA and to make procedures identical for all, the bill as introduced included the first attempt by the Bureau of the Budget to deprive the Board of an essential tool guaranteed in the statute, the right to use its proceeds as the Act directed. The Bureau adopted the position of Senator McKellar. Hearing followed hearing, conference was added to conference, essential exemptions were laboriously obtained, and in the end the bill as adopted was acceptable to TVA.

The same patient and persistent effort obtained adjustments in the Federal Property and Administrative Services Act of 1949.

That legislation was developed to provide a centralized service for some of the housekeeping functions of government—the leasing or construction of office space, the procurement of equipment and supplies, and the disposal of surplus property. The bill was an Administration measure, and interagency consultation preceded its introduction. It was agreed that TVA must be exempt from many of its provisions. Clearly, it would violate the intent of the TVA Act to remove such important responsibilities as the purchase of generating equipment from the Board, but obviously there was room for cooperation and mutual benefit in the acquisition of such standard items as office equipment and supplies. One proviso to which there was no objection directed that TVA should "to the maximum extent that it may deem practicable, consistent with the fulfillment of the purpose of its program and the effective and efficient conduct of its business," coordinate its purchasing with the policies and regulations set out in the new statute.

TVA purchasing policies and its regulations for the disposal of surplus property do conform to generally accepted government standards, although its procedures differ in detail. Relying primarily upon competitive bidding, from the beginning through fiscal year 1971, agency purchases had reached a cumulative total of $8 billion and required the preparation of more than 1.3 million separate contracts. Purchasing is a vital function in TVA. The staff responsible is not only committed to the goal of efficient acquisition, but to the total program, and although its measure of independence from the General Services Administration continues to cause some pain to the disciples of centralization, it has not been seriously challenged.

It is natural that bills should be drafted to apply to the government as a whole, with provisions developed to meet the requirements of centralized agencies. Measures that government departments or bureaus desire to have introduced are supposed to be "cleared" among interested agencies by the Office of Management and Budget. Comments on proposed legislation may be solicited from TVA. Sometimes they are not requested or are ignored, and except in a few cases like that of the Federal Property and Administrative Services Act, the effect on the agency is rarely considered prior to introduction. This is, of course, almost invariably the case when bills are introduced by an individual member of Congress on his own initiative or at the request of some non-governmental group. Then, if the measure might affect TVA adversely exemption must be sought. Often the objectives of the proposed legislation are wholly desirable, approved by TVA, and already promoted under its charter. Additional legislation is not only unnecessary; it might result in administrative confusion.

That is why, when the Tort Claims bill was introduced early in the 1940's, TVA requested exemption, and was excluded from coverage in the measure adopted in 1946. The bill was designed to permit citizens to sue agencies of government in certain circumstances. TVA was not hostile to its purpose, but in some respects broader rights had been included in the TVA statute and the Board sought exemption from the general legislation to make certain that the provisions of the Act of 1933 would prevail.

Again, in 1956, when a bill was introduced to inaugurate a government-wide safety program to be administered by the Department of Labor, TVA requested an exemption. Not that it opposed safety programs. On the contrary, TVA already had well developed procedures which had earned it a series of awards from the National Safety Council. Heavy construction work is hazardous, the operation of a chemical plant has its peculiar perils, and there are a greater number of vulnerable positions in the operation of a power system than in the sedentary occupations of most government departments. The safety program developed by TVA is a cooperative effort between management and workers, tailored to meet the special problems inherent in its work. The Board wanted to assure its continuance, and it remained an integral part of job training and supervision although a general statute was not adopted until ten years later.

Just as legislation was not required to permit citizens to sue TVA, nor for TVA to inaugurate a safety program, none was needed to institute a system to encourage employee suggestions, and exemption from legislation establishing a government-wide program of cash awards was obtained. The program, administered by the Civil Service Commission, is generally regarded as successful, but if it had been applied to TVA it would have disrupted a system long in use and approved by employees as well as management. It would have substituted individual for group recognition, and competition for cooperation. A great many employee suggestions have improved procedures at every project undertaken by TVA. They come up to management through the committees established as one feature of TVA's employee relations arrangements. They are not submitted by individuals. There are some advantages in the TVA system. An employee with a good idea might be inclined to keep it secret until it could be perfected if a cash award were to accompany its acceptance. Under the TVA system, he shares his proposal in its infancy with his colleagues. It is discussed, frequently improved, and its presentation is not delayed. Recognition is limited to citation of the group involved, not the individual, at the annual meeting of management and employees. There is no evidence that good ideas are withheld because of the lack of monetary incentive, and the implication that they would be is more than a little disturbing. Suggestions are expected from TVA employees. They are received because job improvement is a constant goal at every level of responsibility and no extra inducement is required.

Exemptions such as those cited are sought in an effort to avoid fragmentation of responsibility, to protect the principles of management set out by Congress in the TVA Act, and to safeguard programs under way. They are sought even when TVA is an enthusiastic advocate of measures proposed. When a bill to provide a health benefits program for government employees was introduced, TVA's Director of Personnel was the first witness presented by its sponsors in support. Nevertheless, the agency was exempt in the statute of 1959, in recognition of the fact that its own pioneering program was already successfully operating.

Requests for exemptions that are not expressions of dissent from purposes are confusing to a student unfamiliar with the total record. They are sometimes puzzling to members of Congress. One warm friend of TVA was horrified to discover that he was about to vote on a bill providing pay raises for government workers "except employees of TVA." Only the intervention of a more knowledgeable colleague saved him from the embarrassment of offering an amendment to remove what he had interpreted as a discriminatory provision. He was unaware that TVA is usually exempt from general government pay raises. Congress fixes the salaries of the Board members, and the Act provides that no staff member can receive an amount larger than the compensation of a director.

It further provides (Section 3) that in determining the wages of "laborers and mechanics," the quaint phrase used in 1933, the prevailing wage in the vicinity shall be paid, and that consideration shall be given to the rates secured through collective bargaining. In the up-to-date language of TVA, these are called "Trades and Labor" employees (elsewhere in the government they are usually described as "blue collar" workers). They build and operate dams and generating plants, erect and maintain transmission lines. They work at the chemical plants. Their number varies with construction demands, but, over the years, Trades and Labor employees have comprised more than half of total employment. TVA deals with them through their unions, which, for the purposes of negotiation with TVA, have joined together in the Tennessee Valley Trades and Labor Council.

In the autumn of every year, the Personnel Division of TVA working jointly with construction and operating management surveys the region to determine the wage levels prevailing. The Trades and Labor Council conducts its own study at the same time and discrepancies in the data collected in the two investigations are resolved through a joint labor-management wage data committee. Based on its conclusions negotiating sessions follow, and in December the Board must act on the recommendations submitted by the Director of Personnel to determine the rates of pay for Trades and Labor employees during the following year. Some time in the spring similar procedures bring to the Board proposals relating to the Salary Policy employees, a group comparable to those generally identified, for what must be historical reasons, as "white collar" workers in the federal establishment. The salaries of economists, engineers, scientists, managers, and the clerical staff of TVA are reasonably comparable to the schedules approved for similar positions in the federal classified service. But they are fixed by the Board as Section 6 of the TVA Act directs. They are not determined by Congress, and the independence of TVA's personnel system occasions exemptions from legislation proposed every year.

When Senator McKellar offered his amendments to the TVA statute in the 1940's, his effort was an open assault on the authority of a Board that had incurred his displeasure. When he proposed to repeal Section 26 of the Act and deny the agency the use of its proceeds, and when the Bureau of the Budget approached the same objective first in the Government Corporation Control bill and more resolutely in the amendments it pressed when the bond authorization was pending in the 1950's, those were direct and hostile acts. The objective was to remove authority to manage TVA from the Tennessee Valley to Washington, to establish political control as a substitute for nonpolitical management. The dozens of bills that would have taken bits and pieces of responsibility away from the Board of TVA were different. They had no such destructive intent. They were simply expressions of the acceptance of uniformity as a goal, and of belief in centralized control. They varied in importance, but taken as a whole and if adopted without amendment they would have demonstrated that a unified approach to resource development and a decentralized administration is impossible for the federal government to maintain.

Just to preserve the ability to do the job as its charter intended requires ceaseless vigilance on the part of TVA. Every bill introduced in Congress, and there are thousands every year, must be examined. That tedious chore is assigned to the Law Division. It is the responsibility of the legal staff to bring to the attention of other divisions any proposed legislation that may be of interest to them. A request for comment may go to the Manager of Power, to the foresters, the chemical plant, the Personnel Division, or to any of the others—sometimes to several. When comments have been received and agreement in analysis has been reached among the staff, a memorandum is prepared and presented to the Board for discussion and approval. Then files are established, by the Law Division in Knoxville and at the Washington office of TVA. The progress of the bill is charted. If the committee to which the measure is referred follows the practice of sending the bill for comment to all government agencies presumed to have an interest, the statement already approved becomes the basis of a letter signed by the Chairman of the Board. Under government procedures, such letters are submitted first to the Office of Management and Budget, which clears them for presentation to the requesting committee with a sentence indicating whether the position stated is consistent with that of the Administration. TVA may be asked to provide testimony before committees to supplement its official report, but in a good many cases no letter is requested or submitted, testimony is not required, and the analysis is used simply to provide information to members of Congress interested in discovering the position of TVA. During a recent Congress, files were maintained on almost two hundred bills. Selecting one Congress (the Seventy-ninth) at random, TVA files disclose that during its life, eleven public laws enacted contained provisions requested by TVA after the bills were introduced.

The pressure to alter the TVA statute does not invariably come from Congress. In the 1930's Harold Ickes, then Secretary of the Interior, concluded that TVA ought to become a part of the Department he headed. He expressed no hostility to any of its objectives. He was simply annoyed by its independence. He pushed his case with President Roosevelt, arguing as pundits in the field of public administration often contend that the President's time should not be mortgaged to the demands of an independent agency. His position might have been more persuasive if a study had not revealed the inordinate amount of the President's time consumed by the Secretary in promoting his design as contrasted to the relative reserve of the Board of TVA. Ickes and his representatives lobbied on Capitol Hill. They were strangely deaf to the argument that Congress intended TVA to be sheltered from partisan politics and that incorporation in a Department headed by a political appointee would violate that precept. The Secretary was scornful of the notion that it was important that decisions should be made in the region and that the judgment of the Board should be final with no supervisory layer inserted between it and the President and the Congress. He treated as absurd the contention that many TVA activities had a closer relationship to other departments than the one he headed. In the end, the firmness of the President frustrated Ickes' plans, and TVA continued as an independent non-political agency, but from time to time the creation of a new department to include TVA is suggested.

Many such proposals rely upon semantics to justify what is gracefully described as coordination, that elusive mirage of administration intended to promote common purposes while protecting jurisdictions and confirming separation. If any agency has a title indicating a concern with electricity, it appears to be assumed that it might function more effectively if it were associated with other agencies whose nomenclature or activities indicate a similar interest. That is, no doubt, why suggestions have been made to combine under one administrative umbrella the Federal Power Commission, a regulatory body, and the Rural Electrification Administration, a lending agency, with TVA, the only federal instrumentality that owns and operates a power system and does it as one part of a regional program of resource development. It is difficult to see what benefits would accrue from such a misalliance. Evidence that the administration of huge government departments is without flaw is not overwhelming. Clearly, there should be a free flow of information between government agencies having common interests and responsibilities, and coordination, whatever its definition, should be achieved whenever it is desirable. Both objectives can be accomplished without administrative association, and neither is guaranteed by such a relationship. Even a casual acquaintance with government in Washington reveals the rivalries and even enmities existing between different bureaus long associated in the same department. Togetherness is not a cure for maladministration, and conglomerates are not always effective tools for achievement. Yet faith in shuffling to achieve success in government administration remains unquenched.

A Commission on Organization of the Executive Branch of the Government, under the leadership of former President Herbert Hoover, was created on the recommendation of President Harry S. Truman in July, 1947, and made its report to Congress in March, 1949. The conclusions of the Commission itself were not disturbing to TVA. When the Senate Committee on Expenditures in the Executive Departments asked for comment, the Chairman of the Board of TVA in a letter of June 27, 1949, replied:

As you know, the Commission recommended no changes in TVA's organizational status. . . .

The recommendations in the Commission's report on general management emphasize the necessity of strengthening executive responsibility by making clear and adequate delegations of authority, holding accountable for results those to whom such authority has been delegated, and providing adequate staff services to the President and to agency heads. TVA is in full agreement with these basic recommendations, and the TVA Act of 1933 is in conformity with them. The act not only defines the broad program for which TVA is responsible, but provides the TVA Board of Directors with adequate authority to discharge these responsibilities while at the same time holding the Board fully accountable to Congress and the President for results.

In refraining from urging Congress to adopt legislation affecting TVA, the Commission had ignored a variety of recommendations received from its subordinate task forces. The Senator from Vermont, George D. Aiken, a member of the Commission, felt compelled to file a comment pointing out that the suggestions of two of those groups "follow so closely the arguments which the private power interests present in opposition to public water-resource development that the general welfare viewpoint does not seem to be properly represented." He added:

A permeating assumption in these reports is that public projects are to be evaluated by the same criteria as those valid for private business enterprise. This confronts us squarely with the question of whether the primary purpose in developing our water resources is to serve first the common welfare of the people, or to provide profit for business enterprise.

One story carried by the Knoxville (Tennessee) *News Sentinel* and the Paducah (Kentucky) *Sun Democrat* reported that former President Hoover had rejected certain task force suggestions adverse to TVA and had stated that the agency "had the advantages of flexibility of management, budgeting, and accounting that efficient modern business requires . . ." Further, he was said to have pointed out that TVA had an "excellent labor and production record."

In view of the pessimistic view of government operations expressed in his message vetoing the Norris bill of 1931, this described position betrayed a generosity of spirit unhappily not reflected in the reports of the second Hoover Commission created in 1954 and reporting in 1955. Its charter was broader than the first although the title and the Chairman were the same. Five fields of inquiry had been identified for exploration by the first Commission, with the purpose of reducing expenditures, eliminating duplication, consolidating services, abolishing unnecessary activities, and defining and limiting executive functions. To these five, two more were added in the charter of the second Commission— the elimination of "nonessential services, functions, and activities which are competitive with private enterprise" and "relocating agencies now responsible directly to the President in departments or other agencies." Twelve members were appointed to each Commission, four by the President of the United States, four by the President of the Senate, and four by the Speaker of the House. Two of each of the four were to be selected from "private life," joining in the task with members chosen from the Senate and House and the executive branch of the government.

Again, a Hoover Commission organized task forces, which in turn were shattered into work groups. Some of them visited the Tennessee Valley. The Task Force on Water Resources and Power held hearings in Chattanooga. And as a result of its deliberations a report was issued, which, if accepted, would have accomplished the annihilation of TVA. Destruction of the power system was of course the major goal and its sale was recommended, but other activities did not escape the attention of the Task Force. A remarkable sentence in its report commented: "It [TVA] is however, still engaged in many of the miscellaneous [*sic*] activities provided for in the 1933 TVA Act such as fertilizer research and development, watershed development, mineral resource development, reservoir development and topographic mapping, and importantly, flood control and navigation." "Group A," the report continued, "recommends transfer of these miscellaneous activities to the other [*sic*] appropriate Federal or state agencies."

Not all the hostile suggestions of the various work groups and task forces were included in the Commission's report to Congress, and there were dissenting members, but the majority accepted a sufficient number to achieve TVA's demise. There was no evaluation of the work accomplished by TVA, no suggestion that other agencies might do a better job. The Commission simply objected to the agency's existence. It was different. In Congress, reports of the various task forces and the Commission itself were referred to the Committees on Government Operations, and a subcommittee of the House Committee held hearings on the recommendations at a number of places throughout the country, one at Muscle Shoals in Alabama. There Lister Hill, in 1955 the senior Senator from Alabama, raised his eloquent voice in comment. He said:

> . . . I was one of the authors of the legislation creating TVA when it was considered by the Congress in 1933, and a member of the Conference Committee which adjusted the differences between the Senate and the House before the measure was finally enacted into law.

With my colleagues I watched when the President of the United States affixed his signature in approval of the measure, and this great undertaking began. Ever since, first as a member of the Committee having jurisdiction over legislation affecting TVA in the House, and in more recent years participating in the annual review of TVA's appropriation requests as a member of the Committee in the Senate, I have been concerned with the problems and the progress of TVA. I am the only member of that Conference Committee of 1933 now a member of the Congress, the only one who can bear witness now to the way in which an act of faith stands justified by works.

For the enactment of the statute creating TVA was an act of faith. We created a new type of agency. For the first time in the history of federal legislation relating to resource development a single agency in a limited area was told to look at the job as a whole. This had never been done before. Then, as now in other river valleys, the traditional pattern of federal administration divided responsibility, encouraged jurisdictional rivalry, increased red tape, assured delay and confusion. We were trying to do something about that problem when we created TVA, when we gave one agency control of the whole river system, and directed it to see the river in relation to the total resource base.

We made this new agency corporate in form, independent of the centralized departments of the federal establishment, and we tried to give the Board authority commensurate with its responsibilities, so that its fidelity and competence could be judged by results. We authorized it to acquire the land the program required, to purchase its own equipment and to negotiate its contracts. We told the Board to select its own employees and to establish their rates of pay. We wanted the Board to be able to control its costs, manage its schedules and be itself responsible for all its acts. We permitted TVA to sue and be sued in the courts.

We were uneasy then, as now, about the dangers of administrative centralization. We recognized that too many decisions had to be made in Washington by men remote from the problems and far from the people their decisions affected. So we determined that in the case of TVA the power to decide would be placed in the field, and in the law we directed the Board to establish its headquarters away from Washington and in the region it was to serve.

We set up objectives in the Act, and laid down the general policies to be followed, but we did not intend that Congress, or other branches of the Executive Department should interfere with the day to day decisions of the management of TVA. One thing we made crystal clear. Like a watermark on every page of the statute the basic intent of the Act is plain. The objective of the TVA was not simply to create a navigation channel, to control the floods of a capricious river, nor to furnish low-cost power to the people. No project and no program was to be considered an end in itself. The objective of the TVA Act was to build a region, to expand the economic opportunities of the people, to the end that the region and the nation might be stronger and so more free. If we were successful in this area, if this new device for the administration of federal functions in the field of resource development proved to be effective, we hoped that other rivers and other regions might reap the benefits of the pioneering program undertaken in this Valley.

The enactment of the TVA statute was a milestone in federal resource legislation. Yet nowhere in the report of this Commission do I find any analysis or any appraisal of the magnificent record of more than 20 years. Some of the very problems of administration which we were endeavoring to solve when we created TVA are discussed. . . . But no mention is made of the brilliant record of TVA, the single example in the nation of what can happen when one agency is created to develop and to execute a unified plan for a whole river basin, when decisions are made in the field, when responsibility is fixed, when one management can be held accountable for results.

So far as the power system was concerned, the lack of analysis of objectives, methods and results which infuriated the Senator may be explained by examining the conclusions of the half dozen men who formed the "work group," which reported to the Task Force which in turn advised the Commission. They had decided that the TVA power system was "not socially desirable," a finding that appears to involve considerations somewhat beyond the limits of the inquiry, but which eliminated the necessity for study of the record. A point of view with respect to a specific activity accounts for the recommendations with respect to power, but only devotion to the principles of centralization can explain the casual disposal of fertilizer development and other "miscellaneous" activities including "flood control and navigation" which the Commission seemed surprised to find TVA still promoting.

Nothing short of a cherished preference for central control can illuminate the recommendation of the Subcommittee on Transportation, which did investigate the results of TVA's use of its statutory provisions. On page 15 of its report, one reads an approving sentence: "The traffic management organizations of the Tennessee Valley Authority . . . were found to be outstandingly good and their functioning almost beyond criticism." And later,

"Its Traffic Branch, being on the ground, in an area of limited operations, distinctly on a regional basis, is fully acquainted with traffic needs of the agency and is in a position effectively to work out solutions to problems." Then, curiously, the next paragraph begins "It appears TVA traffic management could be made subject to the general supervision and control of GSA [General Services Administration] traffic management without impairing the already effective functioning of its Traffic Branch." It is hard to fight the notion that everything can be managed a little bit better from Washington. It is difficult for an agency to be different.

The venom toward TVA displayed by the second Hoover Commission, in contrast to the relative restraint of its predecessor group, may have been due more to the differing judgments of the men comprising the Commission and staff than to the enlarged purposes set out, although there was temptation enough in the suggestion that "nonessential services . . . competitive with private enterprise" be eliminated and that agencies "responsible directly to the President" be relocated. Most of all, the recommendations responded to the climate of the mid-1950's. The Commission was created in the month the President of the United States reportedly advised his Cabinet of his judgment of TVA by saying, "I'd like to see us sell the whole thing." It assembled in a season when the bounty hunters were in hot pursuit of an agency regarded as outlaw. None of the recommendations adverse to the interests of TVA was adopted by Congress, but the reports provided a convenient arsenal of weapons for foes to use during the four-year consideration of the legislation authorizing TVA to issue revenue bonds. They are worth remembering now, not for the vicious attacks on the TVA power system, but for the mindless advocacy of centralization. There have been, and there doubtless will be, other reorganization proposals in which, it is reasonable to predict, the neatness of organization charts will seem more important than performance in the field. Conformity, not excellence, will be the goal.

For nearly four decades, TVA has requested exemptions from bills that, if enacted, would impede its ability to do the job it has been assigned. It has contended stoutly in the councils of the Administration and before Congress. That obligation it must continue to meet, for the love of uniformity does not diminish, nor faith in centralization. As long as TVA remains an independent agency, free of politics, treating the resources of a region as a unit, and in the Valley it serves applying the principles of management encouraged by the provisions of its charter, it will be a target— just because it is different.

X

The Legislators and the Managers

Whether they are soliciting exemptions from pending legislation, testifying before Appropriations committees, or urging amendments of the organic Act, witnesses from TVA demonstrate the agency's belief that facts are convincing, that if its recommendations are supported by full disclosure of the problems and the goals, they will be approved. Their presentations may lack diplomacy, sometimes they are boring to committee members, but they are complete, for facts are all the agency has to offer as persuasion. It has no favors to give, no honors to bestow. There are no jobs to be dispensed by members of Congress. No projects will be located to please or named to exalt them, and they are even denied the satisfaction of announcing the beginning of new projects or the award of purchase contracts to suppliers in their states or districts. Unlike many organizations of the federal government TVA makes such announcements itself. The credit or the blame for decision accrues to the agency, it is not shared, and the line dividing the responsibility of the makers of policy in Congress and the managers of the enterprise in the region is not blurred. To keep it clear has been a continuing effort throughout the life of TVA.

Resisting the attempts of legislators to breach the boundaries by intervening to determine technical questions is only one part of the problem. There is a companion obligation, for the agency that denies participation in management to politicians must itself eschew the intrusion of political considerations into its recommendations. That becomes a matter of self-discipline. If administrators make no private commitments, the efforts of politicians to control management are open to view, but neither Congress nor the public knows when technicians, engineers, and scientists include political factors as elements in their analyses and recommendations, and few are competent to recognize the occasions when administrators advance proposals designed to lubricate approval rather than to promote objectives. These trespasses are silent and concealed, but when they are tolerated Congress is denied the opportunity to consider the most effective solutions for problems and the public never knows what has been sacrificed in an attempt to meld administrative judgments and legislative wisdom.

From the beginning, the Board of TVA has made a conscious effort to discourage the dilution of technical or managerial recommendations with infusions of political sagacity. In the early years, the directors would admonish the staff about it, reminding its employees that their recommendations should be restricted to the area of their competence, that judgments about the acceptability of programs and projects were not theirs to make. The controversy over Douglas Dam taught the staff how completely the Board respected its technical decisions, and how much the directors would endure to achieve their acceptance. They learned that prognostications with respect to the attitude of Congress were not so warmly received. When one enthusiastic division head ended a presentation with the unfortunate comment that the project he proposed was sure to be attractive to the legislators to whom it must be presented, he was sharply rebuked by the Chairman who pointed out that the Board wanted to be certain that his proposal deserved approval because of excellence, not popularity. The directors needed to know what the technicians determined to be right, not what they believed to be feasible. Congress would decide that.

The policy has not made things easy for TVA's supporters in the Senate and House. Consideration of some legislation the agency has requested would have been less abrasive and its passage easier had the recommendations been adjusted to meet the real or fancied position of influential legislators. Although the political acuity of administrators who consider such factors is generally praised, the directors of TVA have always believed that concern about the acceptability of proposals would involve some inherent disadvantages for the agency they headed. Modification of desired provisions to avoid conflict could betray the objectives sought and create a chasm between the rhetoric of promise and the actuality of achievement. Legislation drafted to ensure support rather than accomplishment might not be worth the effort of enactment. There was a further consideration. Political forecasts might be wrong, sacrifices might be needless, and, if it were given the chance, Congress as a whole might accept what the agency believed to be the soundest proposals even though some members were known to disagree.

Committees do repudiate the leadership of their chairmen, and committee recommendations are rejected by the membership of House and Senate when the facts are presented. TVA learned that early. In 1935, the Military Affairs Committee of the House had jurisdiction over legislation affecting TVA. The chairman and some other members were hostile to important amendments to the Act sought by the agency and pending before the committee. In the opinion of the Board the bill as reported by the majority would have been disastrous if enacted. The prospects were grim until a rebellious minority of the committee organized to reverse the decisions. On the floor of the House, they defied their chairman and his allies. By patient exposition, they won approval of their position, the committee proposals were not accepted, and the measure as adopted accomplished the purposes desired. It was a lesson TVA remembered.

Twelve years later, in 1947, when the Senate Committee on Public Works recommended against confirmation of the President's nomination of Gordon Clapp to be a director of TVA, knowledgeable friends expressed their indignation and regret, but added that the Senate would never approve the President's selection when the vigorous opposition of the senators from Tennessee was supported by an adverse committee report. They forecast insulting debate and humiliating defeat, and suggested that the dignified course would be for Clapp to request the President to withdraw his name. Their advice was not accepted. The Senate debated. Some of the comments were demeaning, but when the record of the nominee was presented and his qualifications discussed, the judgment of the committee was overruled, the tradition of senatorial courtesy ignored, and the President's selection confirmed. Again, in 1953, the decision of the Senate Committee on Appropriations denying funds for the continuance of a variety of important activities was reversed when the facts were presented to the whole chamber.

Like every other federal agency, TVA must accept the decisions of Congress. There is no question about that. When Senate and House agreed with the engineering judgment of Senator McKellar and approved the substitution of Watauga and South Holston Dams for Douglas, TVA began construction of those two dams. But it did not change its recommendation in accommodation. That is the point. TVA continued to press for Douglas, and Douglas was built. Altering a recommendation to make it palatable might make matters more agreeable for some members of Congress and quiet compromises could reduce the incidence of conflict. Concealment of problems might promote harmony, but TVA has never adopted those devices. It presents the facts as it sees them, prepared to abide by the result. If compromises must be made, they are made by members of Congress and in full knowledge of the results.

Insistence upon responsible statements to Congress was the basis of one disagreement between Arthur Morgan when he was Chairman of the Board and his colleague David Lilienthal. It was the subject of testimony before the Joint Committee investigating TVA in 1938. The record of that Committee's hearing shows that in May, 1935, when a request for an appropriation to begin construction of Chickamauga Dam was under consideration in a subcommittee of the House Appropriations Committee, Chairman Morgan, who was then TVA's Chief Engineer, had responded to a question by stating that the cost of the dam would be "probably $15 million." Three years later, testimony at the Joint Committee hearing indicated that, after the bill had passed the House and was pending before the Senate Committee, Lilienthal had learned from a TVA engineer that the estimates were in fact considerably higher. The Chairman's memory had been faulty. At the urging of his colleague, Arthur Morgan wrote a letter of correction to the committees of the House and Senate. The Congressional representative of the district in which the project was to be located, and the people of Chattanooga, near the site of the proposed structure, were disturbed when the letter was made public, fearing apparently that the higher estimate might adversely affect the chances for initiation of the project. The appropriation was approved, however, the dam was built, and the incident was of no consequence, forgotten until Morgan cited the episode as one of his many examples of alleged misconduct on the part of Lilienthal.

Apparently, the Chairman had bitterly resented his colleague's insistence that a letter of correction was required. He feared that it had impaired his relations with the representative and the people, and his accusation against Lilienthal rested on the fact that he believed the latter had not made clear to those who protested that the correction had been made as a result of his urging; that it had not been the Chairman's idea. To the Joint Committee, Lilienthal explained that he would have been glad to take credit for rectifying the error but "I supposed, at that time, that Arthur Morgan would not wish me to claim greater concern for his own reputation for reliability, or for the integrity of the Authority's official statements, than he himself displayed." Later in his testimony he said "My point was . . . that the TVA must make its recommendations to the Congress on the basis of our best engineering and administrative judgment free from political considerations." This is the rule TVA has followed. It has urged its friends to fight for what it believed to be right. It has ignored the advice of those who regard themselves as experts in political maneuvering.

There are always advisers who counsel acquiescence to avoid conflict and expedite action. When a handful of landowners organized a furious protest against Land Between the Lakes, the exemption from acquisition of their individual holdings was urged as a device to make project approval certain. The gross favoritism involved in such a proposal, the limitation on development it would cause, and the myriad problems associated with tolerance of privately owned enclaves in public areas—all these objections were brushed aside as inconsequential compared to the desirability of securing prompt approval of the project. TVA refused to yield to the protestors. It rejected the argument that it was worthwhile "to get a nose under the tent," a phrase often used to justify decisions calculated to enable a project to start even when conditions imposed tend to prejudice its successful conclusion. The furor died, the plans of TVA were approved, landowners were treated alike, and today the project is flourishing.

When, in the long and arduous effort that preceded enactment of the bond amendment in 1959, weary friends in Congress would consider the compromises offered, they were told just what the effects would be. Decisions were theirs to make, and in the face of dark and daily predictions of defeat they determined to struggle on, to get a good bill or none at all, and in the end they were victorious. Adoption of that legislation by Congress did not end the necessity to resist advisers who counseled surrender. The case for the amendment had to be presented to the President. Members of the White House staff advised the Board of TVA that the bill was about to be vetoed. All three directors (Chairman Herbert D. Vogel, A. R. Jones, and Brooks Hays) had been appointed by President Eisenhower, and with considerable firmness the Chairman of the Board insisted that the chief executive owed them the courtesy of an opportunity to present the consequences of his disapproval to the agency he had selected them to head. Reluctantly, an interview was granted.

With stout but heavy hearts, the directors arrived at the White House, discouraged by the spiteful comment of a Presidential aide who assured them they were wasting their time. In fact, the visit proved to be time well spent, for, in the course of the discussion it was discovered that the President's major objection was directed to one provision of the measure that could be eliminated without damage. The Board agreed to recommend the change, and upon assurance from the sponsors of the legislation and the leadership of both houses of Congress that the offending portion would be deleted promptly by amendment, the President signed the measure into law. Once more, tiresome persistence had been rewarded. Again, the oracles were wrong.

Firmness in resisting the injection of politics into its recommendations, insistence on presenting the facts as it sees them, and going ahead with its job at all seasons has endowed the agency with an unrivaled reputation for political ineptitude. To sagacious observers, it was incredible that TVA should turn to foreign suppliers of electrical equipment and under pressure refuse to change its decision when the bond amendment was pending before Congress. The reason was simple. TVA was not indifferent to the problems of legislators, but a generator had to be ordered, and domestic prices had become intolerable. The agency could not wait for a more auspicious time to act. When Memphis encountered difficulties in construction of its steam generating plant, and the city's contract with TVA expired before its completion, interim rates, those applied to short-term arrangements and somewhat higher than the wholesale rates of long-term agreements, were applied. Understandably, Memphis protested. There was sympathy for the city within TVA and consternation in Congress, for the representative who was managing the bond amendment on the floor of the House was a resident of Memphis. Politically the decision was unforgivable. Under the TVA Act, it had to be made. The contract had expired, short-term rates had to be applied, and in spite of understanding of the problems of one hard-pressed distributor, established procedures were honored.

1953 was a bad year for TVA to announce that its administrative headquarters would be moved from Knoxville in Tennessee to Muscle Shoals in Alabama. It was not a sudden decision on the part of the Board. The move had long been discussed. In 1933, Congress itself had established the legal headquarters, the "principal office" of the corporation. Under the Act it was to be "in the immediate vicinity" of Muscle Shoals. The location of Norris Dam, the first major construction project to be undertaken by TVA, made Knoxville a suitable site for administrative headquarters in the beginning, and the University of Tennessee offered the new agency the use of certain laboratories and the library of its law school. Those were compelling considerations in the first hectic weeks of TVA's life, and counsel advised the Board of its authority to establish its own offices wherever it desired.

In selecting Knoxville, the directors surrendered a personal advantage, for in addition to their compensation the Act made available to Board members three residences built on the Muscle Shoals reservation by the Army for officers' use in World War I. Knoxville was considered a temporary location, and spokesmen for Alabama continuously urged the Board to move to Muscle Shoals. Both senators and one representative from the state appeared before the Investigating Committee in 1938 to urge the transfer as essential to compliance with the statute. The Committee, however, agreed with counsel of TVA and held that the Board had authority to decide on the place of its residence and the location of administrative offices as distinguished from the legal headquarters, which was fixed in the Act.

In 1939, with the investigation over, litigation settled, and the acquisition of utility properties accomplished, the Board decided to review the headquarters question. The internal reorganization undertaken in 1937 had been completed and the General Manager was directed to explore the matter. His report recommended that the headquarters offices be moved to Muscle Shoals. It was located near midpoint rather than at the beginning of the navigation channel, nearer to three state capitals, including that of Tennessee, and closer than Knoxville to many TVA activities. One impediment prevented prompt action. There was no office space available in the area. Construction of facilities would have to be undertaken. In the autumn of 1940, in the next budget submitted after the General Manager's report, the Board included a request for funds to construct an office building at Muscle Shoals. The request was denied by the Bureau of the Budget. Defense requirements were rising, soon critical materials were rationed, new office buildings postponed and plans for moving set aside for the duration of World War II.

After the war, attention turned again to agency organization. The problem of headquarters location was surveyed once more, and in 1946 a new General Manager repeated the recommendation of 1939. The Board and central management should move to Muscle Shoals. The problem of providing space remained. A building would have to be constructed, and the bill appropriating funds for TVA to use in fiscal year 1947 provided money to make the necessary plans. As obtaining funds from the Treasury for capital investment grew increasingly difficult, the General Manager in 1950 recommended exploration of an alternative to construction by TVA itself. He proposed a lease-purchase agreement, and after careful exploration the idea was approved, bids were invited, one offer was accepted, and an agreement negotiated. Once again, national priorities intervened to delay action. Eruption of conflict in Korea limited the supply of steel and postponed construction. Not until the steel shortage appeared to be easing could arrangements go forward. Finally, in March, 1953, the Board announced the plan to move.

Whenever government offices are moved there are likely to be objections. It is disrupting to staff and opposed by communities. In this case, the protests were strenuous, which in a way was surprising, for there had never been any secret about the possibility of the transfer. Some five hundred jobs, only a third of TVA's total employment then in the Knoxville area, would be involved, but leased space would be vacated and payrolls reduced, and the real estate and commercial enterprises of the city organized effective opposition. They were strengthened by the addition of partisan to parochial pressure. Knoxville was located in the traditional Republican stronghold of eastern Tennessee, Muscle Shoals in Democratic northern Alabama, and a Republican Administration had just been inaugurated.

The representative from the district in which Knoxville was located urged intervention by the House Committee on Appropriations, and although no funds for the move were requested in the bill then pending, hearings were held and later, when the measure containing TVA's appropriation was reported from the Committee, an odd proviso was attached. It directed that no funds should be expended by TVA for the acquisition of new headquarters at a new site as long as the amount appropriated annually for construction of power facilities was greater than the amount paid into the Treasury. The power staff of TVA was not involved in the projected transfer. That group had been moved from Knoxville to Chattanooga some years earlier. The provision might have no basis in logic, but the intent of the Appropriations Committee was clear. The headquarters were not to be moved. The Senate Committee also considered the question and adopted a more relevant provision. The bill as finally reported by the Conference Committee and adopted by both houses provided that the move should not be made until the Director of the Bureau of the Budget had studied the matter and reported his conclusions to TVA and to the Committees on Appropriations of the House and Senate. The Bureau with the aid of the General Services Administration did conduct an inquiry. The House Appropriations Committee dispatched a special committee to investigate, but no report was ever made to TVA or to Congress.

In January, 1954, the sudden death of the individual with whom TVA had contracted terminated the first agreement, and a search for another builder began. A second lease-purchase arrangement was developed, but it never became effective for on September 16, just two weeks after the new Chairman of TVA's Board had taken office, he wrote the Director of the Bureau of the Budget recommending that action by the Bureau "be deferred indefinitely." He disagreed with the majority of the Board about the desirability of the move. The Acting Director of the Bureau replied that no decision "as to the advisability of the move" had been reached, and that discussion about the matter would be welcome. If conferences were held, they were private. No public comment ever came from the Bureau.

The fact that the Board had selected a peculiarly bad time to advance such a proposal was cited as evidence of the failure of its policy of ignoring what are referred to as political realities. It was not a good time. It was simply the time when honest efforts came to fruition. There had been no unreasonable delay, but moving the headquarters was not the only project before the Board in the postwar years. Work on Watauga and South Holston dams had been resumed, and when they were completed two smaller dams downstream were built, Boone and Fort Patrick Henry. The extended hearings on the President's nomination of Gordon Clapp had required a good deal of attention. He was appointed during the recess of Congress in October, 1946, but not confirmed until April, 1947, and due to the enterprise of Senator McKellar the whole history of TVA was reviewed in the hearings. In 1948, the struggle for funds to start the Johnsonville steam plant had begun, not to be ended until the spring of 1949. Efforts to move the headquarters were only one part of the total scene, but they were continuous.

They were described at the special hearing conducted by a Subcommittee of the House Committee on Appropriations in 1953. It was a typical TVA presentation. Nothing was omitted. The reasons for the proposed transfer were set forth, the history reviewed. Statements of Board members before the Joint Committee investigating TVA in 1938, before Appropriations Subcommittees in 1941, 1944, and 1946 and the Senate Public Works Committee in 1948, were cited in response to the suggestion that the move had been planned in secrecy. The committee members may have been impressed, but the position of the majority was unchanged. Privately, the lease-purchase agreement was described as excellent, and TVA's General Manager, who had testified in the absence of the Chairman, was complimented on his presentation, but it failed of its purpose. There was no ill feeling, but there was no move of headquarters. All efforts were abandoned. Action of Congress had delayed accomplishment and the appointment of directors who preferred to live and work in Knoxville ended the matter. There was no occasion for a clash between Congress and the agency. The matter was, in the end, administratively determined, as TVA believed it should be, and by the decision of its predecessors, the Board of TVA still has its offices in the undistinguished building where the first directors selected space for temporary occupancy in 1933.

Only some seventy, the Agricultural Relations Staff, were moved to Muscle Shoals, a few in 1955, the rest in 1961, when the newly appointed Board members were convinced of the necessity of their transfer. Fortunately, no substantial construction was required to receive them. An administration building had been built on the reservation at Muscle Shoals. Until the chemical staff moved into the new structure in the summer of 1950, temporary quarters built by the Army in 1918 had served as their headquarters. By enlargement of the new building, space was made available to accommodate the transferred personnel. There was opposition from within the staff itself and from the community, but they moved. There was no intervention by Congress.

Muscle Shoals is still the legal headquarters, the "principal office" of the corporation. The chemical operations and agricultural staffs are located there. Two laboratories—one investigating reservoir ecology, the other air pollution—are maintained near the reservation, and a power service facility where repairs and major maintenance jobs are undertaken has been constructed on the government property. Including power personnel at Wilson Dam and other nearby facilities and a few other small offices, a total TVA employment of over 2,300 was registered in the area in the summer of 1971. At Knoxville, the Board and central management reside, and the engineering staff. With some smaller units, TVA employment in the vicinity now totals about 3,000, including the Division of Forestry, Fisheries, and Wildlife Development, which has headquarters at Norris. Chattanooga is home for over 3,000 employees, those employed by the Office of Power, in the Divisions of Purchasing and Property and Supply, the Maps and Surveys Branch, and the main Office of Health and Environmental Science. These three locations have been the major employment centers throughout the life of TVA. Construction forces move from project to project and there are a few small offices at other locations in the region, mainly for the management of reservoir properties, for forestry, or power use. There is now an office at Golden Pond, Kentucky, for employees assigned to Land Between the Lakes, and a small office is maintained at Washington, D.C., with a staff of three full-time employees and one part-time clerk —an illustration of the consequences of a genuinely decentralized administration of a federal program.

The locations of small offices in the region are changed whenever efficiency and economy dictate. Employees complain, communities protest, and members of Congress object, but they are moved, jobs are reassigned, staffs increase or diminish with a single purpose—to serve the people of the region more effectively. That was the objective of the proposed move to Muscle Shoals, but when it was clear that no immediate transfer could be accomplished, leases in Knoxville were renewed and the interior of the headquarters building renovated and refurbished. The offices look better than they did before the improvements, and are more efficiently arranged, but the administrative headquarters of TVA is not distinguished by luxury or style.

There are no private elevators for the directors' use, there is no executive dining room, none of the accepted status symbols confirm the eminence of the Board. TVA has contributed new concepts of architecture in its dams, and most of its steam plants are handsome. The bridges it has designed and built have received awards, but with the exception of the administrative office at the chemical plant and a few small structures serving power needs TVA has done nothing to upgrade the level of commercial architecture in the area. Some years ago a handsome structure was designed to be located on the Chickamauga reservation. Power operations required it, and other administrative units would be housed there, too. Construction has had to be deferred because of budget limitations, and whether government-owned or leased, TVA offices continue to be uniformly unimpressive. It has always been this way. The agency was created in the midst of the Great Depression to promote development of an area then one of the poorest in the United States and the personal preferences of its first three directors were ratified by the circumstances prevailing. No limousines are assigned to Board members, no chauffeurs are at their service. Only in recent years have they had the convenience of reserved parking space near their offices, a distinction received with some initial embarrassment.

The lack of ornament in the life of TVA has led to a kind of retroactive mythology. Some years ago one of the agency publications contained the interesting historical note that at the first Board meeting the directors sat on upended crates. To this writer it seemed incredible that three intelligent men would endure such discomfort, while they labored in a room at the Willard, then one of the leading hotels in Washington. A check with David E. Lilienthal reveals that he has no recollection to support the story. In some astonishment at the inquiry, he said, "Not for eight hours on crates. I would remember that." Perhaps he would, and the account is doubtless apocryphal, but thinking great thoughts and making vast plans while sitting on derelict boxes is in a way symbolic of the way TVA began. There was no time or taste for glorification of the agency or its personnel. The region demanded total concern.

That concern for the region has had an effect on the nature of the agency's relationships with Congress. When directors or members of the staff testify before committees, they are not relying on analyses prepared by unknown subordinates affecting areas strange to them. The studies of technicians are supported by their personal knowledge. They are close to the problems. When Oliver Springs, a community not far from Knoxville, was inundated by a flash flood a few years ago, the waters had barely subsided before TVA cars came splashing through the mud. The Board of Directors with senior water control engineers had come to inspect the damage. Later, when TVA witnesses appeared before subcommittees of the Appropriations committees seeking funds to begin a program of flood protection for the town, they were describing a situation they had witnessed themselves. Observation is not often so immediate, but areas under discussion are always familiar. Communities and their problems are understood. It makes a difference. The Directors of TVA are deeply committed to the programs they advance, and they are convinced that Congress will care too, if the facts are fully presented. They are right. In more than thirty years, the recommendation of only one major project, the Fulton plant, has been rejected. A wartime proposal to build a phosphate plant at Mobile, Alabama was not accepted, and there have been postponements and stretched-out schedules increasing the cost of others, but TVA has experienced only that one significant defeat.

Hundreds of exemptions to pending legislation have been obtained, and these require considerable effort. For TVA itself, each such request involves the same review of programs, of goals, and achievements that the investigation of 1938 required. It is a wholesome exercise in self-examination. The division head must be convinced himself and he must persuade others, the Law Division, and the General Manager's office, that the program he directs deserves the recognition implicit in exemption from a general statute. He must obtain approval of the Board. Then the facts must be presented to members of Congress individually, and to committees. It is understandably exasperating to legislators proposing measures to deal in comfortable uniformity with federal employees or fish or wildlife across the country to be advised that one area, one agency, desires exemption from central control, but over the years they have been generous in understanding and adjustment. Thirteen times, amendments to the basic charter have been adopted by Congress (major changes have been discussed in previous chapters), and only one was enacted in the face of TVA disapproval.

That was in 1968, when an amendment was adopted that deleted those portions of Section 25 of the TVA statute which required the initial determination of the issue of just compensation to be made by a three-man commission in all condemnation actions brought by the agency. The original provision had been drafted by the Land Branch in the Department of Justice in response to a request from TVA's sponsors for "the best system you can devise." TVA believed it had worked well, and that associated with the "no-trading" policy adopted for purchase it had provided an acquisition program fair alike to landowners and government. Unlike many innovations embodied in the TVA Act, its results had been surveyed by qualified and impartial critics.

In 1951, in connection with the promulgation of Rule 71A of the Federal Rules of Civil Procedure, the Supreme Court Advisory Committee made an extensive study of the condemnation provisions of the TVA Act and advised the Court of its approval. The Committee pointed out that they relieved overcrowded court dockets and served the convenience of landowners because hearings could be conducted at a variety of locations. It noted that commissioners made a practice of inspecting property on the ground, which juries rarely are able to do, and that the overwhelming majority of judges (seventeen of twenty-one) having had experience with the TVA system expressed their approval of its procedures. Not only did the Advisory Committee and the Court conclude that the TVA statutory provision should be retained, but Rule 71A(h) provided that a similar system should be made available to other federal agencies desiring to adopt it. The commendation was gratifying to TVA, but, in spite of the official endorsement, pressure from landowners desiring a jury trial increased. Congress was responsive and the effect of the amendment enacted is to apply Rule 71A(h) of the Federal Rules of Civil Procedure to TVA. This means that any party requesting a determination by jury of the issue of just compensation is entitled to it unless the court, for reasons set out in the rule, orders trial by a commission. It means that TVA is restricted to procedures that were a liberalization when they were applied to other agencies and were developed as a result of the experience of TVA. This curious result of TVA's pioneering is the only substantial change in the basic statute not approved by the agency.

For almost four decades, Congress and the management of TVA have worked together to promote the regional program. They are not adversaries. They are companions in the process. At arm's length, each respects the sphere of the other. Members of Congress have accepted the recommendations of TVA. They have used the information it offers in prodigious amounts. Senators and representatives are aware that TVA will resist their intrusion into management, but they know that it will leave political judgments to them. If, in the course of a bill's consideration, compromises have to be made, legislators will make them. TVA will provide the information required, but the decision is theirs. They understand that, often awkwardly and sometimes with skill, TVA is doing the best job it can to advance the objectives of the statute Congress entrusted to it. Its timing may make matters difficult, its proposals may spark controversy, its stubbornness merit irritation. Then members of Congress can reflect, as Thomas Mann observed, that "opinions cannot survive if one has no chance to fight for them."

TVA and its advocates in Congress have been given a multitude of such chances. The opinions on which its program is based have been repeatedly defended, and they have survived. They will have to be protected in the future, and for the advocates of TVA in Congress life will not be easy, for it is unlikely that conflict will cease. One factor has changed. The men who interpret TVA in the Senate and the House today have an advantage over those who defended it in earlier years. The pioneers talked of desperate problems and crying needs. They told of their hopes and dreams. Their surrogates of the present have tested methods to describe, and a record of accomplishments to report. They know the story to be summarized in the following chapter.

XI

A Brief Accounting

In the 1930's Congress debated about measures to control the floods of raging rivers, to heal erosion of the damaged soil, to shelter the dustbowls of the prairies. Ecology was never mentioned. The word environment was rarely used. The vocabulary of the 1970's is different, but respect for resource interrelationships is not new and concern for the surroundings in which men live is not an innovation. Almost forty years ago both were reflected when TVA was created to see the job of development as a whole, and to make certain that its results contributed to "the well-being of the people." Today, a review of accomplishments in the watershed of the Tennessee River suggests the multitude of problems that must be confronted, the variety of opportunities presented, and the time required for progress when improvement of the total environment is the objective, rather than development of a single resource or conservation of one asset without regard to others.

Congress was confident about some measures required to halt the Valley's spiral of resource depletion. The TVA Act was explicit about certain remedies to be provided, but in a singular display of modesty the legislative body revealed its expectation that other problems and solutions would be discovered, and the statute invited recommendations of additional measures to promote "an orderly and proper physical, economic, and social development" of the area. By the terms of the Act fortified by the executive order of the President with respect to sections 22 and 23, the Board was encouraged to explore, to probe for problems unrecognized and benefits unmentioned in the statute, to propose new projects and programs.

Because of that encouragement, TVA has been able to foster development of the recreation asset created by steamflow control, and adopt procedures to abate malaria. It has contributed to reduction of pollution, designed waste disposal systems, undertaken economic studies, demonstrated improved methods of forest management and wood utilization, and advanced the changes in farm practices required to restore fertility to the soil. Because it could face the total job, the habitat for fish and wildlife has been improved, recommendations affecting the transportation system have been submitted, and methods of restoring land damaged by strip mining have been demonstrated. Those activities, and others, were undertaken after investigation disclosed their importance. No study was required to determine that the threat of floods had to be removed before men could live in safety, and development could flourish. The record was well known. In the century before TVA's creation, the Valley had experienced six of catastrophic size, and the new statute made clear that one of the primary purposes of the river control it authorized was reduction of flood menace in the future.

In 1933, as today, one school of conservationists opposed the building of dams as a method of flood control, deploring the resulting change in the watercourses. The critics contended that, by farming practices that deprived the soil of cover and by destruction of the Valley's forests, man was responsible for the inundations and that changes in his use of land would solve the problem. It was true that the acts of men had added to the danger, and that better land management would help to reduce the peaks of some floods. In a few of the watershed's small valleys, it could lower the crests substantially, particularly in summer. But floods in the Tennessee Valley had occurred before the forests were ravished by axe or fire, and when relatively little of the land had been deprived of protective cover. The flood of 1867, the most devastating ever reported for the basin, occurred when the Valley had been settled less than a hundred years and the magnificent forests were in their prime. Not until the turn of the century did lumber production become important in the watershed and the record year for timber harvesting was 1909. The great floods on the Tennessee

River were the consequence of nature's cycle of rainfall, and her pattern of delivery to the drainage basin. Fifty-two inches of rainfall are received in an average twelve-month period—more than half in winter and early spring when vegetation is sparse and evaporation rates are low. In those months, the runoff to the rivers is heavy and when downpours occur in the mountainous eastern portion of the Valley the water rushes from the rugged slopes to all the upstream tributaries. Only mighty dams can hold back the torrents. They cannot be restrained in any other way.

The plan of streamflow management that achieves control of regional floods is simple. It has not changed since it was described to the court which considered the "eighteen-company" case in 1937, and explained to the Investigating Committee in 1938. Every year, the reservoirs behind the high dams on the upstream tributaries are drawn to their lowest level by January 1 and space for 12 million acre-feet of water is ready to hold the runoff from the winter rains. Until April, these tributary reservoirs are managed primarily for flood control. When heavy rainfall occurs their level rises swiftly, then the water is released to make room for the downpours expected in the days to come.

When it rains at the same time in all the upper tributaries as it did in 1957, the operations must be precise and skillful. According to a TVA report:

> Late in January of that year the rain began. It poured down in the Holston valley, in the Clinch and on the Little Tennessee. It fell on towns and cities, on highways and on airports, in the mountains and the hollows. Forests and winter pastures slowed the runoff for a day, or even two, in the beginning, but for 20 days of 21 the rain continued. More than 25 inches fell on Clingman's Dome in the Great Smokies, over 23 at Flat Top in the headwaters of the Ocoee. In the rugged watersheds of Tellico, Cheoah and Nantahala there was no respite. Gauges in the Hiwassee basin, in the French Broad valley, and on the Powell all reported the swelling volume of runoff and the relentless rise in stage as the water ran to the rivers from land soon soaked beyond its capacity to hold.

The men who manage streamflow from the central point of control in Knoxville stayed at their posts all day and night throughout that crisis period, collating reports from more than 600 stream gauges—three times as many as listed in the annual report for fiscal 1938—relating them to forecasts from the Weather Bureau, and sending out the orders that held the waters of the Clinch and Powell behind Norris Dam, released the rising Little Tennessee through Fontana, and restrained the surging streamflow at Watauga while the discharge from Hiwassee was rushed downstream to make room for the rainfall approaching. Hour by hour, the orders went out, and, like a giant orchestra responding to the baton of its conductor, the rivers obeyed. It was the major test of the system, and there was no flood. The Tennessee stayed within its banks. Without the protection of the dams that kept it safe, Chattanooga alone would have suffered damages of over $200 million in those frightening weeks.

High dams on the upstream tributaries do the major job of flood control. They regulate the rate at which the water is released to the Tennessee, but the main river structures have a role, too. As streamflow moves down the channel, precision in management is added at each one until the huge reservoir behind the last in the chain, Kentucky, is reached. That dam stands guard at the mouth, barring passage of the waters of the Tennessee whenever their release would endanger communities down river on the Ohio and Mississippi. Already, losses of over $390 million have been averted by TVA's management of the waters of the Tennessee, and benefits will continue.

Today, a system of thirty-three major dams on the Tennessee and its tributaries controls the river's flow. Six of these and several minor structures are owned by the Aluminum Company of America, but, under a contract with TVA, release of the water they control is coordinated with discharges from the twenty-seven owned and operated by the federal agency, and private enterprise has joined in the common purpose of managing the river to advance the security of men. Tellico Dam, now under construction on the Little Tennessee, will add to regional protection, and as the local flood program advances, the Valley of the Tennessee approaches the day when it will be free of fear of serious floods. Then, one congressional purpose will have been achieved, one obstacle to the well-being of the people reduced. Flood control, however, was never a single goal. It was one of the three primary benefits for which the river system was to be managed, and all three were part of the general program of development. The major water control projects built by TVA are multipurpose. They prevent flood damage, generate electric energy for the region's use, and provide a year-round navigation channel from Paducah in Kentucky at the river's mouth to Knoxville where the Tennessee begins.

In spite of the fact that efforts to improve the waterway were a significant part of pre-TVA history, development of a navigation channel sparked little excitement in the debates preceding enactment of the statute of 1933. Flood control was dramatic, the devastation along the lower Mississippi in 1927 was fresh in memory, and power production was controversial and exciting. By contrast, navigation seemed a little old-fashioned. For the transportation of goods, railroads and trucks were favored in the year when TVA was born. Fewer than a million tons of commerce were carried on the river in 1933, mostly shipments of low value—sand, gravel, logs, and railroad ties—moving seasonally and in short hauls, a total of only 33 million ton-miles of traffic. Everyone was a little skittish about estimates of the use of the river for transportation. There were scornful comments challenging the wisdom of investing federal funds to provide a channel.

Even when the desirability of developing the waterway was conceded, there were no very optimistic prognostications about its use. No one foresaw the day when barges from the Midwest would bring grain into this deficit area to be processed in flour mills established in the Valley or to stimulate the ascendance of poultry raising in the agricultural economy. TVA itself was cautious. In 1940, before the channel was completed, the agency estimated that seven million tons would be carried in 1960, for an estimated total of 1.5 billion ton-miles. The 20-year forecast was considered bold. Even within TVA, there were doubters who thought the predictions a little giddy. In fact, the actual tonnage that rode the river in that target year reached a total of 12.4 million, more than 5 million tons above the estimate, and over 2.3 billion ton-miles were logged, not 1.5 billion as predicted. By 1970, over 25 million tons moved in long tows, some entering the river at its mouth and traveling all the way from Paducah to Knoxville, 640 river miles, making a total of over 3.5 billion ton-miles in all, a hundred times the ton-mile figure recorded in 1933. The river is used, and to a greater degree than anticipated. New and larger locks have been installed at three dams—Wilson, Wheeler, and Guntersville—and will be placed in others when budget considerations permit. The channel has been extended to some tributaries, and will be developed in others.

Navigation is a big thing in the Tennessee Valley today. It is difficult to appraise its importance. Shipper savings provide the conventional measure of navigation benefits. Already they are estimated to have passed the half billion dollar mark on the Tennessee, almost four times the total of investment in facilities and operating costs over the years. Under the cost-benefit system of justifying federal expenditures for navigation improvement, the government investment has been sound and happily its advantages have been widely diffused. For the TVA Act required of the agency something more than creation of a channel. To be an effective tool to aid the economy of the region, it had to be open to small shippers as well as to large enterprises able to construct their own terminals. Facilities had to be provided for general service, and in 1942 TVA obtained appropriations to build four public-use terminals to demonstrate that the benefits of water transportation need not be denied to the small businesses of the area. The four modest projects located at Decatur and Guntersville in Alabama, Chattanooga, and Knoxville in Tennessee, served their purpose. By 1951, all had been turned over to private operators. Today, more than a hundred terminals, large and small, public and private, facilitate the increasing use of the waterway, and the shipper savings reported are widely distributed.

Even though substantial in amount and broadly disseminated, such savings are an inadequate measure of the value of the navigation channel to the region. The existence of the water highway has been a major attraction to many of the industries that have located along the river shores. Some of the installations needed large amounts of water for processing, and streamflow control guaranteed that. All required flood-free sites for building, and the availability of power was important. But water transportation was decisive for many of the new plants which represent about $2 billion in private investment today, providing jobs directly in their operations for more than 37,000 of the Valley's labor force, and indirectly supporting the employment of as many more. Once considered least promising of the major benefits expected to be achieved by the system of river control, navigation has confounded its critics and surpassed the hopes of its friends. Its record has rewarded the efforts of more than a century.

There was precedent for constructing dams to create a navigation channel and to reduce flood danger, and dams were built to generate electricity. But in 1933 there was no precedent for treating a river system as a unit and accomplishing the three purposes together, and there was, not unnaturally, considerable skepticism about the possibility of achieving the several benefits by a single system. Congress established priorities for TVA to observe. The Board was not to locate, design and operate dams to provide the greatest amount of electricity, but to achieve the maximum of flood control and to guarantee a channel for navigation. Only as much power as could be generated after these two requirements had been met would be available for use in the region. So far as river control was concerned, power was subordinate in the statute, although foremost in public attention.

When TVA was created, there were some 230,000 residential consumers of electricity in the area it now serves, and in their homes they used an average of about 600 kwh a year, then close to the national figure for domestic consumption. They paid about the national average, too, 5.7 cents per kwh. They lived in towns and cities, for only a few farms (about 3 per cent) had service, those fortunate enough to be located on the edge of municipalities or next to cotton gins. Congress was firm in its instructions to the Board. Electricity provided by TVA was to be used by the people in their homes and on their farms, and while there could be no evasion of the obligation, there was no guarantee of success. The entire power program was an experiment. No one could measure the effect of a deliberate effort to provide electricity "at the lowest possible rates," to establish prices not to assure profits, but to encourage use. The low rate–high use theory of electricity marketing had never been tried on such a scale before. Even among those who believed the project should have a fair trial, there was some doubt. The private companies then serving the area made converts when they contended that 540,000 kw, the total installed in 1933, was enough to supply the energy requirements of the Valley. In 1935, the late Eugene Yates, of the Commonwealth & Southern Corporation and later coparent of Dixon-Yates, testified before the committee considering amendments to the TVA Act that a

6-year surplus of capacity was in place. He predicted that the additions already under construction and those contemplated by the government would be idle, a waste of public money. On rural electrification he stated his company's position: "We do not consider any farm customer a prospect unless his income is in excess of $1,000. They just cannot pay for the equipment and the wiring of the houses."

In spite of such advice from those assumed to be most knowledgeable, Congress persisted, and the Board of TVA undertook the task assigned. The installation of capacity, the establishment of rates—these were acts of faith. Their justification lies in the record. Today, over 2 million electricity consumers are served by the 160 local distributors that buy their power from TVA. Those distributors, 110 municipally owned systems and 50 rural cooperatives, have grown to be substantial institutions, reporting total assets of over $1.3 billion on June 30, 1971. Electricity use has increased throughout the nation in the years since TVA was established. Most of all it has grown in the TVA area, where the average annual household use of consumers served by the distributors was 14,400 kwh in fiscal 1971, about twice the national average for that year.

Basic resale rates are agreed to by the distributors when a contract with TVA is signed, and lower levels are adopted as operating experience permits. Despite increasing costs, the trend of rates was consistently downward until most recent years, and in 1961, TVA offered the Norris rate in appropriate recognition of the centennial anniversary of the Senator's birth. It was the lowest rate for residential service in the United States, and over the next few years sixteen distributors were able to apply it in their operations. Now, costs have risen sharply, both for TVA and the distributors. TVA's wholesale rates have been adjusted upwards, and retail rates have been increased, but the region served by TVA is still an area where homes and farms are served at the lowest possible rates that will cover costs, and as long as the statute of TVA is unchanged, it must continue to be. The average cost per kilowatt-hour paid by the domestic consumer of power provided by TVA today is something over a penny, about half the national average of more than two cents.

The use of electricity for space heating has climbed since the

1930's when the all-electric homes in the town of Norris excited interest in the region. Over 637,000 homes in TVA's power service area were heated by electricity in 1971. Together with the demands of industry and commerce and of government installations the expanding requirements of domestic users have resulted in growth that has made the TVA power system the largest in capacity in the United States; nearly 20 million kilowatts were installed by 1971 to meet the needs of the region which had only 855,000 kw* in 1933 and an additional 16 million kw will be added when plants now under construction or on order are completed.

Since 1950, most of the capacity additions have been in coal-fired steam plants. Nuclear plants are under construction now, and to those planned by TVA to meet normal system load growth, an experimental facility will be added. On January 14, 1972, the Atomic Energy Commission announced that TVA and the Commonwealth Edison Company had been selected together to construct and operate a demonstration liquid-metal fast-breeder reactor plant to be located in the TVA area. These new sources of energy offer great possibilities, but they can never challenge the role of hydro projects in initiating the TVA system. Although very little remains to be developed, hydroelectric energy made available by streamflow control made the demonstration of low cost–high use pricing possible. It started the region on the way. The politicians who drafted the statute were right. The experts were wrong. Use would grow as rates were lowered, and revenues would rise. Farmers would prove to be substantial consumers of electricity. They would use it in their homes, and it would enable them to increase the productivity of their land while at the same time it lightened their chores. Electricity would have a major part in halting erosion and saving the Valley's soil for future generations. By 1950, rural areas in the TVA area consumed as much electricity as the whole region had used in 1933 in all its towns and cities, and every year use on farms has grown.

Flood control. Navigation. Power production. These were the three primary objectives of streamflow control, and their results

* The figure of 540,000 used in testimony quoted in earlier paragraphs referred to the Tennessee Valley proper. The larger figure relates to the present area where power from TVA is now available.

have surpassed expectations. At the same time, other benefits have been realized as a river once swollen and dark in winter and early spring, a shallow stream in autumn, has been transformed into a series of lovely lakes, with homes and parks and playgrounds as well as industries along its banks. The beauty of the tributary reservoirs is diminished for a few months every winter when they are drawn down to make room for the storage of flood waters, but they are magnificent in summer, filled with the runoff of fresh rainfall, and there is little variation in the level of the main river reservoirs. They add charm to the landscape in every season. Throughout the year, they are hospitable to fish and wildlife, and to the public that is enjoying them in greater numbers every year.

The growth of water-based recreation has proved to be one of the most significant incremental benefits provided by the system of river control. It is not mentioned in the Act. There was no mandate, but there was encouragement for the agency to develop all the potential values of the water resource, and recreation was identified as one. TVA is responsible for recognition of the asset and early demonstrations of its benefits, but with the exception of Land Between the Lakes, the agency now operates no recreation facilities itself. Areas around its projects are attractively landscaped and equipped for visitors to rest, and at more than a score of shoreline sites, parking places, picnic tables, sanitary facilities, and boat launching ramps are provided for public use. Beyond those modest improvements, however, TVA has relied upon the public or private agencies of the localities and the states to manage and maintain the recreation asset created by the federal program of water control.

Fishing is a popular form of recreation in the Tennessee Valley. People fish from banks, from bridges, and from boats. There is commercial fishing too. Early in its history, TVA employed specialists whose particular concern was to explore the effect on fish and wildlife of the changing watercourses. Some expert opinion held that when the construction of huge dams transformed a flowing river into a series of quiet lakes a biological desert would result—an ecological damage the Board of TVA was determined to prevent. Two hatcheries were built in the belief that stocking of the waters would be required and studies and investigations were undertaken. In only a few years it was clear that fishing on the

Tennessee would be better than ever and the hatcheries were closed. Years ago, on the recommendation of TVA, the states abolished the traditional closed season. Today, fishing for sport and for commerce is a year-round activity in the Tennessee Valley. Although a hundredfold increase in catch has been recorded since the program of water control began, technicians report that even today in the waters of this river system more fish die of old age than as a result of their encounter with men.

The lakes have not only encouraged an increase in the population of fish, they are hospitable to waterfowl. The annual midwinter census now reveals more than twenty-five times the number of ducks and geese observed in the Valley some thirty years ago. Such results are not the inevitable by-product of streamflow control. Nor are they inadvertent. They require planning, and the knowledge of experts in the field must be applied. Just as identification of appropriate sites by TVA must precede the location of recreation areas for people to enjoy, so attractive habitats have to be made available for wildlife. TVA has contributed suitable reservoir land to the state and federal agencies that manage areas for their protection, and on property it must retain for program purposes the demands of wildlife have been considered. Some land, including areas subject to intermittent flooding, is licensed to state or local agencies to be managed for the benefit of waterfowl and wildlife. These agencies in turn arrange for farming of part of the land, with the planter agreeing to leave a portion of the grain unharvested as food for the migrating birds that have established their flyways through the area or find it an attractive wintering ground. Other kinds of wildlife have found the Valley a better place to live since the regional program was undertaken. In 1936, TVA biologists introduced seventeen deer on an isolated peninsula in Norris reservoir, part of a 24,000 acre tract later transferred to the State of Tennessee for management for upland game, timber development, and recreation. Thousands of deer now inhabit the area from which they had vanished, and the annual hunts supervised by the state provide the population control customarily exercised by man over wildlife.

While TVA's concern for fish and wildlife has elicited general approval its limitations have been criticized. Agencies and individuals devoted to one use of the water have protested when development of streamflow for multipurposes has threatened their continued enjoyment of a single benefit. In 1965, vociferous objections were registered by trout fishermen and by the Game and Fish Commission of Tennessee when TVA requested the appropriation of funds to commence construction of a multipurpose project on the Little Tennessee just above its conjunction with the main river. It was not a new proposal; the dam had been included in TVA plans for many years. During World War II, Congress had appropriated funds to start construction, but the shortage of critical materials prevented building then and later other projects claimed priority. Now named Tellico, in earlier plans it was called the Fort Loudoun Extension because of its proximity to the main river structure, with a canal between the two reservoirs permitting the dams to be operated in concert. The benefits to be provided by Tellico are substantial. Storage of Little Tennessee waters will add to flood control above vulnerable Chattanooga, additional energy will be produced at the Fort Loudoun powerhouse where equipment was installed earlier to utilize the anticipated increase in streamflow control, and the navigation channel will be extended some thirty miles up the tributary. This last result is of particular consequence to an area where development has lagged, and where the forced emigration of youth has been a matter of desperate local concern, for, together with other favorable factors, use of the river for the movement of commerce is expected to stimulate a repetition of the industrial growth recorded on other stretches where navigation already flourishes.

Against this impressive potential for benefits, opponents argued that trout fishing would be impaired. To a degree, the complainants were right. The reach of the river affected is not a natural trout stream, and the coveted fish do not propagate there. It is not included in the reported total of some 4,700 miles of trout waters flowing in the Valley, but as in other areas in the tailwaters of dams, about 120 miles in all, the fish will flourish in the cold water flowing from the turbines or rushing over the spillways when the stretch is stocked from hatcheries. The Little Tennessee has been generously treated by the Game and Fish Commission of Tennessee. In 1964, for example, 460,000 trout of various sizes were released in the river to provide about fourteen miles of excellent fishing. It is true that construction of Tellico will reduce the attractive mileage, but specialists on the staff of TVA predict that trout fishing will not be eliminated if stocking continues and that other kinds of fishing will be improved. Their forecasts did not reduce the energies of those who opposed the project. They fought hard, importing distinguished anglers to dramatize the struggle and winning support from national organizations interested in wildlife. In the beginning, they accused TVA of the ruthless destruction of a free-flowing stream, and free flowing streams were enjoying a renaissance in popularity.

The rhetoric was somewhat extreme. The river was not free flowing in 1965. Counting only those with a drainage area of over twenty-five square miles, there were then, and there are now, more than 9,400 miles of open streams in the Valley.* The Little Tennessee is not among them. For decades, its waters had been controlled by dams built by the Aluminum Company of America, and since 1944, by TVA's majestic Fontana (it is, in fact, the cold water released from the deep reservoir behind Fontana that permits trout to survive long enough to tempt the downstream sportsmen). Congress heard the opposition. The committee considering TVA's appropriation request listened to those who lamented any loss of trout fishing and to their allies who objected to construction of the dam because the former sites of several Indian villages would be covered with water when the reservoir was filled. The area involved was not Indian land in 1965. For generations, it had been in private ownership. One site had been farmed by a single family for over fifty years and the present owners commented that until it was celebrated to fight Tellico, there had been no prior recognition of the romantic heritage of their croplands and pastures.

TVA is not indifferent to the claims of the past, although it builds for the future. Beginning with Norris and excepting only wartime projects on which the pressure of construction speed limited investigation, every reservoir area has been surveyed by archeologists before the waters rise, and under an arrangement with state universities and the Smithsonian Institution in Washington, promising sites have been explored. In 1938, 1939, and 1942, Smithsonian publications financed by TVA reported the findings

* There are, in addition, more than 30,000 miles of small free-flowing streams, creeks, brooks, and rivulets.

in the reservoirs behind Norris, Wheeler, and Pickwick Landing dams. The Tellico reservoir is now being systematically explored in the hope that there may be valuable additions to the artifacts discovered in prior diggings.

In April, 1972, aroused by reports of conflict, a group representing the Oklahoma-based Cherokee Nation visited the Little Tennessee to discover for themselves precisely what the development proposed by TVA would mean to their historic homeland. They were impressed with the investigations under way, and the conclusions of the group included a recommendation that ". . . The Cherokee Nation should not become involved in any way in the current controversies over future development of the Little Tennessee River basin." Like TVA itself, they were concerned that the site of Chota, reputed to be the ancient capitol of the Cherokees, should be protected, and they expressed hope that some of the artifacts recovered from current excavations might be made available to the Cherokee National Museum.

Earlier finds are now displayed at a number of locations in the Valley, and items already recovered from the Tellico reservoir are lodged at the museum at the University of Tennessee, but it is possible that recollection of Indian lore may be more stirred by the names TVA has chosen for many of its projects than by the additions such excavations have added to collections. Watauga, Chickamauga, Hiwassee, Shawnee, and Cherokee honor the first residents of the Tennessee Valley. Tellico can be added to the memorial list, for the dam is under construction now. Under a stretched-out schedule delaying benefits and escalating costs, but imposed by limitations on the federal budget, it is scheduled for completion in 1975.

Congress recognized the difference between the judgment of those who defended a limited resource interest and the recommendations of an agency whose concern with the environment was boundless. It endorsed the larger approach. Both Senate and House approved construction of Tellico, but the project is still under attack. Following the pattern set by the private power companies in earlier years, opponents have moved from the Congress to the courts—to challenge legislative as well as executive decisions. TVA believes that if its judgment is upheld, construction of the long-planned dam will expand economic opportunities for the people of the area and at the same time scenic beauty will be enhanced and historic sites remembered. The pre-Revolutionary Fort Loudoun will be protected from flooding by a grassy dike with a landscaped pathway. When the reservoir is full, the Fort will stand on an island to which access will be provided by construction of a bridge, and which the state of Tennessee plans to develop as a major park.

Historic buildings along the river are being identified and plans for their preservation and maintenance are well advanced. One house already acquired by TVA has been added to the National Register of Historic Places, and efforts to preserve natural landmarks are extensive. Foresters are working to extend the life span of one of the largest known American elms, which stands 160 feet high on land purchased by TVA. It is estimated to be about 300 years old, and, although it will not be touched by water, to protect its future cattle must be prevented from grazing nearby, a road must be relocated, and the tree itself treated. All these precautions will be adopted as TVA strives to preserve and to increase the attractions along the river, and to harmonize the requirements of the future with remembrance of the past.

Unlike the rich promise inherent in development of the Little Tennessee, the benefits of streamflow control of some of the Valley's rivers would be meager. TVA is now studying a number to discover how their natural beauty can be safeguarded and enhanced, and their contribution to the well-being of the people expanded by protecting their scenic qualities from the encroachment of industry and commerce. The agency is committed to realization of all the many benefits inherent in the resource, and at the same time it is determined to reduce the damage to which the rivers are exposed by pollution of the water.

In the 1930's, there was little interest in the subject of pollution. Then the major use of the Valley's rivers was to carry away the waste of communities along their banks. At the same time, they served as catch basins for the top soil washed by the winter rains from the unprotected land. Although the range of TVA's concern about resource use is not restricted, its authority to regulate the conduct of others is limited. Just as it could not compel farm and forest owners to adopt new land management procedures, it could not require the cities of the Valley to install adequate sewage treatment facilities. Nor could it by decree abate existing industrial pollution. It could, however, use its ability to survey and investigate, to inform and persuade, and in 1936 the new agency undertook its first survey to determine the facts about the water quality prevailing in the watershed. Upon the basis of the situation revealed, it identified polluters, endeavored to arouse public interest, urged action by the municipalities and the states, and offered technical assistance. Progress was slow and as late as 1950, in spite of increasing public concern, only sixty-eight municipalities had installed sewage treatment plants, and many of those were inadequate. Today 175 municipalities are equipped with treatment systems. More than half come up to the standards advocated by TVA. Improvements are scheduled for others, and in 1971 only seven small communities in the Tennessee River basin discharged untreated sewage to their neighboring streams.

Financial assistance from other agencies of the federal government has hastened solution of the problem of pollution caused by municipal sewage discharges and because of that help and in spite of population and industrial growth the Tennessee as a whole is cleaner today than it was when TVA's first survey was reported. To make it really clean throughout its course, municipal sewage treatment systems must be improved and industrial pollution must be ended. TVA has a measure of control over new plants that locate along the shore. When land, or a discharge line easement, is purchased from the agency, a covenant runs with the deed forbidding the release of waste which will lower water quality, and when, under Section 26a of the TVA Act, permits are granted for structures along the shore, certificates of approval from the appropriate agency are required if waste discharge is involved. No such control can be exercised by TVA in the case of industries located in the watershed long before it was created. They are the worst polluters. It is more than a decade since TVA published a list of major offenders, and few industries have been stricken from the list. One long-established paper mill in North Carolina has destroyed the beauty, the aquatic life, and much of the usefulness of a once lovely tributary of the French Broad. Darkened waters a hundred miles down river attest to the defilement, and waste from a 75-year-old chemical plant in Virginia has lowered water quality for a similar distance on another tributary. At Knoxville in Tennessee, users have paid more than $200,000 every year to soften the water made unnaturally hard by the saline discharge of this one industry.

Such problems go beyond ecology. They involve economics. They present social as well as technological difficulties. To enforce penalties that would result in closing the installations would deprive hundreds, even thousands, of people of jobs and at the same time deprive the localities of revenues required for public services. By a dreadful kind of irony, the pollution the plants have caused has given them a kind of protection, for it has prevented the growth of other water-using industries, and their isolation as employers invests them with an inflated value to areas where jobs are limited. Technicians are working on the problems involved, men from TVA, from the companies concerned, from other federal agencies and the states. Until solutions are discovered or the industries are closed down, water quality of some reaches of the Tennessee River system will be impaired, and communities downstream from the polluters will continue to subsidize the offenders and the communities where they are located.

Technology for the treatment of municipal and other sewage is adequate. Only the will to act and money are required to protect the quality of streamflow from debasement from that source. But some industrial pollution appears to be beyond relief at the present level of knowledge. A balancing of good and evil is required, a determination of priorities on the part of the newly created agencies invested with authority. In the case of the Virginia chemical plant, a decision has been reached. The offending operations are being phased out, and there is a good deal of encouragement in accounts of community efforts to readjust to the loss of jobs and revenues. Other judgments are expected to follow and, in the meantime, TVA's investigations continue, and its efforts to arouse the public in support of regulations adopted and enforced by others. More than 70,000 water samples are analyzed every year. State, local, and federal agencies concerned, as well as landowners and businessmen, are advised whenever quality impairment is disclosed, and technical advice is available to help them. With the increased interest and greater public support expressed in new state and federal legislation, the goal of pollution-free water in every reach of all the Valley's rivers may be attainable, and soon.

TVA's continuous effort to protect and improve the quality and expand the use of the water flowing in the Valley's streams has been matched by a program to restore fertility to its soil. Although the wasting of this basic resource was a matter of major congressional concern in the years when Muscle Shoals was a controversial question, the debates reveal little understanding of the complexity of the problem of the land, nor appreciation of the time required for change. The discussions appeared to assume that more and cheaper fertilizer would be an instant remedy. Yet the steady decline in fertility was acknowledged, and TVA was charged with a specific responsibility to control erosion, one of its results. TVA had two major tools: the new kinds of fertilizer produced at Muscle Shoals and the electricity made available by streamflow control. It could provide technical advice, but the problem was immense.

In 1933, about half of the people of the Valley lived on farms with an average size of only seventy acres. Unlike the task of streamflow management, the acts of TVA could not determine whether the purposes of the statute could be fulfilled. The private decisions of farmers would control the pace of progress and the test-demonstration program described in an earlier chapter was the heart of the effort to encourage the conversions required. One thousand volunteer farmers were in the program in June of 1935, the first year it was offered, using new kinds of fertilizer to facilitate changes in land use. By the same date in 1971, more than 57,000 had participated throughout the Valley, and the practices they adopted had spread to their neighbors. That was the objective of the program, and results have been substantial. There are impressive success stories of individual farmers, but the measure of progress lies in the record of the Valley as a whole. Over the years soil-exhausting row crops have been reduced by more than 3 million acres, and over 1.5 million acres have been added to the land used for hay production and for pasture, as livestock have been introduced into the agricultural economy. By 1965, for example, the farmers of the area realized revenues of some $357 million from the sale of livestock and their products, a source of revenue negligible in the 1930's, and by 1970 it was estimated that livestock provided over 70 per cent of farm income in the Valley.

The combination of electricity, new plant food, and the patient application of technical knowledge has reversed the cycle of soil depletion that threatened the Valley's land resource in the 1930's. The battle against erosion has been won. Cotton has been brought down from the hillsides, and today the silt carried by the rainfall to the river is more likely to be washed from highway construction or suburban developments than from the Valley's farms. The test-demonstration program continues, but it has changed. From the pioneering introduction of the phospate-lime-and-legume formula, essential to restore fertility, it has expanded, not only testing new forms of plant food but emphasizing techniques of management and the adoption of procedures to meet the specific problems and opportunities of different areas. In connection with the TAD groups, or separately, groups of farmers are experimenting in the cultivation of new kinds of crops. In one location, for example, where soil and climate and proximity to markets combine to encourage a favorable prognosis, farmers are growing specialty crops —vine-ripened tomatoes, peppers, strawberries, cucumbers, and ornamental shrubbery. To ensure success, irrigation may be required, for even in this area of high rainfall, showers in the growing season are erratic in many localities. Small systems from farm ponds are supplying the pioneering farmers, with larger facilities anticipated if the enterprise succeeds.

The changes are reflected in rising farm income. Twenty years ago only 1.1 per cent of the Valley's farms reported sales of over $10,000. By 1964, the date of the last agricultural census, the proportion stood at 8.5 per cent. Tenancy has declined. Between 1934 and 1964, it was reduced from 43 per cent to 12 per cent of operating farms. As in the rest of the United States, the number of farms has decreased. There are some 170,000 in the Valley today, fewer than half of the total in 1933, with an average size of 105 acres, not 70 as when TVA began. But in spite of these improvements, and although this area may be able to demonstrate the continued viability of family-sized farms, agriculture has lost its dominance of the economy in the watershed of the Tennessee river. There is a vast improvement in soil management, there are greater comforts in farm homes and higher incomes, but today agriculture must yield primacy to industry. That is the sharpest change in resource use appearing in the fourth decade of TVA's life.

Even though the preamble of the Act mentions "industrial development" as a purpose to be achieved by TVA, expectations of such growth were not high in TVA's beginning years. The power program was not to be managed with a view to attracting manufacturing plants. Priorities were clear in a provision relating to power rates. It reads "that sale to and use by industry shall be a secondary purpose, to be utilized principally to secure a sufficiently high load factor and revenue returns which will permit domestic and rural use at the lowest posible rates . . ." In 1933, service to farms was regarded as more important than supplying power to industry. Three years later, in its 1936 report to Congress on its plans for "The Unified Development of the Tennessee River System," a document now out of date and out of print, TVA itself commented "It is reasonable to assume that agriculture . . . will continue to be the occupation of a large fraction of the population." There was talk about achieving a better balance between agriculture and industry. The Act itself directed the Board to use electricity to achieve "the fuller and better balanced development of the resources of the region," and at one of its early meetings, the minutes report that the first Board discussed the problem, but the balance desired was never defined. There are references to the necessity for encouraging "small local industries" in early documents, and the Board considered the possibility of providing "combined industrial and agricultural training so that small enterprises . . . could be promoted." The adjective "small" was repetitiously employed. Expectations were modest. Even as late as 1951 one author, Herman Finer, in a report for the International Labor Organization, "The TVA Lessons for International Application," wrote of the necessity to increase "small industries" to supplement agriculture.

It turns out that in the past twenty years the situation has been exactly reversed. Now agriculture supplements industry. Today, fewer than 10 per cent of the Valley's labor force is employed on farms as compared with 62 per cent in 1933, not the "large fraction" TVA anticipated in 1936. Over 33 per cent have jobs in manufacturing, and this once underdeveloped region has a greater proportion of its workers employed in industry than the average of 27.4 per cent reported for the country as a whole. The growth has been slow but persistent. Much has been the result of TVA programs, but none as a consequence of solicitation by the agency.

In general, TVA has limited its activities to providing information to companies exploring the question of plant location, and making its analyses available to local groups—the TAD organizations and others—to encourage wisdom in decision. Its technicians appraise the requirements of various kinds of industries for building sites, water supply, raw materials, markets, labor, and transportation in an effort to discourage the random solicitation that characterized the activities of lagging regions in the immediate post-war years, when inducements such as tax abatement, free land, and even buildings were relied upon to promote industrial growth. As a result, a good many plants were poorly located, often impermanent, contributing little to the community. Such ill-advised efforts continue, but in the Tennessee Valley they are being superseded by activities based on more careful analysis and prudent judgment. In part because of these more sophisticated methods of solicitation and in part due to programs of municipal improvement, a recent change in the pattern of industrial location within the region has been recorded. During a three-year period, 1966 through 1968, for example, 89 per cent of the growth in manufacturing and 56 per cent of the increase of employment in trades and services occurred outside the five largest metropolitan centers. Population growth has followed a similar pattern, and the decentralization of opportunity is not only a goal in the Tennessee Valley. It is a fact.

Some new industries are based on changes in agricultural production. Food processing plants have appeared. A cheese factory in Alabama was one of the first to recognize the opportunity implicit in better land use. Other enterprises are based on the revitalized forest resource. Modern pulp and paper mills have been established, and the public is beginning to appreciate the relation of the forests to economic growth. It took a long time. When boys from CCC camps began to plant seedlings in the 1930's, the objective was erosion control, and they left the Valley a heritage of 110,000 newly wooded acres. When the CCC camps were disbanded in World War II, the rate of planting fell, not to rise again until payments for retiring land from cultivation were made as a part of the Soil Bank program of the Department of Agriculture provided by legislation in 1956. Then trees were planted to put a brake on the overproduction of certain agricultural commodities.

Reforestation for erosion control is traditional, and adding to forest reserves for the protection of agriculture is a familiar goal. Planting trees to create jobs and earnings expresses a relatively new incentive. It provided the push for the third stimulus to reforestation in the Tennessee Valley. In 1960, it was estimated that about 1 million acres remained in need of planting in the watershed of the Tennessee, but they were scattered across the Valley in the relatively small holdings of more than 200,000 private owners, and the outlook was discouraging. The Soil Bank was phasing out. There would be no more payments to reward the planters, and a landowner could not expect a prompt return from his labor when he planted seedlings. He had to work for a profit that would not be realized for fifteen years or more, a prospect not particularly invigorating to middle-aged or elderly farmers, and studies reveal that today, as in the 1960's, the average Valley farmer is in his mid-fifties, while over 20 per cent are sixty-five or older.

There was encouragement in some localities when the harvesting of trees planted as seedlings by CCC forces could be observed. Surveys now indicate that landowners in the Valley are receiving and will continue to realize over $1 million a year from their careful thinning of CCC plantations. Year-round employment for some 730 men is provided and about $3 million added to the region's industrial payroll as a result of the work of the young men of the Depression. But in spite of continued efforts and clear demonstrations of value, tree planting faltered, until 1963 when TVA, in cooperation with the seven Valley states, launched an intensive campaign to overcome the continuing apathy and accomplish the prompt reforestation of all idle land suited for the purpose. Then, for the first time, reforestation was urged as an aid to economic growth, not to control erosion or to retire land from cultivation. Foresters had always included estimates of economic return in their analyses and their forecasts were familiar to the owners of large holdings, but to the farmers and the public generally only the traditional objectives had been emphasized. This campaign was different. "Plant Trees—Grow Jobs" was the slogan and when it ended a net increase of more than 600,000 acres of woodland in the Valley was recorded. Although, even during the campaign,

some woods had been lost because of highway construction, suburban developments, or industrial building, the increase was
enough, according to a TVA report, to promise some 4,300 new
high-wage jobs before the end of this century.

It is expected that tree planting will continue in the Valley, although at a slower pace, and the volunteer growths that used to be
uprooted or burned now are tolerated, even welcomed—a measure
of the change in attitude. High-quality seedlings are now available
from state and industry sources, and the TVA nurseries that started
the program are devoted to research and experiments in forest
genetics. After years of search, foresters have identified 198 superior hardwood trees from which seed orchards have been established to begin the slow process of upgrading the basic resource.
This takes time. These trees grow slowly. The men who labor at
the task today will never see the fruits of their endeavor, but, if the
program is successful, their children and their grandchildren will
view forests on the way to becoming the majestic asset the pioneers
surveyed.

Nearly 2 million acres of new woodland, over 1.5 million acres
of fresh pastures, and more than a score of broad lakes have
changed the landscape of the Tennessee Valley. It is more beautiful than it was in 1933. The scars of erosion are being healed.
Patches remaining here and there are only reminders of the desolation threatening before the program of soil protection began. They
are no longer menacing omens of the future.

Some years ago, a thoughtful visitor asked the editor of a Valley
newspaper if the changes might not have occurred without TVA.
He reflected a moment before he made his oft-quoted reply. Then
he said, "Well, they didn't." And it is just possible that in 1933
when the Congress created a new instrumentality to carry out the
purposes it endorsed it hit upon the best means of achievement.
When it endowed one agency with responsibility to promote the
development of all the values of all the resources, and to consider
the relationship of each one to all the others, it advanced an idea
regarded as novel more than three decades later. In a time when
ecology has become a familiar word and the environment a challenge, from the Valley of the Tennessee the method is the message.

XII

The People and Their
Local Governments

On a summer day in 1969, billions of dollars invested in space exploration enjoyed instant justification. Millions of taxpayers, comfortable in the security of their homes, watched an intrepid team of astronauts make their clumsy descent from vehicle to lunar surface, and suddenly the spectacular was worth whatever it cost. Two men from earth were walking on the moon. Their fellow earthlings could see it. Only a few viewers were competent to judge the enduring value of the achievement, but for the moment skeptics were silent. Whatever might happen to space exploration in the future, no matter what the astronauts who followed might accomplish, that day is the one remembered. Euphoria was complete.

It is not that way with a program created to deal with resources and with people on this familiar planet. For TVA, there never has been and it is unlikely that there will ever be one moment of triumphant affirmation that everything has been done just right. Probably there never will be a single occasion when all the battles in the courts and in the Congress will be vindicated, when without a shadow of doubt the wisdom of the Act and the fidelity of management to its principles will be validated by consensus. The development of the resources of a region is bound to be a slow and complex process, and no accomplishment is an end in itself. The job is never done, and there is no moment of truth.

A vast amount of scientific and technical knowledge has been invested in the Tennessee Valley over the years, and considerable skill in management has been applied to the program. Changes in utilization of the region's resources can be summarized, methods adopted can be described, problems remaining and emerging can be outlined, but the real measure of achievement involves some appraisal of the effect on the people who live in the area. For the objective of the total effort was to widen their opportunities, to strengthen their institutions, and to improve their prospects for the future. The Act creating TVA was clear about that, the point was emphasized again and again.

It is difficult to judge the effect of a program of resource development on human beings. There is no way to measure enhancement of serenity, increased joy in life, or to know whether the people of the Valley are happier today than they were in 1933. It can only be reported that some of their burdens are lighter. The woodburning stove has given way to the electric range, the balky pump in the backyard to the faucet in the farm kitchen. Electric appliances reduce the housewife's drudgery in the home, and new equipment is at the farmer's service in the barn. Antennae rise from roof tops and people who live in the country are no longer denied communication with the world outside.

Surveys show the people are better housed. They are healthier. In 1933, a third of the population living within a mile of the river in northern Alabama suffered the debility of malaria. With treatment of reservoir areas and manipulation of water levels to disrupt the life cycle of the carrier mosquito, that source of human misery has been eliminated. For more than two decades, not a single case of malaria of local origin has been discovered. Refrigeration on the farm has encouraged a better diet as well as a change in land management, and studies of water quality have helped to alert the public to the hazards to health implicit in pollution. To those program results which have created an improved environment for health TVA has added another element, a byproduct of service to its own employees that has enabled the agency to contribute to better medical care for the people of the area.

Over the years, preemployment physical examinations have been given to more than 240,000 men and women in the region, applicants for jobs with TVA. For many, it was a first encounter with preventive medicine, and by June, 1970, 1 million routine examinations of those who were employed had been conducted. Employee health services have been expanded and improved. In 1942, a trailer was outfitted to facilitate the examination of workmen at scattered locations. In the beginning, it was fairly simple, but equipment and services have been perfected and today the mobile clinic offers a sophisticated battery of medical tests, using modern methods of diagnosis. Electronic recordings of heart actions are analyzed by a remote computer, blood samples are collected for a dozen different analyses in a central laboratory, a chest x-ray is part of the routine. All the usual tests of a complete examination are available as the unit moves from project to project throughout the region.

Knowledge of the service spread, and in 1968 the Memphis Regional Program* requested a demonstration of its use in a campaign to promote health care in five rural and low-income counties of northeastern Mississippi. Some 500 people were given the same series of tests offered to TVA employees. Most of the patients had never had a thorough examination before, many had never experienced medical service of any kind. As a result of the demonstration two of the counties determined to inaugurate a similar service for their citizens, and TVA agreed to give consultative and laboratory assistance during the initial period of operation. Later, in the summer of 1970, the unit and staff participated in "Project Community Outreach," a plan developed by medical, nursing, and other students of Vanderbilt University to offer, under faculty supervision, examinations and related services to residents of certain impoverished counties in Appalachian eastern Tennessee. More than 6,000 patients were examined. One town decided to establish its own clinic when the demonstration was over, with a mobile facility loaned by TVA providing service until the new building could be completed. There are other examples of spreading adaptation.

Automated equipment and computer programs developed by TVA have been used successfully by a Knoxville hospital and a plan to offer a regional network of service to smaller institutions is under study. It will involve the use of closed television circuits and

* Operated by the College of Medicine of the University of Tennessee, local hospital and medical societies, and the Mississippi State Board of Health.

when it is installed rural hospitals will be able to have the advantage of diagnosis and advice from specialists unavailable in their communities. Through such cooperative enterprises the equipment and procedures developed by TVA for the benefit of its own employees are reaching people in areas where adequate medical services have never been provided, a contribution TVA can make because in the summer of 1933 the first Board determined that its construction program should be carried out by force account and not by contract.

Today, because the choice of jobs is greater throughout the region, individual freedom is increased, and the variety of leisure time activities has multiplied. There is more and better fishing, and a vast increase in the enjoyment of water sports. Parks and playgrounds abound. There are sailing regattas and motorboat races on water that covers the land where cotton used to grow. Observers may differ as to the value of these new assets to the people, but one measure of change is generally regarded as decisive in appraising well-being. Incomes have risen as impediments to enterprise have been reduced and opportunities expanded. In 1933, average per capita income in the Valley was only 45 per cent of the low figure then prevailing in the nation. Now it hovers around 75 per cent of the much higher national average, an improvement accomplished without discovery of new resources, but more effective use of the region's basic assets. Economic growth is reflected in the fact that out-migration of workers from the Valley to the industrial North and East has been halted. It took years to accomplish that result, but it has been achieved. Today there are prospects for work and a satisfactory life in the region, and emigration of the jobless no longer compounds the problems of urban centers in areas earlier industrialized. Many factors contributed to the change. The work of TVA was one.

Local units of government are stronger than they used to be and they serve the people better. This is an important part of the environmental change, for their competence and commitments affect the quality of life. TVA's deliberate effort to increase their involvement in the administration of a federal program, and to invest its own presence with a consistently low visibility has been persistent and unqualified. It is probably true, as many have argued, that progress would have been more rapid in some areas if the federal agency had chosen to go it alone. At times, members of the TVA staff have found the prospect of reliance on local enterprise frustrating to their hopes and have urged an expansion of the powers and activities of the federal agency. The foresters were the first to contend for an extension of TVA's statutory responsibilities and although their 1934 recommendations in this respect appeared to have tacit Board acceptance for a time, they were in fact ignored, modified in 1937, and specifically rescinded in 1941.

In 1940, in their turn, technicians in the field of recreation were convinced that the full development of shoreland required additional authority for TVA. When a Section 22 report surveying the region's recreation asset was submitted to the President on January 8 of that year and a week later transmitted by him to Congress, it contained a recommendation that TVA be given authority to construct and operate recreation facilities beyond the extent necessary to demonstrate their effectiveness. An authorizing bill was drafted, approved by the Administration, but never introduced in Congress. Neither files nor memories provide an explanation of failure to pursue the matter. The fact that other amendments to the Act were pending may account for inattention to this proposal. Hearings on the important in-lieu tax amendment began in the month the report was submitted and the measure was not passed until July. By that time, rising defense demands for power shoved other questions to the background. Perhaps the Board had second thoughts.

At any rate, the suggestion was never renewed, and, always excepting Land Between the Lakes, the role of TVA in the development of the Valley's recreation resource has been to demonstrate its potential contribution to the area, to provide technical advice, and to make land available for its use by sale to private persons or grant to public agencies. Just as the initial impatience of the foresters proved to be unwarranted as landowners and wood utilization industries accepted the job of forest improvement, so the doubts of recreation specialists turned out to be unjustified. By 1949, the transfer to state auspices of TVA demonstration areas was under way and states, counties, and cities, public and private organizations began the job of utilizing the recreation resource provided by the TVA system of river control.

Today on land made available by TVA, more than ninety

municipal, county, and state parks serve the public along the reservoir shores and 400 smaller areas provide convenient access to the water. In all, TVA has transferred more than 54,000 acres to state or local governments to be used for public recreation or to be incorporated in wildlife refuges, now twenty-one in number, and some 40,000 acres have been reserved for similar disposal in the future.* In addition to the areas managed by public agencies, over a hundred quasi-public organizations, churches, scout groups, YMCA's, and the like have developed facilities for the enjoyment of their members, and over 350 private recreation establishments are flourishing. TVA construction centers have been the basis of some of the developments. Fontana Village, one of the largest resorts, is operated under lease from TVA, and the town built in wartime to house the families of workmen at the dam is now a popular vacation spot in the mountains of North Carolina. In addition to the resorts and parks and boat docks operated by public agencies or private persons, more than 13,000 cottages along the shores provide vacation homes or year-round residences for their owners, the land purchased at auctions conducted by TVA. To date, more than $300 million from nonfederal sources have been invested in recreational facilities on the Tennessee or its tributaries, and there is no longer any doubt about the competence of local agencies to manage the asset.

Sometimes, but not always, benefits may be postponed by waiting for local interest to generate, but there are rewards in the method, too, which may be lasting. It is possible that the people of the Tennessee Valley are more acutely aware of their relation to their resources than most populations, and more accustomed to share in decision making. Power consumers themselves decided to participate in a government program when they marched to the polls or council meetings in towns and cities and organized cooperatives in rural areas in TVA's early years. Farmers who have joined in the test demonstration program and forest owners who have taken part in campaigns of tree planting, organized in support of improved fire protection, and attended timber management demonstrations have learned a good deal about the relation of their

* In addition, TVA has conveyed over 121,000 acres to other federal agencies, principally to add to the Great Smoky Mountains National Park, other park and forest areas, and for wildlife refuges.

private decisions to the public welfare. The Tributary Area Development groups that span the Valley know the resources and the problems of their communities in greater detail than residents of most areas, and they have become a driving force in the assumption of new responsibilities by their local governments and the improvement of existing services. They have learned that progress reveals new problems.

No longer is there confidence that if flood danger is reduced instant prosperity will flourish, or that a new sewer system alone will cure all community ills. In January, 1971, when the Bear Creek Watershed Association mailed a brochure conveying the highlights of its work the previous year, the president's letter of transmittal pointed out "We have come a long way and still have not scratched the surface." The people of the Valley have found that enhancement of the environment is a job of considerable complexity. Industrial growth emphasized the need for more intensive educational efforts. The stream clean-up projects directed attention to the necessity of devising systems for the disposal of solid waste and emphasized the responsibility of the community to substitute measures of control for the haphazard habits of individuals. TVA's policy has made it essential for towns and counties to maintain and manage recreation areas if they are to share in the newly created asset, to assume the responsibility of zoning if potential flood losses are to be reduced, to make certain that building codes are enforced. Local agencies are undertaking a variety of once unfamiliar tasks, and the states themselves have accepted enlarged responsibilities.

Only two of the seven states that lie in part in the Tennessee Valley had any kind of park system in 1933. All have them now. All have expanded their activities in forestry. In 1971, more than 500 professional foresters were employed by the states which used the services of only thirty-six in 1933, and higher standards and improved procedures are reflected in the statistics reporting woods lost because of forest fires. The estimated annual burn has been reduced from more than ten to less than one-half of one percent of timbered areas. All the states have enacted legislation to control water pollution, although there were no state regulations in 1933. All have created planning commissions, and the four coal-producing states have adopted strip-mining regulations. Some of these developments might have occurred without the encouragement of a regional agency, but the fact is that they did not, and if it would be bold to claim that all have been stimulated by TVA, at least it is clear that the federal agency has not stifled local initiative. On the contrary, it has endeavored to foster it, to resist the temptation to substitute its will for the judgment of smaller units of government, or to permit its competence to become an excuse for local inactivity. It is not easy. For it is not true that people always feel that local governments, those closest to them, are the ones they would select to solve their problems. On a good many occasions, they would choose federal action themselves, and their pressures must be diverted, sometimes with difficulty. TVA has experienced their preference. It has incurred their displeasure, and endured their criticisms for its adherence to policies of decentralization, in small ways and large.

Some years ago, TVA transferred to one of the Valley states a desirable shoreland area to be developed as a park. Lack of funds prevented its immediate use. The site lay idle, untouched so far as TVA was aware until a citizen of a nearby community complained that trees were being felled under a contract that assured profit to the cutters but meager return to the state and the ultimate ruin of the acreage for park use. Indignation began to run high as knowledge of the destruction spread. Garden clubs and chambers of commerce passed resolutions. Professional conservationists became involved. National leaders joined in a common chorus: "TVA should do something." There were hostile statements in the press, the ceaseless refrain, "TVA no longer cares about conservation. It is just a power system." To irate callers, representatives of TVA responded again and again "Protest to the state government, to your representatives in the legislature. They have the responsibility." Accusations of negligence had to be endured. It was true that under the contract TVA could recapture the acreage if it were not used for the purposes for which it was conveyed, but recapture would not provide a park, which was wanted and needed. Pressure on TVA was greeted with counterpressure. In a small way, it was a test of the method.

TVA foresters went on the property to inspect and appraise the damage, and to put a price on the timber cut. There was, of course, a possibility that recapture might be necessary. In preparation, TVA lawyers met with attorneys for the state, but drastic action was not required. When local groups confronted the state officials and the politicians they held responsible for the invasion, the cutting stopped. Payments for the timber removed were made on the basis of estimates of value made by TVA, and an aroused electorate convinced the legislature that they cared. The entire state park system received new recognition as a result of the controversy. Development began, and the people learned something about their responsibility to act through levels of government close at hand. They discovered that TVA would rather suffer their displeasure than supplant or discourage the authority of the state.

The states were slow to intervene to reduce the blight caused by strip mining for coal, and pressure on TVA to act alone was insistent. The agency had no authority to dictate mining methods, it could not order strip mining to cease, but it was not indifferent to the problem. Strip mining for coal in the area had begun in the 1920's. The devastation resulting was clear by the 1930's when TVA began its first surveys, although it was not visible to many observers before new highways and increased air travel disclosed it. The damage was of two major kinds, pollution of the watercourses by silt and acid in the runoff of the rainfall, and destruction of the aesthetic values that even nonproductive land can offer to the countryside when it has cover. Stripped land, eroded and bare, is desolating to behold. Its extent in the watershed of the Tennessee itself was less than in adjoining areas, and the alkalinity of the Valley's major waterways reduced the problem of acid pollution. Surface mining was, however, recognized as a threat to the environment, a challenge that had to be met.

Unfortunately, neither concern nor outrage equips the critic to correct abuses. Experiments had to be undertaken. In the 1940's, before it became a substantial purchaser of coal, TVA undertook to work with a few landowners and coal producers willing to cooperate in an effort to discover how the harmful results of stripping might be lessened. Seedlings were supplied from TVA nurseries for planting on denuded acres as foresters, agronomists, and engineers combined their talents in the search for remedies. Slowly the program was expanded to include a number of demonstration tracts on which newly developed techniques could be tested. Prior to initiation of these studies, TVA's experience with the reclamation of stripped areas had been limited to the rehabilitation of the phosphate lands it owned and mined in middle Tennessee. Restoration after phosphate recovery is relatively easy, for when it is graded for planting the land is hospitable to vegetation. Growth comes swiftly. Ugly bareness disappears and beauty takes its place. The treated land becomes an asset. Today one city in Tennessee is enjoying a small park on thirty-five acres of land reclaimed by TVA after stripping to recover phosphate.

Rehabilitation of coal lands with their high sulfur content presents a much more difficult problem. Much vegetation is rejected, but patient experiments did afford persuasive evidence that with selective planting, attention to surface drainage, and the use of fertilizer the reclamation of most stripped acres could be accomplished in a few years, and that vegetative growth would continue. At the same time, the demonstrations proved that acid pollution could be sharply reduced if adequate plans for drainage and spoil disposal were made in advance of mining. It was clear that the two principal penalties of strip mining in the area could be greatly diminished if existing knowledge were applied.

As TVA began to purchase coal in increasing quantities, experiments and investigations were expanded. A good deal of information was assembled and technology was advanced, but the pace of devastation accelerated as coal consumption increased throughout the United States. In 1962, a group of TVA staff members was organized to add information from other regions to the data available from the demonstrations conducted by TVA in the Valley. A forester, an hydrologist, an aquatic biologist, and a mining engineer visited every area in the eastern United States where stripping was used to mine coal. Methods of extraction and of rehabilitation were explored. Conferences with experienced persons were arranged. A modest pamphlet issued in 1963 summarized the conclusions of the group; 4,000 copies were circulated to a public at last aroused, but without much information on the subject. Interest grew, but only one state in the Tennessee Valley, Kentucky, had adopted regulations by that date, and it was not unnatural that the familiar refrain "TVA should do something" should increase in volume.

Within the organization, there was a good deal of discussion about the problem. Some members of the staff argued that TVA should add controlling provisions to its coal purchase contracts, not because it would cure the situation but to illustrate TVA's capacity to lead in a vital conservation program. There is no question but that in some quarters TVA's reputation was damaged by its failure to assume a public posture of aggressive action. But the problem before the Board was not how to make TVA look good but how to reduce the damage of strip mining. The difficulties associated with independent action were considerable and results uncertain. Complexities of enforcement were discouraging if TVA demanded that producers accept standards of rehabilitation affecting only the acreage disturbed to satisfy its requirements, and not applicable to coal mined for other purchasers. There was the further sobering fact that such provisions, in the absence of state regulation, would have little effect. For in spite of the fact that by 1960 TVA was the largest single coal buyer in the nation, it was acquiring a relatively small proportion (less than 14 per cent) of the total output of coal produced by stripping in the states from which the fuel was received.

Basic to TVA's reluctance to resort to contract provisions was the fear that state action would be inhibited, that pressure for reform would be reduced in the mistaken notion that the federal agency could achieve results alone. Slowly, the states did respond to citizen concern. Kentucky led the region. It improved its statute, and Virginia and Tennessee followed with legislation. Later, Alabama acted. TVA technicians worked with the staffs of state agencies, members of the Board conferred with officials and testified before legislative committees, and gradually the knowledge TVA had accumulated was communicated to the states. Now all the Valley states where stripping for coal presents a problem have enacted regulations of varying effectiveness, and since 1965 TVA has required premining plans for restoration as a condition of its coal contracts. Kentucky, the state that supplied much of TVA's needs, had adopted improved standards by that date and legislation was under consideration in other states. The contract stipulations are designed to supplement and support state regulations, not to supplant them. Twice they have been strengthened as technology has advanced, but they are not now and they never can be a substitute for standards that must be applied to all producers and in every area to be effective. Their impact is limited, and so far as is known no other major coal purchaser has developed similar contract provisions.

TVA will have an opportunity to develop and test methods for pollution control and rehabilitation beyond those now required under its purchase contracts or state regulations as it is presently recovering coal from mineral reserves in its ownership. Agreements for mining the areas include provisions that will permit the operations to be used as a proving ground for improved techniques. It is unlikely that all these efforts will subdue the criticism directed at TVA for what is alleged to be its part in encouraging surface mining. Neither contract provisions, described as excellent by impartial observers, nor the research and demonstrations that have yielded generally promising results can quiet the clamor.

A good many critics appear to be indifferent to reclamation efforts. They simply want all surface mining stopped. Some, perhaps most, appear to suggest an increase in underground mining as an alternative method of coal extraction. Damage to the environment would not be prevented by such a substitution. Acid seeps from deep mines to pollute the waterways just as it drains from surface mines if it is not controlled, and there are other adverse effects, including the heavy costs borne by miners in this, the nation's most hazardous industry. TVA is now endeavoring to develop contractual provisions to aid in reducing the environmental damage caused by underground mining, but even if successful the problems associated with the recovery of coal will not be eliminated. They are great, and require increasing vigilance and improved technology for solution.

While some critics recognize the importance of coal in producing the electrical energy essential for the nation and urge a different method of mining to avoid stripping, others ignore the basic problem. They offer no alternatives. They do not favor deep mining, nor do they suggest greater utilization of water power to satisfy the need for energy. Some of the same organizations that protest strip mining have endeavored to halt dam construction by TVA, and many have opposed the building of nuclear plants. In fact, some of the most vocal opponents of strip mining appear to be against the production and use of electric energy from any source, heedless of the environmental damage that would cause. Without electricity, millions of acres of farm land in the Tennessee

Valley were eroded. They are green with cover today. Without electric heat, the air in urban centers of the Valley would be heavy with smoke once more. Without electricity, job opportunities would be reduced, life in the watershed would be harsh again. The position of TVA is clear. An abundant supply of energy is vital to the region but continuous effort must be devoted to the relief of every adverse effect its production may have upon the environment. It insists that strip mining be controlled, and the land reclaimed. Technicians of the agency believe that with improving technology, more experienced administration, and wider public support for effective regulation, surface mining can be made progressively less damaging, and that reclamation of areas stripped in the future will be achieved more promptly than in the past, often to a more productive state than they previously enjoyed.

The problem of orphan mines remains. These are reminders of past sins, areas mined before state regulations were invoked, some of them including terrain on which stripping would not be tolerated under the most permissive regulations prevailing today. Many of them were stripped years ago, long before TVA was a purchaser of coal. The mining companies have moved on, ownership has changed, no one will accept responsibility for reclamation. Present landowners are unwilling to undertake the rehabilitation, which would cost more than the value of the land to them. It is a public problem, for public indifference fostered the emergence of these ugly and nonproductive polluters. In 1964, TVA proposed a program for the rehabilitation of some of these orphan mines as a joint federal-state demonstration. TVA would plan the program and provide general supervision, but the work would be undertaken directly by the states with grants of funds from the federal government. Officials of the states endorsed the plan, but the then Bureau of the Budget in Washington disapproved, and nothing came of the proposal.

In 1969 and in 1970, the request was renewed, again rejected. If TVA persists and the $8 million requested is allowed in some future year, or if financing from some other source becomes available, 90,000 acres now unreclaimed can be treated. They lie in twenty-five Valley counties of Tennessee, Virginia, and Alabama and an adjoining twelve-county area of southeastern Kentucky. Employment and some training for the unskilled idle in these Appalachian communities would be provided, and methods of restoring lands to usefulness can be demonstrated. There is hope that some acreage can be reclaimed to provide attractive habitat for wildlife. One large-scale demonstration of this concept is under way in southwestern Virginia, where TVA, state agencies, and a private company are endeavoring to combine timber management, strip mining reclamation, and wildlife development on 10,000 acres. The smaller demonstrations undertaken earlier stimulated this large-scale experiment. They were effective although not widely noticed, and in time their benefits may be immense.

Whether it is control of strip mining or the management of parks, the continuous effort to assist and encourage rather than to replace the activities of local governments meets resistance. It is questioned by citizens who distrust their neighbor politicians, by specialists deeply concerned about some particular achievement, and by state and local officials reluctant to face new responsibilities. In spite of difficulties TVA's commitment to decentralization has been constant. It has produced results, and throughout the Valley local public agencies and private organizations are assuming a growing share of responsibility for the regional program of more effective resource use. Neighboring counties are working together in the Tributary Area Development programs, one of the most encouraging of the many by-products of the methods.

For a long time, political scientists have been writing about the often obsolescent and costly system of county governments. To eliminate them or reduce their number, to reorganize the structure of the states, would require major political surgery, but in the Tennessee Valley some of the disadvantages of multiple jurisdictions are being overcome as counties and towns pool their resources and work together to upgrade community facilities. A few multicounty services were initiated when TVA was building its first river control projects, and some new activities were undertaken. Library service was one. By arrangement with county governments, the resources of libraries at TVA construction villages served the surrounding countryside and bookmobiles climbed mountain roads long after the dams were built and the workmen had departed. Their maintenance had become an item in county budgets, and from that beginning the organization of regional library facilities was accomplished. Health services were improved in some areas, but although there were expanded activities, and a few co-operative enterprises, there was no real change in the structure of local governments, and specialists in the field expressed some disappointment. Later, when the new in-lieu tax provisions were under study, scholars pointed out that another opportunity to promote the reorganization of local governments might be at hand. At the time, however, TVA believed that its information was inadequate to recommend major alterations, and that the urgently needed legislation should not be burdened with ill-considered proposals. There has been no revision of local political organization, but in recent years, in large part due to the influence of the Tributary Area Development program, there have been substantial improvements in services as towns and counties combine their efforts for common goals.

A tricounty health service now replaces the inadequate services previously offered by the individual counties. A common water treatment system is being developed by the municipalities in one TAD area, and in still another a pioneering water grid is proposed to extend service to communities in a four-county area. Three counties and one town have joined with two federal agencies and the State of Virginia to develop a centrally located industrial center. Two counties are cooperating in an ambitious stream restoration program organized by one tributary development group. Two multicounty systems of trash disposal have been organized, and a number of counties are working together in the collection of abandoned automobiles. The pattern is spreading, and the change is striking. Parochial interests and jurisdictional jealousies are set aside as a variety of governmental units combine to promote environmental change. Illustrations include activities which the federal agency once undertook alone.

In 1933, TVA built the town of Norris. It was designed, constructed, and, until its sale in 1948, operated by TVA. Like the villages at Muscle Shoals built by the Army in World War I and inherited by the new agency in 1933, it was intended to provide housing for employees, in the case of Norris, principally the construction forces engaged in building Norris Dam.* When the proj-

---

* The Muscle Shoals houses built by the Army and turned over to TVA were sold in 1949, those on the reservation removed, those located at some distance sold on site.

ect was completed the town lived on as a suburban community. Until its sale most of its residents were TVA employees located in Knoxville. Today, its population is less than 1,500, its residents still largely employed in Knoxville or Oak Ridge, but a smaller proportion associated with TVA than in the beginning. Now a new city is being planned to rise on the shore of Tellico Lake. It is different from Norris. For one thing, it will be larger. It will be designed to accommodate a population of some 50,000, the figure expected to be reached in a quarter century, and it will not be a bedroom community, but a self-contained municipality with industries and commercial enterprises as well as homes.

TVA is not planning it alone. That is the major difference. State and local agencies are participating from the beginning. Organized by the Tennessee State Planning Commission, a Tellico Area Planning Council composed of representatives of neighboring towns and cities is working with TVA on a plan for shoreland use and a design for the new city, to be called Timberlake in honor of a British soldier who lived with the Cherokees for a period, and left, as a legacy to the future, a record of their lives, together with the earliest known maps of the area. A joint public and private demonstration of how a new urban environment can be created is contemplated, to show how economic growth can be accomplished without the disadvantages often associated with it. Problems of access and education, waste disposal and noise control, are being explored long in advance of construction, and major attention is being devoted to aesthetic factors, for these are increasingly a matter of local concern in the Tennessee Valley. Today, they are applied to the delivery of power.

For several years, distribution lines have been going under ground, and in a good many communities electricity consumers are willing to pay the extra costs involved to eliminate overhead wiring. In its service area, TVA has proposed 1973 as a target date for new distribution lines to be concealed in the earth. Replacement of existing systems will require a longer time, for although adequate techniques have been developed, the procedure is costly. The problems associated with burial of the high tension transmission lines owned by TVA itself are more complex, and except for use in very limited areas satisfactory methods of underground placement are not yet available. Until solutions for the difficulties are discovered, concern for aesthetic values will continue to be expressed by emphasis on the design and placement of the towers, the treatment of rights of way, and the use of extra high voltage (ehv) lines to reduce the number required to carry energy from the generating plants to the distribution systems. TVA has pioneered in this development in the United States, and today one ehv line delivers as much energy as ten of customary voltage could carry.

Not every observer finds transmission lines and towers ugly. To many eyes, there is a certain grandeur of design as well as symbolic beauty as they march over hills and valleys, carrying energy to the people. Admittedly, proliferation reduces their appeal and that TVA is endeavoring to prevent. Distribution lines rarely offer beauty of design, and in an area and at a time when an abundant supply of electricity is taken for granted their pioneering grace is forgotten. A member of Congress who spent his boyhood on one of the Valley's small farms recognized the change with a nostalgic comment. "If my mother were alive," he said, "you would have a hard time convincing her those lines are ugly. She thought they were beautiful. They changed her life."

Awareness of environmental problems is general in the Tennessee Valley today, and the habit of accepting local responsibility for improvement is established. For that achievement, TVA deserves some credit. It takes more than the rhetoric that is in abundant supply to strengthen state and local institutions. Their competence is not promoted by the abandonment of federal responsibility but by the way in which it is administered. Grants of money are not enough. Expert advice is vital, for few counties or municipalities can afford to employ professional assistance in the variety required to meet every current problem, and the supply of specialists themselves is not inexhaustible. Even states are limited in their ability to attract professional staff in all the needed disciplines. In the Tennessee Valley, technicians from the regional agency play an important role as consultants to state and local agencies. They work not to enlarge the sphere of TVA activities but to enhance the skills of local institutions and therefore the people's confidence in them, for local units of government will never be effective unless citizens learn to demand responsiveness from them.

If there is a permanent strengthening of state and local agencies in the Tennessee Valley, and a steady increase in the resolution of citizens to require excellence in performance from them, that achievement will be a substitute for one blazing moment of triumph for the federal agency. Instant acclamation will forever be denied to TVA. There will never be anything to compare with a walk on the moon. New problems will appear as old ones are solved. The task to which TVA is committed is never ending, and its goals will always move ahead of accomplishment.

XIII

"If We Are Successful Here . . ."

In 1933, much of the excitement generated by adoption of the new approach to resource development was related to the final sentence of President Roosevelt's message recommending the creation of TVA: "If we are successful here we can march on, step by step, in a like development of other great natural territorial units within our borders."

There was no doubt that the President and Congress had joined to challenge prevailing methods of federal administration in resource matters. They offered something different, and assumed that if it proved to be successful the organization envisaged in the new Act would be copied again and again. Their hopes were vain. The structure of TVA has never been duplicated in the United States. The Tennessee is still the only river system developed as a unit in spite of recommendations made more than half a century ago. Its watershed is the only drainage basin where a single agency can consider the resources as a whole and make its decisions close to the problems and the people.

The advocates of change tried to extend the plan. They early concluded that TVA was successful, and in 1937 the President recommended the creation of seven regional authorities popularly described as "Little TVA's." Bills to accomplish their initiation were introduced in Congress, but the measures were never adopted, nor were later proposals to create TVA-like agencies for individual river basins such as the Missouri and the Columbia. For some there was considerable support in Congress and fairly widespread

234

public interest in the areas concerned. But no bill was ever enacted and visitors, particularly those from other nations, profess to be mystified that TVA is still unique in the United States, while in more than a dozen foreign countries it has stimulated efforts to use it as a pattern.

There are several reasons why TVA has never been copied in its native country. The proponents of the idea underestimated the size of the task. After all, it took a long time to get TVA, and in no other river basin was the utilization of surplus war investment a compelling prod toward action. In addition, a new element had been added to the opposition. Although none of the regional agencies proposed was a replica of TVA there was sufficient similarity to arouse the hostility of some of the traditional agencies of the central government. They were determined that there should never be another TVA, or anything resembling it. One such enterprise could be tolerated, and with relatively few exceptions relations between TVA and more conventional federal organizations have been cooperative and mutually helpful. They have been established by letter agreement, by memoranda, and by contract. These were essential in some cases, for TVA was not given exclusive jurisdiction over resource activities in the Tennessee Valley. The range of its responsibilities was wider, and it was authorized to undertake certain activities not conducted by other agencies, but general programs were available in the area, too, and to avoid waste and duplication a number of agreements were negotiated to define relationships.

In later years, many cooperative arrangements have been developed and maintained through informal conferences and communications, but the use of written agreements has continued to some extent. In the beginning, they helped the bureaus and departments of the central government to accept the existence of TVA, but they did nothing to quiet doubts about the results if a bevy of such oddities emerged. Then the jurisdiction of centralized agencies dealing with resource problems would be threatened and their clientele might be reduced. So the creation of regional entities having any resemblance to TVA was opposed by a number of federal organizations, most effectively by various bureaus in the departments of Agriculture and the Interior, and by the U.S. Army Corps of Engineers.

Although the Corps of Engineers was the only organization that in a sense yielded jurisdiction when development of the Tennessee and its tributaries was assigned by Congress to TVA, relations between the Engineers and TVA have been relatively good over the years. TVA designs and builds the locks and does the dredging required to create a navigation channel. The Corps then operates the locks as it does on other rivers, maintains the channel and compiles the statistics that reveal use of the river for navigation. TVA manages streamflow for flood control within the Valley, but at times of high crests on the lower Ohio and Mississippi release of water from the Tennessee depends upon advice from the Corps. There is a record of cooperation between the two agencies, but it is not a record that would encourage the Engineers to surrender plans for other waterways, and the fact that TVA has used force account to carry out its construction program has ensured the hostility of the Corps' stout allies, the Associated General Contractors of America. With the same concern for jurisdiction, the Bureau of Reclamation in the Department of the Interior opposed the establishment of regional organizations that might take over the development of Western rivers. Agencies less directly challenged expressed their apprehension. These were the new recruits who joined the private power companies to prevent any spread of the regional idea. It was a formidable and resourceful army, and there have been no more TVA's.

There were, of course, other critics. Their doubts may have had little influence on the fate of the proposed new agencies, but there were scholars in the field of public administration skeptical of the wisdom of extending the regional concept of federal administration. Even among those who favored the general principle of decentralization there was uneasiness about the viability of river basins as "territorial units." Although they were clearly desirable for programs of water control, their general effectiveness for the administration of other resource activities was questioned. In some ways, the Tennessee Valley was unique, and its watershed was a particularly suitable unit for such an arrangement. It will be remembered that when Harcourt Morgan spoke to the Investigating Committee in 1938 he described its selection as "providential." Not only were the problems and opportunities of the economy closely related to the water resource, the size and shape of the basin itself contributed to ease of management.

The Tennessee, fed by its major tributaries, which drain the mountainous and forested eastern part of the Valley, begins near Knoxville. It flows southward through the foothills of the Smokies, then turns west moving through the flat land of north Alabama until it touches Mississippi. From there, it streams north and finally west again to join the Ohio in Kentucky. Like the river, the watershed forms a kind of crescent, and its boundaries enfold a relatively homogenous area. There are, of course, variations in resources and differences in their use within the Valley. TVA's early surveys revealed contrasts in soil and terrain, rainfall, climate, and ground water supply. Local economies were not alike, but compared with some other river basins common problems prevailed, and control of the river to reduce floods, provide a navigation channel, and generate electricity was vital to development of the whole area. The more effective use of water on the land and in the streams was the key to progress throughout the basin. Whether the plan would have worked as well in other watersheds is a matter of speculation. It was never tried.

No other such regional agency of resource development has been established, but that does not mean that the experience of TVA has been without effect on other areas of the nation. The very threat of its replication stimulated a degree of change. When bills to create a Missouri Valley Authority (MVA) were pending, one of the most compelling arguments for enactment rested on the controversy then existing between the Corps of Engineers and the Bureau of Reclamation. The Engineers' plans for development of the lower Missouri conflicted with Reclamation's plans for the upper river. It was a classic example of the frustration caused by divided jurisdiction, and the proponents of an MVA made the most of it. Until suddenly the controversy was ended. Agreement between the two agencies was reached through what the press described as a shotgun marriage, and a scheme popularly called the Pick-Sloan plan for the development of the Missouri River was initiated in 1944. It bears the names of the two men then heads of the agencies involved. It fell considerably short of the principle that responsibility for the development of a river system should be in the hands of a single agency, it was divided, but at least the plan quieted the open warfare between two federal instrumentalities, and development of the Missouri went forward.

In some river basins, modest recognition has been given to the principle of resource unity. Interagency committees or commissions have been created and representatives of various federal and state agencies meet together to discuss and counsel and to plan for the future. Such arrangements are a pale reflection of the procedures in TVA where specialists in every major resource meet together to make their recommendations to a Board that has the power to decide, and their limitations have been noted. Of the Missouri Valley committee, a Task Force of the first Hoover Commission commented:

> The present system may also be criticized because there is no single administrative center in the region which can take leadership in pulling together the many segments for a comprehensive resources program for the entire basin. . . . They do not assure a basinwide and active consciousness that the basin is a unit for coordinated management.

Even though not wholly effective, the various interagency devices probably represent some improvement in the administration of federal resource development functions. To that extent, we may have "marched on" a little, "step by step," but not very boldly. Pressure for extension of the unified concept of regional administration was not extinguished until the 1950's, when the survival of TVA itself appeared to be in doubt, and new such agencies clearly unachievable. There was no revival of interest in the 1960's, and while it is likely that in its early years TVA did act as a prod to reform because of the threat that a similar act might be substituted for old-line procedures, that value has been reduced. Its contribution to federal administrative practices must be measured by the extent to which adoption of some of the innovations its charter encouraged has resulted in a kind of piecemeal progress. Some results are direct and documented.

In 1933, for example, the first countywide electric cooperative was organized in Alcorn County, Mississippi, to purchase power from TVA and distribute it to consumers. From that beginning, the electrification of rural America sprang, for Senator Norris was stimulated by the experiment, and, after a trial period authorized by Executive Order 7037 in 1935, he sponsored the legislation that a year later created the Rural Electrification Administration and extended to the nation the program under way in the Tennessee Valley. The record is just as clear with respect to the program of local flood control inaugurated by TVA in 1950, and summarized in a Section 22 report presented to Congress in August of 1959. There is no doubt that its success was responsible for the 1960 authorization for the Corps of Engineers to undertake similar activities.

Much of the experience of TVA's personnel system is acceptable elsewhere, too, and it has been studied by a considerable number of experts in the field. From the beginning, there was a conscious effort to make the independent merit system a model of excellence as the men who framed the statute had intended. To the provisions of the Act forbidding political consideration in appointment, the Board, before adoption of the Hatch Act by Congress, added regulations limiting partisan activity on the part of its staff. Restrictions with respect to nepotism and to "moonlighting" were developed early, regulations affecting employee relations with contractors were formulated, and in some areas its policies have been stimulating to others.

There is no doubt, for example, that TVA's labor policies have had some influence in advancing the principle of collective bargaining within the federal government. Progress was not swift. In 1934, TVA first recognized the right of employees to organize and to deal with management through their unions. Twenty-eight years later President Kennedy signed Executive Order 10988 authorizing a similar policy for federal employees generally, a plan revised and confirmed in Executive Order 11491 signed by President Nixon in 1969. Today, agreements between management and unions are a respected medium for establishing viable relations in the public service and TVA's experience has been a factor in the change. It has been surveyed and commended by skeptics and by friends. In 1949, a Joint Congressional Committee on Labor Management Relations conducted a study of TVA's procedures in the field of labor relations, and issued a generally favorable report. In 1960, in

Power Magazine, the late James P. Mitchell, then Secretary of Labor, commented on the apprentice training program developed by TVA and the unions with which it deals. He wrote:

It has assisted private industries and other agencies to develop and improve apprenticeship through contributing its experience and materials. . . . This program is a fine example of what a well-thought-out training program can mean to management, the individual, community and the nation as a whole.

Just as TVA's employee health program encouraged adoption of a plan for all government employees, the 1955 adjustment of its independent retirement system to give members coverage under the Social Security system may result in similar benefits for other federal employees. As these and other experiments have been studied, the once insistent pressure to bring TVA employees under the jurisdiction of the Civil Service Commission has lessened somewhat, although it has not disappeared. There is a more general understanding that, although TVA personnel policies are keyed to the specific requirements of its program, its experience can be shared, and that there may be some advantage to the government as a whole in the preservation of its independent merit system.

It was in the Tennessee Valley that the importance of public recreation as a potential advantage resulting from a federal program of water control was first recognized, and while TVA's pioneering may have had some part in stimulating the concern of other agencies, its policy of placing responsibility for development on state and local agencies has not been widely imitated. Apparently, it has not been noticed. There was, for example, no evidence that the experience of TVA had been an encouraging factor when, in February, 1971, President Nixon proposed that federal agencies should transfer to local organizations for recreation use land in their custody but surplus to their requirements. Such a policy had been adopted by TVA more than twenty years earlier, and already over fifty thousand acres had been conveyed. Similarly, it is not clear that the pioneering Smithsonian reports of archaeological investigations of the reservoir areas of TVA's first three dams—Norris, Wheeler, and Pickwick Landing—were responsible for the Institution's decision to undertake archaeological and paleontological studies of reservoir areas in other watersheds, as it did in the 1940's. Now under the general direction of the National Park

Service, the program's genesis may lie in the early studies financed by TVA, although the origin has not been acknowledged. Rule 71A(h) of the Federal Rules of Civil Procedure did recognize the value of the condemnation procedures set out in the TVA Act, and extension of their use was authorized. There may be other examples of adoption or adaptation of innovations embodied in the TVA statute or expressed in its administration. Nevertheless, it is probably true that the authors of the original Act would be disappointed that Congress has never created another such agency, and that TVA's contribution to federal administration in other river valleys has been random and limited.

If they were in Congress today, they might charge their colleagues with timidity. They could point out that none of the fears so loudly voiced by the opposition to TVA had been realized. One by one, they could name the perils predicted, which the years had shown to be chimerical. The regional agency had not become a superstate suffocating the energies of local governments, as its foes had forecast. On the contrary, it had fostered their competence and increased their strength. Flood control, a navigation system, and power production have been accomplished together. They were not incompatible as opponents had argued. A public power system had proved to be well managed, not operated by incompetents as scoffers had claimed to fear, and it was achieving the objectives its sponsors had outlined, proving that their goals were not romantic dreams as skeptics had contended, but reasonable ends to seek. Most of all, perhaps, it would give them satisfaction to demonstrate that the investment of the federal government in TVA was paying out in dollars, as well as in regional strength, for they would remember how the opponents had charged that the appropriation of funds to the new agency was an unwarranted extravagance, a loss to the Treasury.

They could report that by the end of fiscal year 1971 TVA had paid from its proceeds almost a billion dollars in cash to the Treasury of the United States, and, to TVA's direct payments, which are exact and recorded, they could add estimates of the savings in the government's own power bills realized because electricity was available from TVA. The figures would be estimates, but when power is purchased in the amounts required by Atomic Energy installations alone a reduction of only one mill per kwh would in many years accomplish savings of some $50 million. Over more than two decades the total would be substantial. Its size would not be minimized by the men whose efforts created TVA. They might reasonably claim that directly or indirectly the total investment of appropriated funds in TVA facilities would soon be, if it had not already been, returned to the Treasury.

From the record, they could demolish the cliches of long-time foes. They would be entitled to boast a little, for they had endured scorn and gibes. With bitterness edged with mirth, they might recall the antic slogan invented by Wendell Willkie in 1936. Then he said, "The Tennessee River waters four states and drains the nation." The charge was considered sufficiently clever to be echoed, with variations, in future years. In 1945, one writer announced that the river flowed "through five states and drains the nation." The *Wall Street Journal* in an editorial of June 19, 1951, proclaimed that the Tennessee ran through "three states and drained the other forty-five," and as late as 1958 a letter to the editor of the *Washington Post* from an official of the U.S. Chamber of Commerce offered the intelligence that the "Tennessee River flows through seven states and drains forty-eight." The number of states through which the river flowed might be a matter of dispute between the opponents but they were in solid agreement that the rest of the nation was "drained" by TVA. The thesis advanced appeared to suggest that federal expenditures were higher in the Tennessee Valley than elsewhere, and that the taxpayers of the nation were unfairly burdened by the cost of its development.

Now, with statistics, the advocates of TVA could demonstrate the falsity of that contention. They could show that as a matter of record all federal expenditures, including those of TVA, were, on a per capita basis, lower in the TVA region than the average recorded for the country as a whole. In 1965, TVA statisticians studied the records of the three decades of TVA's life. While during that period cumulative federal expenditures across the nation had amounted to just under $12,000 per person, in the 201 counties of what is called the Tennessee Valley region (the watershed of the Tennessee plus the counties outside the basin where power from TVA is available), they had reached a per capita total of less than $7,000, and TVA's share amounted to less than 10 per cent of the regional sum.

So far as federal expenditures were concerned the area had not been favored over the rest of the nation. Perhaps the vocal opponents had always known that, and only hoped that people generally might be deluded by their slogans. What they themselves may not have realized was the fact that the funds appropriated for use by TVA were not all spent in the area. The headquarters of the organization was located in the Valley, and the structures built with appropriated funds were in the region, but expenditures have never been restricted to the locality. From 1933 to July 1, 1971, for example, TVA had spent over $3.5 billion outside the seven states which lie in part in the drainage basin of the Tennessee, more than the total appropriated from the Treasury to the agency throughout its life. Proceeds from the sale of power and bonds as well as funds from the Treasury have been used to purchase supplies and equipment produced in other regions of the nation. Jobs have been created, profits maintained, and tax collections increased in areas far away from the watershed of the Tennessee. States in other regions were not "drained" by the development of this one area. They benefited, as public and private enterprises in the region furnished a new market for their productivity.

The men who framed the statute would emphasize that record. Although they might remind their colleagues that these were results they had expected and forecast in debate, there is no question but they would have to claim surprise as they reported the degree to which the agency they created has aided this government and the international organizations with which it is allied as they strive to stimulate the production of food in countries where it is urgently required.

The major features of the TVA statute were hammered out in the 1920's, a period of isolationism for the United States, and one provision of the original Act reflected the national consensus. It read, "No products of the Corporation* shall be sold for use outside of the United States, its Territories and possessions, except to the United States Government for the use of its Army and Navy, or to its allies in case of war." As fertilizer was the only exportable

---

* Modified in 1959 by inserting the words "except ferrophosphorus" after "Corporation." Ferrophosphorus was a byproduct of TVA's phosphatic operations. There was no market for the material in the United States in 1959, but it was used in steel manufacture in Europe.

product contemplated by the Act, the prohibition clearly was intended to preserve every ton for use by the American farmer in times of peace. The injunction has been obeyed. In World War II, the highly concentrated plant food produced at Muscle Shoals was shipped to Great Britain, and small amounts have been sent for testing by other allies, but although the fertilizer produced at Muscle Shoals is available only in the United States, information about the processes developed there has been exported to every continent and across every sea. Just since 1963, fifty teams have been sent from TVA to twenty-five countries where food production is a pressing problem, and several hundred foreign specialists have studied at the Alabama plant for periods ranging from a fortnight to a year. Seminars have been arranged to meet the special needs of specific countries, and a plant first designed to produce munitions in time of war has become a classroom for men who battle against hunger.

This of course is not the only TVA activity stimulating requests for technical assistance abroad. Some 50,000 foreign visitors have been received by TVA since the end of World War II, and in many instances their observations have resulted in the solicitation of help in meeting problems at their site. Never without the approval of agencies of the U.S. Government charged with responsibility in the field of foreign aid, members of TVA's staff have been dispatched abroad to counsel on power plant operation, electricity rate making, collective bargaining, malaria control, dam construction, and the maintenance of transmission lines. But in recent years the most frequent call is for the help of the technicians who work for TVA in its fertilizer operations at Muscle Shoals.

Today the facilities in northern Alabama include laboratories where scientists work with test tubes, plots where new materials are first tried out, and plants where a variety of products are produced in quantities sufficient for wide-scale tests in actual farming operations. Agronomists, economists, chemists, and engineers have their headquarters there. Every process is open, every improvement disclosed. The experiment stations of the several states, the Extension Service and the Land Grant colleges, private companies that manufacture fertilizer, and dealers and cooperatives that sell to individual farmers are participants in the general program. Its objective is the one laid down in the Act, to improve the quality and lower the cost of fertilizer to the American farmer, and TVA has added another, to encourage its use in soil-conserving practices. When a new product is developed and has been produced in sufficient quantity for testing in the forty-four states now cooperating, when results have been reported and appraised, and a market of sufficient size to interest manufacturers is assured, TVA begins to reduce its production. Using patents issued to TVA which, until the summer of 1970* were available on a nonexclusive royalty-free basis, commercial enterprises then begin to provide a supply and TVA devotes its capacity to the development of new processes and new materials. To date, 196 patents in the field of fertilizer technology have been issued to TVA and the equipment or the process they cover is used in 478 privately or cooperatively owned plants located in thirty-nine states.

The TVA Act provided that ownership of all patents resulting from the work of agency staff should rest in the government itself. In the beginning, the provision was austerely interpreted, and all patent applications resulting from staff efforts, whether related to TVA activities or not, and even if clearly developed on an employee's own time, were filed by TVA. Then, in the case of devices undertaken privately and unrelated to TVA's responsibilities, an exclusive license was issued to the inventor. When an astonished Board discovered that TVA had been granted a patent on a tackling dummy, a more realistic policy was inaugurated, and applications for patents irrelevant to the interest of the agency are no longer handled by TVA. Two committees of the Senate have conducted hearings at which TVA's patent policies have been described. They have been praised but not generally adopted by other federal agencies although they have been effective in achieving wide application of developments accomplished by the use of public funds.

Fertilizer technology has advanced greatly in the years since TVA took over the plant at Muscle Shoals, and its use has become selective and sophisticated. TVA has had a part in the change and it can be argued that the agency's contribution to national experience is more accurately measured by its influence on the private sector of the economy than by its contribution to the art of gov-

* Yielding to a practice imposed by the Office of Management and Budget, a fee is now required.

ernment. Certainly, the biennial fertilizer technology conferences arranged by TVA suggest a general acceptance of its findings and endorsement of the quality of its research. As many as 1,000 persons have attended. The Representatives of farm organizations, teachers at agricultural colleges, delegations from private fertilizer companies, and editors of farm journals come for three-day periods to visit the laboratories and the plants, observe, question, and discuss. The government facility is recognized as a vital educational service for the benefit of agriculture and the enterprises that supply its requirements for plant food.

The TVA power system has had its impact on private companies, too, although not quite in the way the authors of the Act may have expected. The primary responsibility, the purpose of TVA's power program, is, and always has been, to promote the well-being of the people it serves, but a secondary purpose, one much talked about in the 1920's and 1930's, was to provide a "yardstick" by which the fairness of the rates of private companies might be judged. The concept was discussed at length by the Investigating Committee in 1938, but a survey of the hearings conducted by various committees of Congress in the 1920's is required to understand the importance of the function. In those sessions, there was agreement that the rates at which electricity was sold to the consumer should cover all the costs of its production and distribution and in addition provide a return on the capital prudently invested by the owners in facilities. The difficulty was that no one seemed to know what production costs actually were or what they should be, or how rates were established. Representatives of private companies who testified were unable or unwilling to describe their pricing policies. Some of them were candid, and it was clear that their companies charged all the traffic would bear.

To the members of Congress who heard such testimony, some remedy seemed imperative, for this was no ordinary business. Its soundness was essential to the economy. It was and had to be a monopoly, denied the discipline of competition. The regulatory agencies intended to protect consumers when competition is absent were generally ineffective. Not all states had established them and power systems crossed state boundaries. As the 1920's drew to a close, an investigation by the Federal Trade Commission revealed the massive propaganda campaign by which the private companies were endeavoring to reduce the growing displeasure of the public and to frustrate the growth of the movement for public ownership and operation of power systems. Soon the Insull utility empire in the Midwest collapsed. Zeal for reform was high, and accomplishment was not inconsiderable. With the creation of TVA, a device to measure performance was added to other legislative remedies enacted.

The yardstick, as it was called, has been misrepresented and misunderstood. TVA power rates were never intended to serve as a model, although the enthusiasm of some politicians promoted that idea. Their function was to provide a device for judgment with respect to the validity of the various items of cost that had to be covered by rates. TVA would be required to keep its accounts according to the specifications of the Federal Power Commission, exactly as the accounts of private companies are reported, and in turn TVA would require detailed reports from its distributors. This was important, for distribution costs were said to be shrouded in mystery. Ordinarily, the same company generated, transmitted, and distributed energy, and there was a general charge that distribution costs were masked in the total. In the case of TVA, costs could be segregated, item-by-item comparisons could be made, and investigation could be directed to specific charges whenever unaccountable differences invited it. The function of the yardstick was specifically set out in the clarifying amendments added to the TVA Act in 1935. One provision read in part:

> For the purpose of accumulating data useful to the Congress in the formulation of legislative policy in matters relating to the generation, transmission, and distribution of electric energy . . . and to the Federal Power Commission and other Federal and State agencies, and to the public, the Board shall keep complete accounts of its costs of generation, transmission, and distribution of electric energy and shall keep a complete account of the total cost of generating and transmission facilities constructed or otherwise acquired by the corporation.

It was hoped that the experience of TVA would provide the information required to permit customers to judge, regulatory commissions to function, and legislators to act.

It has not worked out quite the way the advocates of the yardstick anticipated. There is little indication that the expected comparisons of individual cost items have played much part in the adoption of more reasonable rates by private companies, but there is considerable evidence to suggest that the public system has injected an element of competition into electricity pricing. Privately owned systems adjacent to TVA began to lower their rates shortly after TVA was created. Those early reductions were reported to the Joint Committee investigating TVA in 1938, and today concentric circles drawn around the area supplied with power from TVA enclose bands of progressively lower rates as it is approached. Perhaps a government agency had to take the risk of proving the soundness of the new pricing policies and exposing the scanty hazard involved in providing electricity to farmers. There is no reason to doubt the sincerity of the private power company officials who advised congressional committees that rural electrification was impractical to consider for the region now served by TVA. But, when TVA undertook such a program, neighboring power companies followed to discover that the financial risks of lowered rates and expanded rural service had been exaggerated. At any rate, they were less fearsome than the threat of more TVA's. That at least was the import of the testimony of Hamilton Moses, Chairman of the Board of the Arkansas Light and Power Company, when he explained to a subcommittee of the House Committee on Appropriations why low rates were offered to rural cooperatives by his company. "Well, we have given a preference to the cooperatives," he said. "They might propose another TVA over in the Southwest."

Whatever the motive, the purpose of the yardstick was achieved and the demonstration was effective. Consumers have benefited and their power suppliers have prospered, as lowered rates have encouraged an increase in consumption and revenues have risen. In the case of the government as consumer, the effect of TVA's example has been direct. When the Atomic Energy Commission began to purchase large blocks of power from combinations of private companies organized as Electric Energy, Inc. (EEI), and the Ohio Valley Electric Corporation (OVEC), it was apparent that existing contracts with TVA were a factor in obtaining rates lower than those usually offered to large industrial customers, a saving to the Treasury of the United States. When the Dixon-Yates contract was pending, the relationship was clear. Then as a result of extensive comparisons between estimates of the costs of power from the projected private plant and actual costs of TVA's Shawnee or estimates for the plant proposed for construction at Fulton, the first offer of the utilities was sharply reduced. Here, at least, the yardstick was used, and as a matter of fact the influence of the government-owned system may have been fairly wide.

To suggest that the example of a government program might have been helpful in achieving improvements in private management is a denial of conventional wisdom. For a long time people have been led to believe that public operations are by their very nature incurably inefficient, and that private enterprise sets a standard of performance. Some recognition that the infirmities of public operation were not inherent but were the consequence of the burdens under which most government activities were obliged to operate was implicit in President Roosevelt's message to Congress in 1933. He recommended that TVA be created as "a corporation clothed with the power of government but possessed of the flexibility and initiative of a private enterprise." Understanding of the problem was echoed when the House members of the Conference Committee reported:

> We have sought to set up a legislative framework, but not to incase it [TVA] in a legislative strait jacket. We intend that the corporation shall have much of the essential freedom and elasticity of a private business corporation. We have indicated the course it shall take, but have not directed the particular steps it shall make.

The statute designed by Congress did assure flexibility and promote initiative. It has been used by TVA to seek the goals set out in the Act. That should be the test of achievement, but expressions of approval or dissent are more likely to be based on comparisons with private business than on measurement of progress toward statutory objectives.

In only one case can a simple comparison be made between performance by TVA and private enterprise, where each one, in the same area at the same time and for the same reason, was engaged in similar activities. It happened in 1953. In 1950, the Atomic Energy Commission had to make arrangements for a supply of power for the new facilities it was about to build at Paducah, Kentucky. TVA was asked to provide it, and a request for funds to begin construction of a steam plant was pending before the House Committee on Appropriations when one of AEC's Commissioners proposed that private companies be invited to supply a portion of the requirement. His suggestion was accepted, and TVA prepared to build a smaller facility, as the newly organized Electric Energy, Inc., composed of five private power companies, would be responsible for supplying a portion, something less than half of the total load. The two plants were to be located in the same area; they drew upon the same labor force. Construction of both began in 1950, the private facility by contract, TVA's by force account. Both would be paid for by funds from the Treasury of the United States. One, TVA's plant, named Shawnee, would be built by public funds directly and would belong to the government. The other at Joppa, Illinois, across the Ohio River from Shawnee, would have the initial private investment retired by AEC's payments for power, also provided by the federal Treasury, but ownership would remain in private hands. Because of the conflict in Korea critical materials were scheduled, and the delivery of equipment was established in advance. By agreement, the EEI plant was to come in first.

The critics of TVA appeared to welcome this kind of competition. One editorial in the *Evening Citizen* of Cairo, Illinois, pointed out that "many companies pooled their ideas and their resources . . . for the expressed purpose of demonstrating to the government that private enterprise could do the job much better for half the cost," and in the same paper a news report added, "It is expected that the Joppa plant will begin producing power ahead of the Shawnee plant." That was the plan. Deliveries were arranged that way. The race was fixed, but something funny happened to Electric Energy, Inc., on its way to the goal. TVA came in first. Power from Shawnee was on the line in April, 1953, some three months before the Joppa plant was in service. The privately owned plant was not only late. It had overrun its estimates by a substantial amount. AEC Commissioner Thomas E. Murray, who had initially sponsored its organization, later testified before the Joint Committee on Atomic Energy. He said in part,

> . . . a section of private power interests was given a fair opportunity to prove what it could do. All knew, everyone knew that an almost identical TVA program was under way across the river.

Competition was out in the open—competition as to time and competition as to dollars—and no one can escape the fact that TVA won the Paducah power contest.

There was little criticism of the private effort. In fact, early in June, before the belated operations began, EEI was given the Charles A. Coffin award, according to the Edison Electric Institute, "the electric industry's highest honor" in a ceremony at the annual convention of the Institute. The citation oddly commended the combine for "its superb example of competitive enterprise." Some weeks later, on July 31, J. W. McAfee, President of EEI, announced cancellation of the combine's contract with Ebasco Services, general contractor for the plant, "in order to permit reorganization of the construction project so that the station can be completed on a more efficient and economical basis," but just as EEI got an award for its performance Ebasco got new contracts. When AEC joined with the Bureau of the Budget to impose the Dixon-Yates arrangements on power consumers of the TVA region it developed that, in spite of what had been described as the "Ebasco fiasco" at Joppa, the company had been chosen to construct the new plant to be built by the Mississippi Valley Generating Company. Over protest from the General Accounting Office the selection was defended and the company's President participated in the ground breaking ceremonies in Arkansas in June of 1955, a celebration which in the end proved to be premature.

There were no awards or citations for TVA, no special recognition of its success in overcoming substantial difficulties in the construction of Shawnee. Everyone expected a responsible performance, and just as cash awards are not given to employees for acceptable suggestions because TVA trusts members of its staff to offer them as a matter of course, perhaps the failure to win plaudits for accomplishment is the highest compliment a public agency can receive. If excellence is taken for granted, there is a value beyond the particular achievement. It demonstrates that, if the statute enacted by Congress permits, a branch of government can perform effectively. It can, on occasion, even better the record of private enterprise. Recognition of that fact could be a contribution to national experience significant in itself, a part of the "marching on" contemplated by the President in 1933.

There will be other contributions, for the results of every experiment and investigation conducted by TVA are available for adaptation elsewhere. Visitors are welcome at the facilities on Norris Lake where research in forestry and fishery is conducted, records of the continuing timber inventory are maintained, and studies of fish life in the reservoirs are both planned and analyzed. They can inspect the chemical plant at Muscle Shoals and the nearby laboratories where scientists probe the life secrets of the vanishing mussel, the proliferating milfoil, and the anopheles mosquito. Demonstrations of the ways in which the scars of strip mining can be healed are available for exploration. The region offers a huge laboratory for study of problems both old and emerging.

When the nuclear plants now under construction begin operation, TVA and the Environmental Protection Agency are prepared to conduct an exhaustive investigation to determine the precise effect on aquatic life of the anticipated rise in water temperature. Conditions prior to operation are being examined and recorded for comparison. Some temperature increase is expected, although the plants are designed to moderate it, and the investigation will identify the results exactly, substituting knowledge for fear and results for forecasts. To date, TVA's experience with the effect of temperature changes resulting from the discharge of heated water has been limited to the stretches of the rivers immediately below its coal-fired plants. Heat discharge from such plants is less than from nuclear plants, and after years of operation no calamitous effects have been reported, and some small benefits have been realized. In winter months, fishermen congregate in the river reaches warmed by the discharge, and at one plant a private company is experimenting in the use of heated water for the commercial production of catfish. Already agriculturalists are considering the possibility of utilizing the discharge from nuclear plants in greenhouses. Only time and research will permit an accurate appraisal of all the effects of what is now called thermal pollution and enable TVA to minimize every potential damage and to take advantage of every benefit in its own operation, at the same time providing the public in other areas with the information essential to sound judgment.

General concern may be channeled into effective relief as a result of investigations going on today in several of the Valley's small watersheds where scientists are at work testing the runoff of the rainfall from farm land in an effort to determine to what extent fertilizers used by farmers contribute to eutrophication of the streams. Measures of correction by changes in product or application will be developed if they are required. At the same time, at a number of TVA steam-generating plants, scientists and engineers are engaged in experiments designed to discover ways to remove the sulfur dioxide from the emissions of coal burning—a problem of concern throughout the nation.

Experiments and investigations such as these deal with issues that are only forerunners to the questions of increasing complexity that will be presented by every technological advance, and which, in turn, technology must solve. Aubrey J. Wagner, Chairman of the Board, talked about the years ahead when he spoke to a group of TVA employees in the summer of 1972. He began by looking at the past. Wagner is peculiarly well qualified to review the years. In the spring of 1934 he was offered a job as a TVA Engineering Aide, and his colleagues have not let him forget that the files record the skepticism of his telegraphic response. He would be glad to accept, he said, if one year's employment could be assured. For an assignment of briefer tenure, he would be unwilling to move his family from Wisconsin to Tennessee. One year's employment was promised, and he came to work for TVA. Today, by appointment of the President, he is a member of the Board and, by designation of the Chief Executive, its Chairman.

In June, 1972, when he spoke, TVA was entering its fortieth year. The agency stood, as he pointed out, on the threshold of middle age.

I have reviewed with you the major accomplishments of past decades, the period of youth, and you have asked me to outline what I see as TVA's future as it moves into middle age. You know the projects, either under way or planned and announced, that we hope to complete in the next few years. You know them because your vision, your analyses, and the application of your technical knowledge prompted the Board to recommend them, and your skills will be devoted to the realization of their promise. I cannot predict what new problems will emerge or what new projects will be proposed. This is a time of rapid change. I can however remind you of the constant factors that must guide the present Board and staff and those that follow, the principles TVA must uphold and the methods I am certain it will use as the problems of the future are confronted.

Our goal will be the same. It is laid down in our charter. Now, as in 1933, TVA is committed to one purpose. All its acts are designed to promote the use of every natural resource to improve the quality of living for the people. In the future, as in the past, TVA must consider the impact of its decisions on the total environment, never a single aspect. That means we must look for balance. In this search, we are denied the easy path of those who would advance only one objective or solve only one problem.

Because strip mining for coal in the past has left a legacy of desolation we cannot join with those who say "Stop it." We have to consider the problem in terms of human well-being, to recognize the benefits of electricity to the people of the region, and instead of trying to stop stripping, we must strive to reduce its damage, to encourage improvement in mining methods, seek more effective restoration of the land, and work to heal the scars of the past. It is a more complex task than simply clamoring to stop the practice would be, but it is essential and it must be accomplished.

Because industrial growth can add to pollution we cannot decide, as some enthusiasts suggest, to discourage growth. Growth in this Valley has assured more rewarding work for the people. It has reduced the misery of poverty. It has halted the emigration of the Valley's work force to the crowded industrial centers of the North and East. It must continue, but at the same time we must invoke the best solutions technology can discover to make sure that it is accomplished without the sacrifice of clean water or pure air and that the environment is improved, not damaged by progress. We cannot abandon a water control project that will add greatly to total area advantages because it will reduce by a few miles the opportunity for enjoyment by a special group of fishermen. We have to base our decisions on an analysis of all the factors, not a selected few, and we must consider all the people, not a single group. Just as we must never forget our goal, we must never weary of the laborious task of fact finding.

In the years ahead, TVA will continue to work with local institutions, public and private, and here I will venture a few predictions. In the next few years I am confident that the pollution caused by municipal sewage discharges will be eliminated throughout the Tennessee River system, that hundreds of miles of tributary streams will be cleared of debris, that derelict automobiles will be removed from the countryside. I am certain that the towns and cities of the Valley will be more attractive, better places to live and that local flood problems will be reduced to manageable proportions. Without reservation I can forecast improvement in the services of state and local governments. I am sure that citizens will make greater demands upon them, and that they will respond with increased effectiveness.

One further prophecy can be added. The years ahead will not be easy. TVA will be attacked. We will know disappointments and frustration. We are accustomed to opposition, and we have learned that the nature of accusations change. A good many of you will remember that just a decade ago we were under fire because certain critics had decided we were not building a sufficient number of water control projects. They were not concerned with the facts we were obliged to consider before proposing a project. They simply called for more dams. Now we are haled into court by those who want to stop all such developments, even those recommended after detailed investigation. They want water control to cease.

Among our new adversaries there are some who appear to be against change of any kind, who seem to long for a bucolic past that most of them never experienced. We must listen to them. Criticism can be helpful. We must never be reluctant to re-examine our judgments nor to present the facts on which our conclusions are based. But we can never agree with those who are simply afraid of change. We can be patient, but to their fears we cannot yield. Those of us who came to this Valley in TVA's beginning years would not return to the past—to a river that contributed little to the well-being of men, to millions of eroded acres, hundreds of abandoned farm houses, to floods, to forest fires, jobless and discouraged men. We are not afraid of the future. Its problems will be complex, but its opportunities immense. There will be conflict, and we will have to fight in the years ahead as we have fought in the past. But I believe that our objectives are worth the struggle, that our methods are sound and deserve defense. To search out the facts and to strive for balance as we stretch toward our goal of a better environment for all the people—those are imperatives never to be abandoned. They affect the lives of people beyond the region.

In 1933, when President Roosevelt sent a message to Congress recommending the creation of TVA, he wrote "It should be charged with the broadest duty of planning for the proper use, conservation, and development of the Tennessee River drainage basin and its adjoining territory for the general social and economic welfare of the Nation." We must remember that, and know that whether it is the design of a new city, construction of an experimental nuclear power plant, work in forest genetics, or the development of a recreation area where learning and play can be combined, the overriding purpose of all our acts is the same. It has not changed since the first Board phrased it almost forty years ago. The inscription on every structure reminds us that as every project is built, so every program must be carried out not only for the enhancement of the quality of life in this region, but

". . . for the people of the United States of America."

Appendix A

TVA Career Opportunities

Individual opportunities to participate in the Tennessee Valley Authority's unified resource development program are virtually limitless. TVA requires a uniquely wide range of skilled professionals—agronomists, foresters, ecologists, economists, planners, and practitioners of a host of other disciplines—all as part of a coordinated team concerned with every aspect of regionwide resource conservation and use. In addition to persons from these many major fields of college training, TVA needs an extensive pool of supporting talent including clerical and service personnel, engineering aides, and technicians. Also available are a variety of jobs for skilled craftsmen and laborers to carry out TVA's massive construction programs.

ENGINEERING, SCIENTIFIC, AND ADMINISTRATIVE POSITIONS

TVA has a broad, continuing need for engineers. Openings involve most major areas of specialization including chemical, civil, electrical, industrial, mechanical, nuclear, safety, and environmental.

Most new employees are recent college graduates, usually at the bachelor's or master's level, with records of outstanding academic achievement and of participation in extracurricular activities on campus. Also considered are graduates with related experience in other companies, industries, or governmental agencies. Most recently graduated engineers employed with TVA participate in an 18-month internal training program designed to develop an understanding of the unusually broad scope and interrelated nature of TVA's many resource development programs.

A limited number of scientific and administrative positions are filled each year, representing nearly every discipline of professional training including, but not limited to, accounting, biology, business administration, chemistry, economics, forestry, law, mathematics, personnel administration, regional planning, and statistics.

256

AIDE AND TECHNICIAN

Opportunities are available for aides and technicians to provide technical support and assistance for engineers and other professionals. Typical assigned duties include: preparation of routine reports and summaries, making calculations and data analyses, drafting and layout work based on engineering data, and inspection and testing of materials and equipment.

TVA conducts a formal training program for electrical engineering aides to provide persons with adequate backgrounds in science and mathematics the additional training necessary to become competent electrical test personnel. The program consists of seven months of classroom work in engineering theory at the college level and thirty months of on-the-job training under the guidance of field test engineers.

The basic qualifications required for these positions normally include training in specialized technical courses or work experience in a related field. Selections are frequently made from graduates of technical institutes or from candidates who have completed two years of college. High school graduates with demonstrated abilities and aptitude for the work are also considered.

CLERICAL AND SERVICES

Many clerical and service positions are filled each year to provide necessary support and services for professional and technical employees. Clerical jobs include all classes of positions that involve general or specialized clerical, secretarial, and office machine operation functions. Reproduction and communication jobs include positions that involve primarily general service functions, such as printing, bindery operations, telephone operations, and attendant work. Custodial service jobs include positions that involve functions related to building operations, such as janitorial, gardening, and elevator operator work. Public safety service jobs involve the safety, security, and protection of all TVA property and of TVA employees during work hours.

PLANT OPERATIONS AND MAINTENANCE

Most of TVA's generating plant and substation operators begin their careers as students in a Student Generating Plant Operator Program. The two-year program combines classroom instruction in mathematics and science with on-the-job training. Students learn the full range of operation of main and auxiliary equipment in fossil-fired and nuclear power plants, hydro plants, and substations. Operators at all levels are encouraged to take advantage of additional training courses offered by TVA.

A craft apprenticeship program is provided by TVA for training maintenance and construction personnel. This training is for a period of four to five years. In addition to extensive on-the-job training, apprentices are given each year at least 144 hours of related classroom assignments, such as mathematics, trade science and theory, and blueprint reading. Upon satisfactory completion of training, trainees are accredited for journeymanship.

APPOINTMENTS AND CAREER DEVELOPMENT

Appointments and promotions are made on the basis of merit and efficiency. Generally, positions above the entry level are filled by promoting employees rather than recruiting from outside sources, thus enhancing promotional opportunities for employees. After present employees are considered, an outside candidate may be selected if his qualifications can be shown to be superior to those of employee candidates. Equal opportunity is extended to every applicant and every employee without regard to sex, race, creed, color, or national origin. No political test or qualification is considered.

TVA recognizes the importance of its employees' professional development. This recognition is given meaning through a flexible policy that enables employees to receive additional education and training in their respective fields with all or part of the expenses paid by TVA. In addition to outside education and training arrangements on an individual employee basis, TVA sponsors internal training programs designed to meet specific needs. Employees are encouraged to participate in civic and in professional organizations to keep abreast of new developments in their fields. The opportunity for employees to combine a program of formal studies with comprehensive on-the-job training speeds up the normal growth process and results in a ready pool of available talent from which most supervisory and management level positions are filled.

Positions are grouped into salary schedules and grades according to type of work and level of difficulty and responsibility. Salary rates for each schedule and grade reflect prevailing rates of pay for similar work in the TVA area.

SUMMER EMPLOYMENT PROGRAMS

Some individuals may be hired for temporary summer positions to substitute for or add to regular staffs. These positions usually are subprofessional in nature, and the appointments are temporary. In addition, there are four special summer programs:

Summer Aid Program

TVA participates in the Summer Aid Program, which is a part of the President's Federal Summer Employment Program for Youth. Candidates must be between the ages of sixteen and twenty-one and be certified as disadvantaged in terms of either economic or educational need. Applicants are obtained through local offices of the State Employment Service, which keeps local registers of candidates who meet the criteria for certification as disadvantaged. They are employed by TVA under a personal service contract and paid the current minimum hourly wage.

Summer College Student Program

This program is designed to interest promising college students in future employment with TVA. Selections are made from students who have completed at least one academic year. Most are hired for engineering work under temporary appointments and are paid at regular annual rates for engineering aides and technicians, depending on the level of the work assigned.

Summer Faculty Program

Faculty members in selected fields who can contribute to and gain insights from TVA's broad scope of programs are frequently sought for summer employment. The level of duties assigned and rates of pay are as close as possible to the level of their academic positions.

Summer Intern Program

TVA conducts a Summer Intern Program for students majoring in management sciences, social sciences, or public administration. Candidates are obtained through established internship programs at selected colleges and universities. Interns are employed under a personal service contract at pay rates competitive with rates for similar positions in other companies or agencies.

HOURLY CONSTRUCTION WORK

A large number of skilled craftsmen and laborers are hired each year by TVA. In filling these trades and labor jobs, people living near the work location are given first consideration. If there are not enough well-qualified people available locally, applicants from other areas are considered. Employees are paid hourly wage rates based on prevailing wage rates for similar work in the TVA area.

Jobs are frequently available for boilermakers, carpenters, electricians, iron workers, laborers, operating engineers, steamfitters, and other craftsmen.

Appendix B

TVA Directors, 1933–72

All Board members are appointed by the President, subject to Senate confirmation. Appointments run for the nine years (except the original unequal periods set up to stagger the terms), or for the remainder of an unexpired 9-year term in case of a vacancy. The Chairman of the Board (*) is designated by the President.

1933–42 Term

ARTHUR E. MORGAN
*Appointed as Chairman
Senate confirmation 5-30-33

A. E. Morgan removed 3-23-38 by Presidential action

JAMES P. POPE
Senate confirmation 1-12-39

1942–51 Term

Sen. Pope reappointed
Senate confirmation 5-12-42

Term expired 5-18-51

1933–39 Term

HARCOURT A. MORGAN
Senate confirmation 6-10-33

*Designated Chairman 3-23-38

1939–48 Term

H. A. Morgan reappointed
Senate confirmation 5-8-39
*Relinquished Chairmanship 9-15-41

Term expired 5-18-48

1948–57 Term

HARRY A. CURTIS
Appointed 5-4-48
Senate confirmation 2-8-49

1933–36 Term

DAVID E. LILIENTHAL
Senate confirmation 6-10-33

1936–45 Term

Mr. Lilienthal reappointed
Senate confirmation 5-18-36

*Designated Chairman 9-15-41

1945–54 Term

Chrmn. Lilienthal reappointed
Senate confirmation 5-21-45
Resigned 10-28-46 to become AEC Chairman

GORDON R. CLAPP
*Appointed as Chairman 11-2-46
Senate confirmation 4-24-47

1951–60 Term
RAYMOND ROSS PATY
Senate confirmation 7-4-52

Dr. Paty died 8-7-57
FRANK J. WELCH
Senate confirmation 7-15-58
Resigned 2-20-59

BROOKS HAYS
Senate confirmation 6-23-59
1960–69 Term
Mr. Hays reappointed
Senate confirmation 2-8-60
Resigned 2-27-61

AUBREY J. WAGNER
Senate confirmation 3-3-61
*Designated Chairman 6-23-62

1969–78 Term
Mr. Wagner reappointed
Senate confirmation 5-23-69

Term expired 5-18-57
1957–66 Term
A. R. JONES
Senate confirmation 7-15-58
Term expired 5-18-66

1966–75 Term
DON McBRIDE
Senate confirmation 5-19-66

Term expired 5-18-54

1954–63 Term
Brig. Gen. HERBERT D. VOGEL
*Appointed as Chairman 8-2-54
Senate confirmation 8-11-54
Gen. Vogel resigned 6-30-62

FRANK E. SMITH
Senate confirmation 7-23-62
Took office 11-14-62 after completing congressional term

1963–72 Term
Mr. Smith reappointed
Senate confirmation 4-26-63
Term expired 5-18-72

1972–81 Term
WILLIAM L. JENKINS
Senate confirmation 9-30-72

Appendix C

Facts About Major TVA Dams and Reservoirs

MAIN RIVER PROJECTS	River	State	County	Max. Height (Feet) (a)	Length (Feet)	Length of Lake (miles)	Lake Elevation (feet above sea level) Full Pool (j)	Construction Started	Closure	Cost of Plant in Service 6-30-70 (d) (millions)	Lock Size (Feet)	Lock Max. Lift (Feet)
Kentucky	Tenn.	Ky.	Marshall (b) Livingston	206	8,422	184.3	359	7-1-38	8-30-44	$118.0	110x600	75
Pickwick Landing	Tenn.	Tenn.	Hardin	113	7,715	52.7	414	3-8-35	2-8-38	45.7	110x600	63
Wilson (i)	Tenn.	Ala.	Lauderdale (b) Colbert	137	4,535	15.5	507.5	4-14-18	4-14-24	107.6	110x600 60x300 60x292	100
Wheeler	Tenn.	Ala.	Lauderdale (b) Lawrence	72	6,342	74.1	556	11-21-33	10-3-36	87.5	60x400 110x600	52 52
Guntersville	Tenn.	Ala.	Marshall	94	3,979	75.7	595	12-4-35	1-16-39	51.2	60x360 110x600	45
Nickajack (h)	Tenn.	Tenn.	Marion	81	3,767	46.3	634	4-1-64	12-14-67	74.9	110x800(k) 110x600	42(k) 42
Chickamauga	Tenn.	Tenn.	Hamilton	129	5,800	58.9	682.5	1-13-36	1-15-40	42.1	60x360	53
Watts Bar	Tenn.	Tenn.	Meigs (b) Rhea	112	2,960	72.4	741	7-1-39	1-1-42	35.6	60x360	70
Fort Loudoun	Tenn.	Tenn.	Loudon	122	4,190	55.0	813	7-8-40	8-2-43	42.4	60x360	80
TRIBUTARY PROJECTS												
Tims Ford (g)	Elk	Tenn.	Franklin	175	1,484	34	888	3-28-66	12- -70	50.9		
Apalachia	Hiwassee	N. C.	Cherokee (c)	150	1,308	9.8	1,280	7-17-41	2-14-43	24.0		
Hiwassee	Hiwassee	N. C.	Cherokee	307	1,376	22	1,524.5	7-15-36	2-8-40	24.4		

Chattuge	Hiwassee	N. C.	Clay	144	2,850	13	1,927	7-17-41	2-12-42	9.1	
Ocoee No. 1 (i)	Ocoee	Tenn.	Polk	135	840	7.5	837.65	8- -10	12-15-11	3.0	
Ocoee No. 2 (i)	Ocoee	Tenn.	Polk	30	450	—	1,115	5- -12	—	3.0	
Ocoee No. 3	Ocoee	Tenn.	Polk	110	612	7	1,435	7-17-41	8-15-42	9.0	
Blue Ridge (i)	Toccoa	Ga.	Fannin	167	1,000	10	1,690	11- -25(e)	12-6-30	5.5	
Nottely	Nottely	Ga.	Union	184	2,300	20	1,779	7-17-41	1-24-42	8.1	
Melton Hill	Clinch	Tenn.	Loudon (b) Roane	103	1,020	44	795	9-6-60	5-1-63	36.2	75x400
Norris	Clinch	Tenn.	Anderson (b) Campbell	265	1,860	72	1,020	10-1-33	3-4-36	33.3	60
Fontana	Little Tenn.	N. C.	Graham (b) Swain	480	2,365	29	1,708	1-1-42	11-7-44	78.6	
Douglas	French Broad	Tenn.	Sevier	202	1,705	43.1	1,000	2-2-42	2-19-43	46.9	
Cherokee	Holston	Tenn.	Jefferson (b) Grainger	175	6,760	59	1,073	8-1-40	12-5-41	36.6	
Fort Patrick Henry	S. Fork Holston	Tenn.	Sullivan	95	737	10.3	1,263	5-14-51	10-27-53	12.3	
Boone	S. Fork Holston	Tenn.	Sullivan (b) Washington	160	1,532	17.3	1,385	8-29-50	12-16-52	27.8	
South Holston	S. Fork Holston	Tenn.	Sullivan	285	1,600	24.3	1,729	8-4-47(f)	11-20-50	31.4	
Watauga	Watauga	Tenn.	Carter	318	900	16.7	1,959	7-22-46(f)	12-1-48	32.5	
Great Falls (i) (in Cumberland Valley)	Caney Fork	Tenn.	Warren (b) White	92	800	22	805.30	-15	12-8-16	8.2	

Technical reports on most TVA dams and several steam plant projects are available at nominal cost. Write for list.
   a. Foundation to operating deck.
   b. River is county line.
   c. Powerhouse is in Polk County, Tennessee.
   d. Original construction or acquisition cost, including switchyard as adjusted by subsequent additions, retirements, and reclassifications. Includes estimated costs of projects under construction.
   e. Construction discontinued early in 1926; resumed in March, 1929.
   f. Initial construction started February 16, 1942; temporarily discontinued to conserve critical materials during war.
   g. Under construction; cost and quantity data estimated.
   h. Nickajack Dam replaced the old Hales Bar Dam 6 miles upstream.
   i. Acquired: Wilson by transfer from U.S. Corps of Engineers in 1933; Ocoee No. 1, Ocoee No. 2, Blue Ridge and Great Falls by purchase from TEP Co. in 1939. Subsequent to acquisition, TVA heightened and installed additional units at Wilson.
   j. Full Pool Elevation is the normal upper level to which the reservoirs may be filled. Where storage space is available above this level, additional filling may be made as needed for flood control.
   k. Construction of Nickajack main lock limited to underwater portion; for completion later.

263

Bibliography

The books and articles listed below include some referred to in the text and additional material of possible interest to the student or general reader who wishes to delve deeper into the story of TVA.

Books

ADAMS, SHERMAN. *Firsthand Report.* New York: Harper & Row, 1965.

BIDDLE, FRANCIS B. *In Brief Authority.* New York: Doubleday, 1962.

CASE, HARRY L. *Personnel Policy in a Public Agency: The TVA Experience.* New York: Harper & Row, 1955.

CLAPP, GORDON R. *The TVA: An Approach to the Development of a Region.* Chicago: University of Chicago Press, 1955.

DONOVAN, ROBERT J. *Eisenhower: The Inside Story.* New York: Harper & Row, 1956.

DUFFUS, R. L. *Valley and Its People.* New York: Alfred A. Knopf, 1946.

GUNTHER, JOHN. *The Story of TVA.* New York: Harper & Row, 1951.

HUBBARD, PRESTON J. *Origins of the TVA: The Muscle Shoals Controversy, 1920–1932.* Nashville, Tenn.: Vanderbilt University Press, 1961.

HUGHES, EMMET JOHN. *The Ordeal of Power: A Political Memoir of the Eisenhower Years.* New York: Atheneum, 1963.

KING, JUDSON. *Conservation Fight from Theodore Roosevelt to the Tennessee Valley Authority.* Washington, D.C.: Public Affairs Press, 1959.

KYLE, JOHN H. *The Building of TVA: An Illustrated History.* Baton Rouge: Louisiana State University Press, 1958.

LILIENTHAL, DAVID E. *Journals.* Vol. 1, *TVA Years, 1939–1945.* New York: Harper & Row, 1964.

————. *TVA: Democracy on the March.* Twentieth anniversary edition. New York: Harper & Row, 1953.

McCraw, Thomas K. *Morgan vs. Lilienthal: The Feud Within the TVA.* Chicago: Loyola University Press, 1970.

————. *TVA and the Power Fight, 1933–1939.* Philadelphia: J. B. Lippincott, 1971.

Norris, George W. *Fighting Liberal: The Autobiography of George W. Norris.* New York: Collier, 1961.

Pritchett, Charles Herman. *The Tennessee Valley Authority: A Study in Public Administration.* Chapel Hill: University of North Carolina Press, 1943.

Schlesinger, Arthur M.. Jr. *Age of Roosevelt.* Vol. 2, *Coming of the New Deal.* Boston: Houghton Mifflin, 1957.

Smith, Frank E. *Politics of Conservation.* New York: Pantheon, 1966.

Tennessee Valley Authority. *TVA—the First Twenty Years: A Staff Report.* Knoxville: University of Tennessee Press, 1956.

Articles

Blee, C. E. "Development of the Tennessee River Waterway." *American Society of Civil Engineers, Centennial Transactions,* CT:1132–46, 1953.

Cole, W. E. "Impact of TVA upon the Southeast." *Social Forces,* 28:435–40, May, 1950.

Menhinick, H. K., and L. L. Durisch. "The Tennessee Valley Authority: Planning in Operation." *Town Planning Review,* 24:116–45, July, 1953.

"A Second Spring Stirs the TVA." *Business Week,* pp. 112–15, October 29, 1966.

Smith, Frank E. "Improving the Southern Environment." *New South,* 25:63–69, Fall, 1970.

"Such a Lovely Green Valley." *Time,* 81:27, April 26, 1963.

Tennessee Valley Authority. "Historical Roots of TVA" (in its *Annual Report,* 1953, pp. 51–82). Washington, D.C.: Government Printing Office, 1954.

Index

Adams, Sherman, 112
Administration; *see* President of the United States
Advisory Commission of the Council of National Defense, 82–83, 87; *see also* War Production Board
AEC; *see* Atomic Energy Commission
Agricultural and Chemical Development, Office of, 66, 144
Agricultural Industries Department, 59
Agricultural Relations Department, 59
Agricultural Relations Staff, 187
Agriculture: cooperation with other agencies, 30, 33, 35, 75, 124, 128; economy, 19, 128, 131, 197, 210–13; farm management, 29, 31, 122, 127–28, 194, 210–11; research, 100, 246; rural electrification, 28, 31, 157, 201, 210, 212; statistics, 9, 130–31, 210–12; test demonstrations, 29, 33, 35, 75, 122, 133, 210–11; *see also* Fertilizer; Forestry
Agriculture, Department of, 29, 32, 66, 104, 213, 235; *see also* Chemistry and Soils, Bureau of
Agriculture, Secretary of, 32
Agriculture, Senate Committee on, 9
Aiken, George D., 171
Alabama, 12, 16, 19, 102, 154, 213, 228, 237; Muscle Shoals, 5–7, 13, 15, 185; TAD, 128, 137, 154, 244
Alabama Power Company, 24, 25, 37, 50
Alcoa; *see* Aluminum Company of America
Alcorn County, Mississippi, 238
Alcorn County Electric Power Association, 27, 238
Allen Steam Plant, 151
Aluminum Company of America, 82–84, 196, 205
American Economics Association, 41
American Farm Bureau Federation, 30

Anderson County, Tennessee, 137
Antimonopoly Subcommittee of the Senate Judiciary Committee, 110, 140
Antioch College, Ohio, 4
Appalachian communities, 228–29
Appalachian East Tennessee, 218
Appropriations Committees, 64, 177, 186, 189; *see also* House of Representatives, Senate Appropriations Committee
Arkansas, 251
Arkansas Light and Power Company, 248
Army, 7, 24, 33, 95, 183, 187, 230, 243; *see also* Civilian Conservation Corps; Corps of Engineers, U.S. Army
Asheville, North Carolina, 84
Ashwander v. Tennessee Valley Authority, 36–38
Associated General Contractors of America, 236
Atlantic City, New Jersey, 119
Atlantic Monthly, 41–42
Atomic Energy Commission, 88, 92, 96, 103, 201, 241, 248–51; Dixon-Yates contract, 104–13; power needs, 94, 96, 103–13

Barclay Hotel, New York City, 147
Barkley Dam, 140–42
Barkley Lake, 140
Bear Creek, 128–29
Bear Creek Valley, 128
Bear Creek watershed, 128
Bear Creek Watershed Association, 128, 137, 222
Beck, Adam, 11
Beech River, 123, 125–31
Beech River watershed, 123, 128
Beech River Watershed Development Authority, 125–27, 129

267